The Agency Book

The Agency Book

Volume II
Gavin Brackenridge & Co., Inc.
Publisher

Oliver Johnston
Editor

Oliver Johnston Design
Design and Production Coordination

Distributed to the trade by Robert Silver Associates, 307 East 37 Street, New York, NY 10016.

Printed in Korea by Creative Graphics International, New York.

Copyright © 1986 Gavin Brackenridge & Co., Inc. All rights reserved. We are not responsible for errors or omissions.

Introduction

Whether you are a product manager, marketing executive, entrepreneur, or student, we hope *The Agency Book* will provide you with an interesting overview of the standard of quality available from leading advertising agencies, both large and small. We also hope its information will answer questions, demonstrate possibilities, and create opportunities.

Advertising agencies included in this 1986 edition are proud of their accomplishments. *The Agency Book*'s spreads convey a sense of each agency's style and its implied desire to do more...more creatively for more people. Together, the agencies offer a diversity of capabilities that should satisfy any specific demands of the user.

Your inquiries to the participating companies are welcome. If you have any suggestions or comments regarding this publication, please contact the undersigned.

Gavin Brackenridge
Publisher

Contents

Introduction v
AC&R Advertising, Inc. 3
Albert Frank-Guenther Law Incorporated 5
The Alden Group 7
Ally & Gargano 9
N W Ayer Inc. 11
Backer & Spielvogel, Inc. 13
Barnum Communications, Inc. 15
Basso & Associates, Inc. 17
Biederman & Co. 19
Bozell, Jacobs, Kenyon & Eckhardt 21
Leo Burnett Company, Inc. 23
Burrell Advertising 25
Calvillo, Shevack & Partners, Inc. 27
Campbell-Ewald Company 29
Campbell-Mithun Advertising 31
Chiat/Day inc. Advertising 33
Cole & Weber, Inc. 35
Dancer Fitzgerald Sample, Inc. 37
David Deutsch Associates 39
Davis, Johnson, Mogul & Colombatto, Inc. (DJMC) 41
Della Femina, Travisano & Partners Inc. 43
Doremus & Company 45
Doyle Dane Bernbach Group Inc. 47
The Earle Palmer Brown Companies 49
William Esty Company, Inc. 51
Font & Vaamonde Associates, Inc. 55
Fitzgerald Advertising Inc. 53
Foote, Cone & Belding Communications, Inc. 57
Grant/Jacoby, Inc. 59
Greenstone & Rabasca Advertising, Inc. 61
Haddon Advertising, Inc. 63
HBM/CREAMER, Inc. 65
Healy-Schutte & Company 67

The Jayme Organization, Inc. 69
The Johnston & Johnston Group 71
Kerlick, Switzer & Johnson Advertising 73
keye/donna/pearlstein 75
Knudsen Moore Schropfer, Inc. 77
Laurence, Charles, Free & Lawson, Inc. 79
The Lempert Company, Inc. 81
Levine, Huntley, Schmidt and Beaver, Inc. 83
Levy, King & White 85
Long, Haymes & Carr Incorporated 87
Lord, Geller, Federico, Einstein, Inc. 89
Luckie & Forney, Inc. 91
MARC Advertising 93
McCaffrey and McCall, Inc. 95
McCaffery & Ratner, Inc. 97
McCann-Erickson New York 99
Nationwide Advertising Service Inc. 101
Needham Harper Worldwide, Inc. 103
Posey & Quest, Inc. 105
Richardson, Myers & Donofrio, Inc. 107
Rosenfeld, Sirowitz & Humphrey, Inc. 109
Rumrill-Hoyt Advertising 111
Saatchi & Saatchi Compton Inc. 113
Scali, McCabe, Sloves, Inc. 115
Schneider Parker Jakuc 117
Scott Lancaster Mills Atha 119
Sudler & Hennessey Incorporated 121
J. Walter Thompson U.S.A., Inc. 123
Tracy-Locke 125
VanSant, Dugdale & Co., Inc. 127
Waring & LaRosa, Inc. 129
Zechman and Associates 131
Index 137

The Agency Book

The 1986 edition of *The Agency Book* offers an important sampling of leading advertising agencies' creative work, clients, and overall style. It is designed primarily as a visual reference for marketing executives and other individuals and companies interested in the advertising industry.

In addition to the informative and colorful agency spreads, there is a comprehensive, three-part index which allows for the quick matching of an agency to either a client, a brand, or a particular state or city.

We're the number one agency in the book

And in the hearts of our friends at right.

AC&R Advertising, Inc.

16 East 32nd Street
New York, New York 10016
212.685.2500
Telex: ACR NYK 62156
Cable: ACARWORD NEW YORK

Contact: Stephen Rose
Chairman of the Board

Employees: 230

Founded: 1965

Annual Billings: $115,000,000

Gross Billings by Media:	
Newspaper	4.4%
Magazine	45.1%
DM	1.8%
Outdoor	0.2%
TV	45.3%
Radio	3.2%

People

Stephen Rose/Chairman of the Board

Alvin Chereskin/President

Louis Miano/Vice Chairman of the Board, Director of Creative Services

Kaz Kudo/Executive V.P., Director of Account Services Group

Sheldon Marks/Executive V.P., Management Supervisor

Mort Weinstein/Executive V.P., Director of Marketing Services

Harry Koenig/Executive V.P., Finance, Administration

Karen Amorelli/Senior V.P., Account Supervisor

AC&R Client List

Advertising Checking Bureau (1985)
Air Jamaica (1985)
Aramis (1969)
The Arrow Company (1979)
Beefeater Gin (1985)
Beefeater Gin & Tonic (1985)
Berkley Publishing (1985)
Bridal Originals (1985)
Burrough's English Vodka (1985)
Clinique Laboratories (1969)
Duofold (1983)
EgyptAir (1985)
El San Juan Hotel & Casino (1985)
Esteé Lauder (1966)
Extrom (1984)
German Nat'l. Tourist Office (1974)
Health-tex (1965)
J.A. Henckels (1985)
The Jacob K. Javits Convention Center of New York (1983)
JAZ—Paris (1982)
Jean Lassale (1981)
Keepsake (1983)
Lassale (1982)
Lauder for Men (1984)
Leslie Fay (1980)
London Fog (1970)
Lorus (1982)
Marx & Newman (1986) (Div. U.S. Shoe Corp.)
Maxell (1980)
 Computer Products Division
 Professional/Industrial Division
 Battery Division
Perkin-Elmer (1983)
Philon Compilers (1985)
Hotel Plaza Athenée, N.Y. (1984)
Prescriptives (1982)
Ron Chereskin (1982)
RPM Fashions (1981)
Seiko Time Corp. (1968)
Stanley Blacker (1985)
Sun Line (1981)
TAP Air Portugal (1972)
3M Thinsulate (1984)
Tiffen (1984)
Trifari (1980)
Trusthouse Forte North America (1982)
UMA Shoe Company (1985)
 Bruno Magli
Westbury Hotel, New York (1983)
Wilkes-Barre Times Leader (1985) (Div. of Capital Cities Communications)
Willowbrook Mall (1985)
The Wines of Bordeaux (1984)
Woman's World Magazine (1981)

Brought to you by the agency that "only does financial."

Of course we do financial advertising. And we do it without parallel, for clients such as Drexel Burnham, Shearson Lehman, The Morgan Bank and Citicorp. But our true speciality is in an even broader category—reaching the high net worth individual.

We've done it for AMBAC, with a human approach to a serious business. For M Magazine, with the best-received new publication launch in a decade. For Clingers, with an award-winning new product introduction. For Hilton's VISTA International Hotel, with a 100% increase in weekend occupancy.

We've created effective memorable messages for each of our clients. To talk about how we can create one for you, call Jack Cowell, President and Creative Director at (212) 248-5200.

Brought to you by the agency

Ambac Indemnity Corporation
Newspaper

Clingers™
Television

AFGL Albert Frank-Guenther Law Incorporated

71 Broadway
New York, New York 10006
212.248.5200

Contact: Jack Cowell
President

Employees: 90

Founded: 1872

Annual Billings: $58,000,000

Gross Billings by Media:	
Newspaper	45%
Magazine	25%
DM	5%
Outdoor	5%
TV	5%
Radio	5%
PR	10%

that "only does financial."

M Magazine
Magazine

Vista International Hotels
Outdoor

Before you select an agency, ask yourself some hard questions:

What kind of advertiser are you?

Do you take chances? Every businessman does. And in all advertising there is risk. Are you ready to surrender your fate to a "Trust-us-we'll-take-care-of-everything" kind of agency? Or will you control your advertising so rigidly that your agency will be little more than an order-taker?

The Alden Group avoids both extremes. We work closely with you because *you know your business* better than anyone else, and we want to learn all we can. On the other hand, *we also know our business* better than anyone else. Our decades of experience in health care, optics, travel/leisure, and other industries reduce the risk element in your advertising. Take risks? Of course! But take them intelligently—by choosing an agency that will minimize your risk through sound marketing strategies and creative solutions that make good business sense.

What kind of client-agency relationship are you looking for?

Arm-in-arm, or at arm's length?
The key to the successes we've created for our clients is that we created them *with* our clients. Because behind any great campaign is a successful client-agency relationship based upon shared knowledge, trust, and expertise. Don't take our word; ask our clients.
Partner or assistant?
But sharing is not enough. You need to decide whether you

The Alden Group

535 Fifth Avenue
New York, New York 10017
212.867.6400

Contact: Jack Casper
Executive Vice President

Employees: 18

Founded: 1956

Annual Billings: $10,000,000

Gross Billings by Media: NA

want a partner or an assistant. Some agencies will do what you ask—no more, no less.

The Alden Group is interested only in the role of partner. We're not interested in piecemeal "advertising à la carte." We design *strategies,* not just ads. Because we understand the business of business. With three decades of experience in every phase of advertising, public relations, and marketing communications, we offer you a complete range of services.

What do you expect your advertising to do for you?

Beautiful ads?

Some agencies point with pride to award-winning ads: graphic masterpieces worthy to be hung in galleries. We've won our share of awards—but frankly, though we want our ads to look intriguing, their real "beauty" is their ability to sell your product or image.

Overnight Sales Increase?

Good advertising's effect is cumulative, and we seek *long-range* benefits. Some agencies boast of overnight sales increases, then neglect to add what happened a month later. We prefer to *earn trust* through an ongoing, strategically designed campaign—rather than dazzle with a "quickie" lure that may be forgotten tomorrow.

Stronger Corporate Image? Long-Range Sales?

Now you're talking! We can achieve both. We function as an advocate—arguing your case in public, in common language, creating a link between company and consumer. The Alden Group strives to win both heads and hearts; it's no longer enough to be just creative or just brilliant. We need both! If *you* aren't receiving all you expected from your current advertising or marketing program, contact Alan Jarosz or Gil Numeroff at (212) 867-6400.

The Clio Awards
Since 1980, one agency has won more Clios and top Clios for National Campaign than any other agency.

The One Show
Since The One Show's inception, one agency has won more Gold Awards and more total awards than any other agency.

The American Marketing Association
Since 1980, one agency is tied for the most Grand Effies won with one other agency.

Ally & Gargano

805 Third Avenue
New York, New York 10022
212.688.5300

Contact: Amil Gargano
Chairman, President & CEO

Employees: 230

Founded: 1962

Annual Billings: $150,000,000

Gross Billings by Media:
Newspaper	9%
Magazine	18%
TV	70%
Radio	3%

The agency is Ally & Gargano.

You can call Amil Gargano at (212) 688-5300, and ask for a television reel of what may very well be the best work in the business.

NW Ayer Inc.
New York, Chicago, Detroit, Los Angeles

International offices:
Argentina, Australia, Belgium, France, Germany, Italy, Malaysia, Netherlands, New Zealand, Spain, Sweden, United Kingdom

Ayer Clients
ABC (American Broadcasting Company)
American Lamb Council
American Telephone & Telegraph Co.
Australian Tourist Commission
Australian Trade Commission
Automobile Club of Southern California
Avon Products, Inc.
The Bahamas Ministry of Tourism
BDP™ Company
Bryant Air Conditioning Company
Carl Buddig and Company
Citicorp Savings of Illinois
Club Med Inc.
Dart & Kraft, Inc.
De Beers Consolidated Mines, Ltd.
Deere & Company
Dremel®, Div. Emerson Electric Co.
E.I. du Pont de Nemours & Co. Inc.
First Interstate Bank of Nevada
General Motors Corporation
The Gillette Company
Globe Life and Accident Insurance Company
Honeywell, Inc. MICRO SWITCH Div.
Iberia Airlines
Illinois Bell Telephone Company
KitchenAid, Div. of Hobart Corp.
Leaf, Inc.
National Council on Alcoholism
JCPenney Company, Inc.
Rice Council
The Sun Company
Toshiba America, Inc.
TV Guide® Magazine
U.S. Army Recruiting
U.S. Travel and Tourism Administration
Yamaha Electronics Corporation
Yamaha International Corporation

LOVE & HONOR
CRIES & WHISPERS
PRIDE & PREJUDICE
COMFORT & JOY
HOPES & DREAMS
BLOOD, SWEAT & TEARS
OOOHS & AAAHS
BRAINS & BRAWN

They're words that identify human emotions. They're emotions that can bring a product and a prospect closer together. They're campaigns where the strategies are built on information and insight, and the consumer benefit communicated with feeling.

It's advertising that not only reaches people, but

NW Ayer Inc.

1345 Avenue of the Americas
New York, New York 10105
212.708.5000
Telex: 177307

Contact: Louis T. Hagopian
Chairman & CEO

Employees: 1,197

Founded: 1869

Annual Billings: $826,400,000

Gross Billings by Media:	
Newspaper	9%
Magazine	22%
DM/DR	3%
Outdoor	0.4%
TV	58%
Radio	8%

You're looking smarter than ever—JCPenney

Nothing runs like a Deere—John Deere

The right choice—AT&T

Be All You Can Be—U.S. Army

Pssst. Whispering colors—Avon

A diamond is forever—DeBeers

Ice cream with that ice cream parlor taste—Sealtest

It's Better In The Bahamas.

I only wear mink—Gillette's Mink Difference

touches them. One person at a time. Because that's the way buying decisions are really made.

At Ayer, we call it human contact. Let us tell you about it.

Ayer & human contact.
Nothing sells harder.

A GOOD ADVERTISING CAMPAIGN IS A CAPITAL ASSET.
IT SHOULD BE BUILT WITH AS MUCH CARE AS A FACTORY.
AND ABANDONED WITH AS MUCH RELUCTANCE.

Miller Brewing Company
Lite Beer

Campbell Soup Company

Helene Curtis Industries, Inc.
Finesse Shampoo and Conditioner

The Paddington Corporation
Baileys Original Irish Cream

Miller Brewing Company
Meister Bräu Beer

Hyundai Motor America
Excel Automobile

Campbell Soup Company

NCR Corporation

Miller Brewing Company
Lite Beer

Helene Curtis Industries, Inc.
Suave Shampoo and Conditioner

The Quaker Oats Company
Celeste Frozen Pizza

Campbell Soup Company
V-8 Juice

The Quaker Oats Company
Chewy Granola Bars

The Quaker Oats Company
Captain Crunch Cereal

Backer & Spielvogel, Inc.

11 West 42nd Street
New York, New York 10036
212.556.5200
Telex: 703 790
Cable: BSV New York

Contact: Carl Spielvogel
Chairman & CEO

Employees: 625

Founded: 1979

Annual Billings: $425,000,000

Gross Billings by Media: NA

The Quaker Oats Company
Gatorade

The Paddington Corporation
J & B Rare Scotch

Philip Morris, U.S.A.
Parliament Cigarettes

Foundation For Savings Institutions, Inc.

**The Barnum Philosophy:
Science, Creativity, Service**

The Science Base. As a science-based marketing communications agency for the healthcare industry, we start with a foundation of science. We maximize the use of existing information and augment it with timely new data under the direction of a professional medical staff in conjunction with a large group of consultants.

The Marketing Challenge. Identification of marketing needs is the challenge that is effectively met by our staff of healthcare and advertising professionals with experience in most product categories. Working closely with our clients, we use our scientific and marketing expertise to meet their specific objectives and goals.

The Creative Process. Our unique contribution is the integration of science, marketing and communications skills in producing a distinctive creative product.

Communications Strategy. Broad-based experience in all standard as well as innovative new media provide the means for developing communications strategies ideally suited to achieving specific objectives. Communications plans include advertising, sales promotion materials, direct mail campaigns, medical education programs, films and audiovisual materials, and public relations.

Dynamics. Communications is a dynamic, interactive process. As a product or service moves through its many phases—pre-launch, launch, growth, maturity—we continue to develop and provide programs, materials, and services that keep pace with the changing demands of the marketplace.

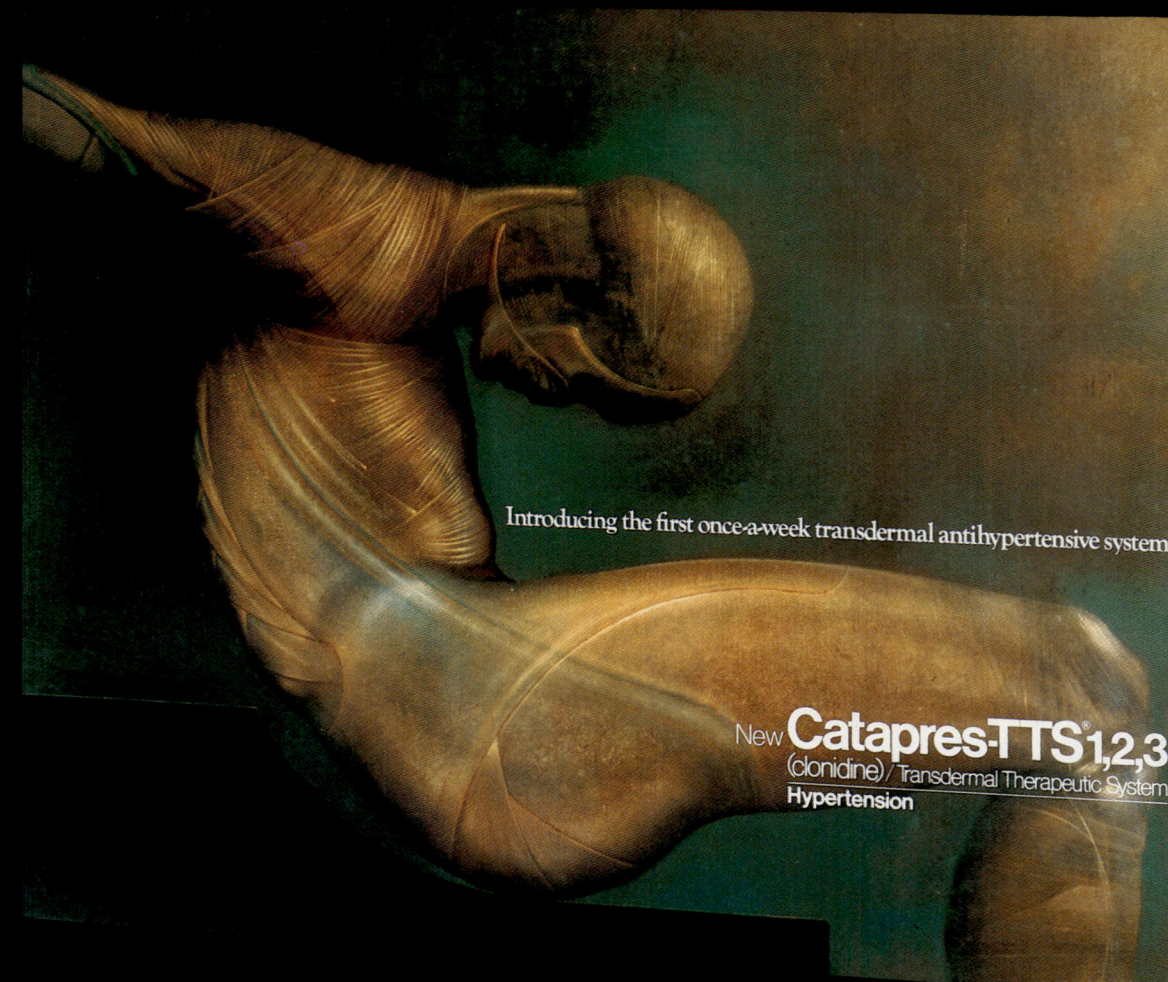

© 1986, BARNUM COMMUNICATIONS, INC.

Barnum Communications, Inc.

500 Fifth Avenue
New York, New York 10110
212.221.7363

Contacts: H.J. Barnum, Jr., M.D.
Chairman of the Board;
Dorothy M. Philips, Ph.D.
President

Employees: 85

Founded: 1975

Annual Billings: $45,000,000

Gross Billings by Media:	
Newspaper	5%
Magazine	12%
DM/Collateral	22%
TV	5%
Radio	1%
Bus/Trade Publs.	55%

...Speaking powerfully to healthcare professionals.

714/641

Basso & Associates, Inc.

Post Office Box 8030
Newport Beach, California 92660
714.641.0111

Contact: Joseph Basso
President

Employees: 37

Founded: 1972

Annual Billings: $25,000,000

Gross Billings by Media:
Newspaper	23%
Magazine	27%
DM	3%
Outdoor	2%
TV	35%
Radio	10%

0111

Call this number for a direct line.

All the Nuts and Bolts... You could easily mistake us for just another small creative agency.

Certainly, we have a strong creative bent.

(The Biederman of Biederman & Co. used to be creative director of one of the country's largest agencies.)

Where we're different from most small shops, however, is that we don't just limit ourselves to creative.

In fact, we have everything the big agencies do...things like highly professional research, media and marketing support services.

But since we're smaller, our management gets involved in your business.

And it doesn't take forever to get us moving.

Some of the Caviar

–Award-winning (and hard-working) creative

–All our senior people come from top 20 advertising agencies. Or high-level client positions.

–In-house public relations, direct response, sales promotion

–We spend as much on marketing support services as agencies two or three times our size.

–Current clients show our range: from Fortune 500 to growing, entrepreneurial companies.

Nuts and caviar.™

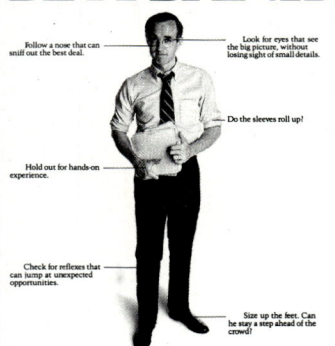

The Agency Book **19**

Our clients

Canadian Imperial Bank Group (U.S.)

Deloitte Haskins & Sells

ITT Corporation
Corporate, International Telecom

State of Israel—Tourist Office

Tower Air

Winsight

Biederman & Co.

100 Fifth Avenue
New York, New York 10011
212.929.7200

Contact: Barry Biederman
Chairman

Employees: 46

Founded: 1984

Annual Billings: $31,000,000

Gross Billings by Media:

Newspaper	10%
Magazine	36%
DM	1%
Outdoor	3%
TV	45%
Radio	5%

bolts and

  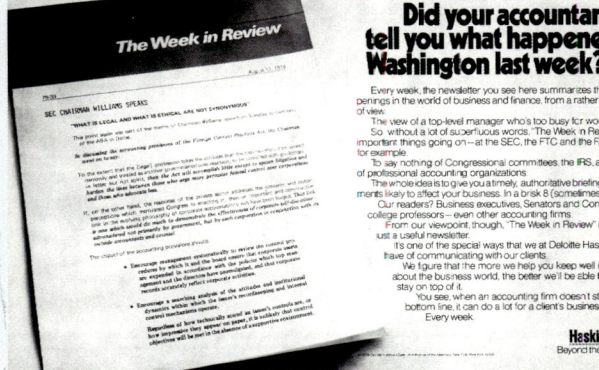

Announcing the birth of Bozell, Jacobs, Kenyon & Eckhardt.

The 12th largest agency in America.

With worldwide billings of 1.2 billion dollars. (And baby, that's just the beginning.)

Fully-staffed offices in 11 major U.S. cities. Plus 18 service offices and an international network in 35 countries.

And a full range of specialized services: Public Relations, Healthcare, Direct Response, Yellow Pages, Co-op. And more.

Our creative approach aims for the heart as well as the brain.

Because reaching people isn't enough. You have to touch them, surprise them, involve them.

That's how we help our clients get close to the customers they're trying to reach.

Find out how we can help you. Call Charles D. Peebler, Chief Executive Officer. (212) 206-5000.

Bozell, Jacobs, Kenyon & Eckhardt

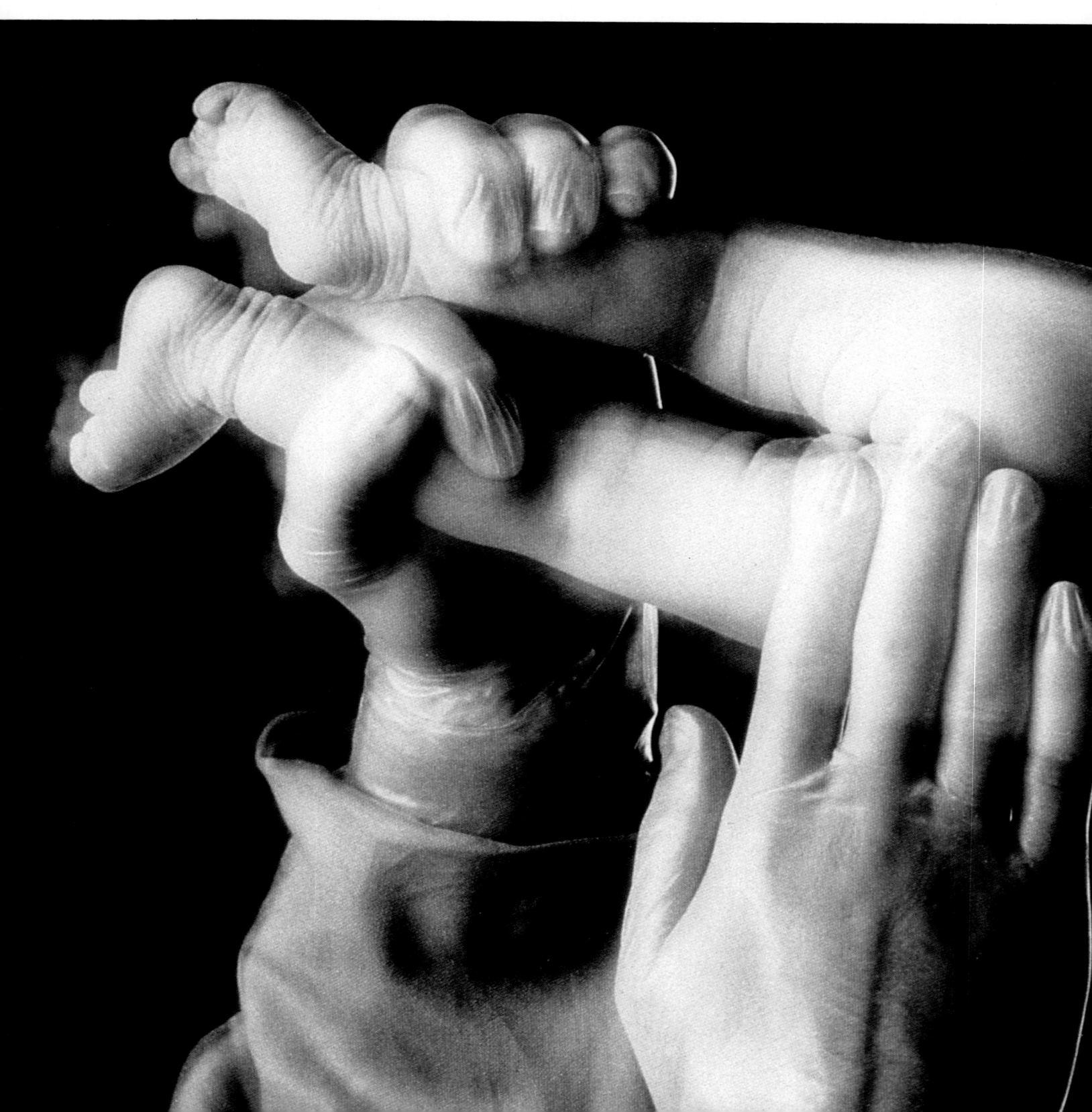

Bozell, Jacobs, Kenyon & Eckhardt

40 West 23rd Street
New York, New York 10010
212.206.5000
Telex: 234904

Contact: Charles D. Peebler, Jr.
CEO

Employees: 2,500

Founded: 1921

Annual Billings: $1,200,000,000

Gross Billings by Media:	
Newspaper	14%
Magazine	23.7%
DM	1%
Outdoor	1.8%
TV	43.3%
Radio	16.2%

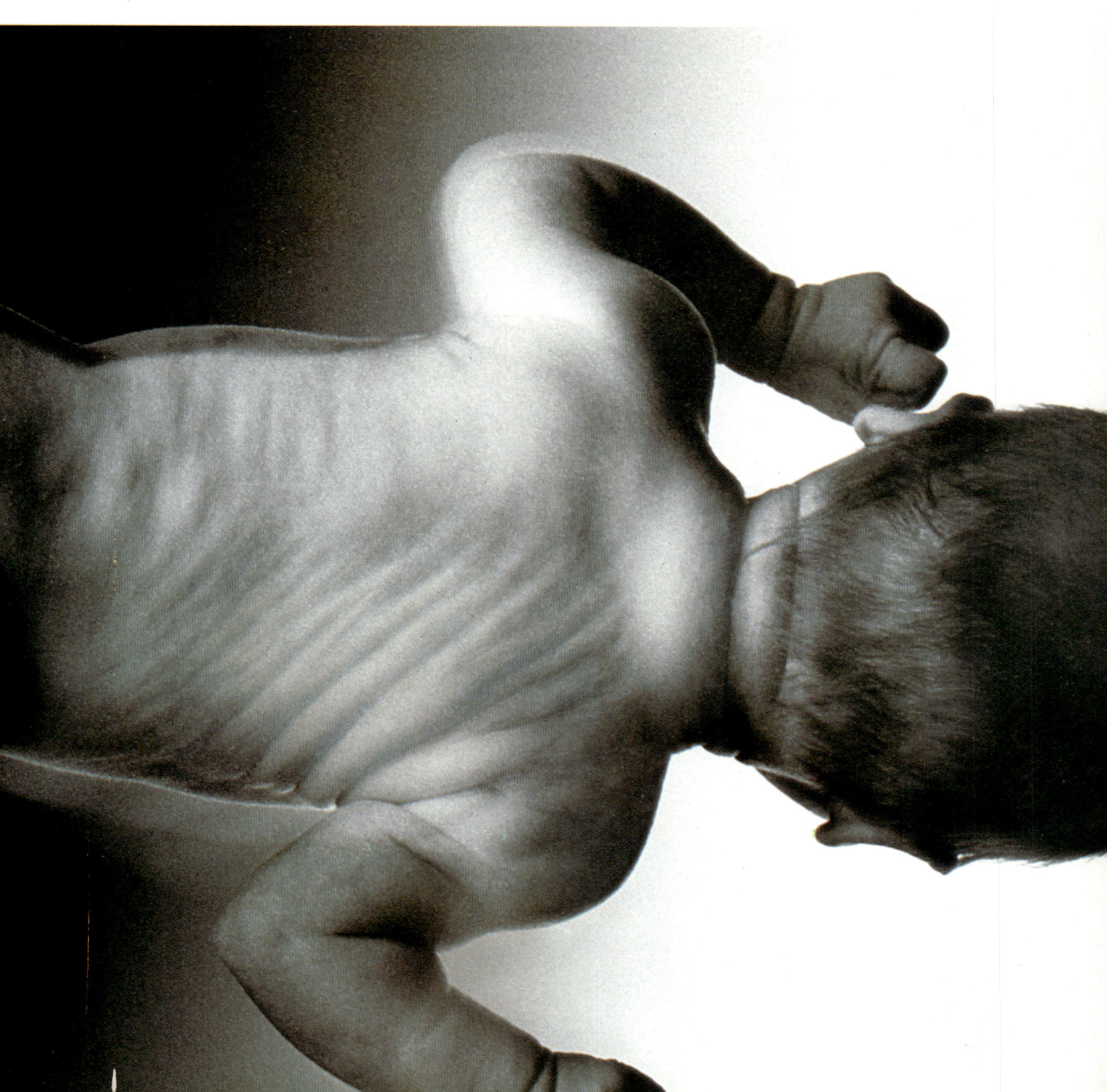

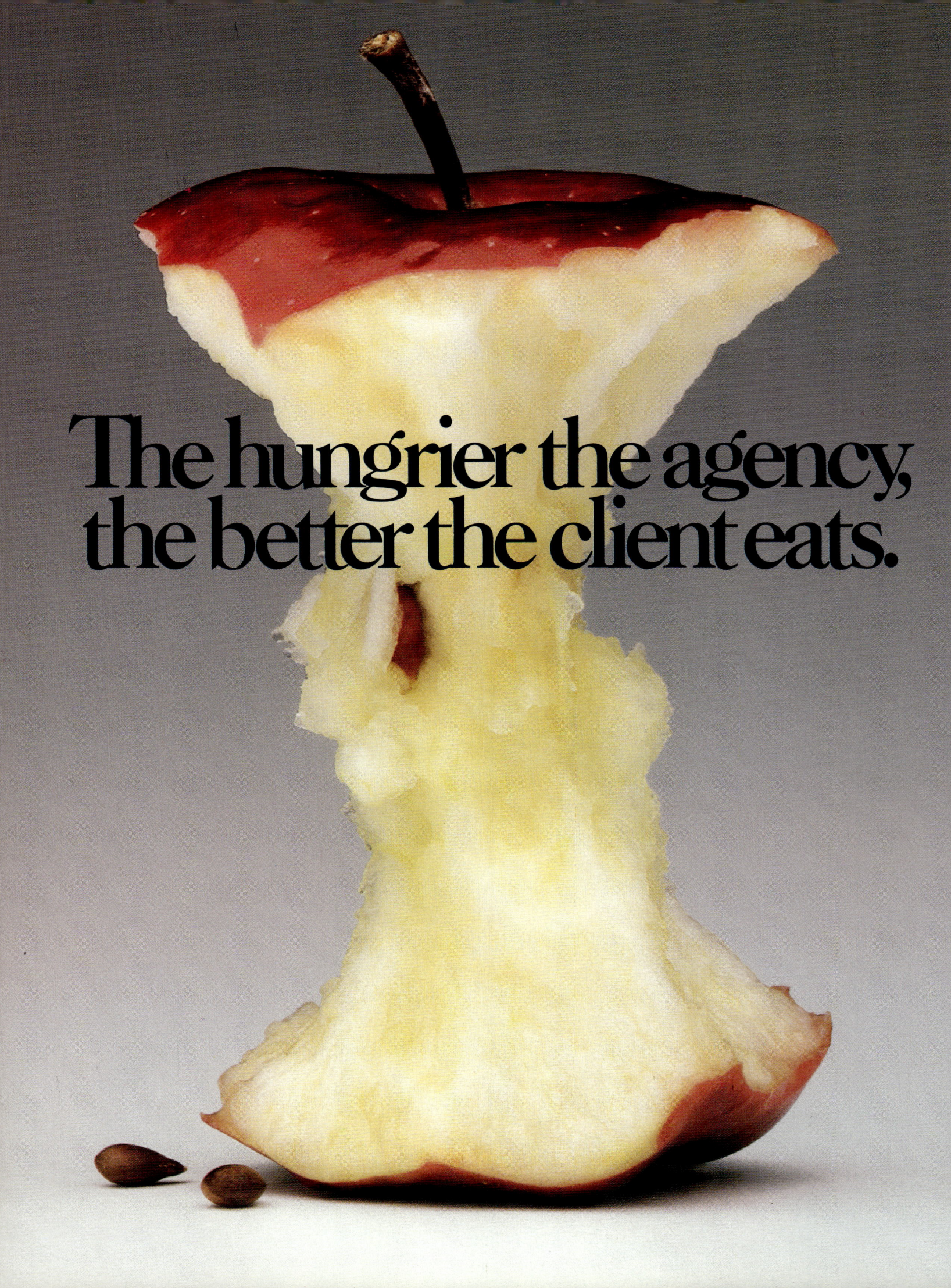

And the longer they stay.

Allstate Insurance Companies	28 years
Association of Chicagoland McDonald's Restaurants	*
Beatrice Companies, Inc.	2 years
Commonwealth Edison Company	31 years
General Motors Corporation	18 years
Harris Trust & Savings Bank	33 years
Hewlett-Packard	1 year
H.J. Heinz Company	11 years
Keebler Company	17 years
Kellogg Company (Including Salada, Whitney's and Mrs. Smith's Frozen Foods Co.)	36 years
Kraft, Inc.	1 year
Mars, Inc.	*
The Maytag Company	30 years
McDonald's Corporation	3 years
Memtek Products (Memorex Consumer Products)	15 years
Miller Brewing Company	3 years
Philip Morris Incorporated	31 years
The Pillsbury Company (Including Green Giant Company)	50 years
The Procter & Gamble Company	33 years
RCA Consumer Electronics	9 years
Schenley Industries, Inc.	17 years
Seven-Up Company	2 years
Star-Kist Foods, Incorporated	27 years
Union Carbide Corporation	24 years
Unocal Corporation (Union Oil Company of California)	47 years
United Airlines	20 years

*Less than 1 year

Leo Burnett Company, Inc.

Prudential Plaza
Chicago, Illinois 60601
312.565.5959
Telex: 254098 or 254514
Cable: LEOBUR CGO
TWX: 910-221-5064 or
910-221-5067

Contact: Hall Adams, Jr.
Chairman & CEO, U.S.A.

Employees: 3,545

Annual Billings: $1,680,000,000

Gross Billings by Media:

Newspaper	9%
Magazine	16%
Outdoor	9%
TV	65%
Radio	1%

Leo Burnett International

Adelaide	Madrid
Amsterdam	Manila
Athens	Melbourne
Auckland	Mexico City
Bangkok	Milan
Beirut	Montreal
Bogota	Panama City
Brisbane	Paris
Brussels	San Juan
Buenos Aires	Santa Domingo
Cairo	Santiago
Caracas	Sao Paulo
Copenhagen	Singapore
Frankfurt	Sydney
Hong Kong	Taipei
Kuala Lumpur	Tokyo
Lausanne	Toronto
London	Zurich

What's Black, professional, worth over 50 million dollars, and not a basketball player?

Burrell Advertising

625 N. Michigan Avenue
Chicago, Illinois 60611
312.226.4600

Contact: Chuck Wimbley
Senior Vice-President/
Director of Account Services

Employees (U.S.): 117

Founded: 1971

Annual Billings (U.S.): $53,000,000

Gross Billings by Media:	
Newspaper	3%
Magazine	15%
Outdoor	4%
TV	63%
Radio	15%

Clients

Coca-Cola USA
McDonald's Corporation
The Procter & Gamble Company
Brown-Forman Distillers
Ford Motor Company
Coca-Cola International
Georgia Power Company

Jack Daniel Distillery
Johnson Products Company
Joseph Garneau Company
L'eggs Products
The Stroh Brewery Company
Beatrice U.S. Food
Johnson Publishing Company

Burrell Advertising Inc.

Our guarantee to our clients: Targeted Visibility

Our Clients
Alno Kitchen Cabinets, Inc.
Argenti
Avis
Drexel Burnham Lambert
The Equitable
Firestone Building Products Company
Goldline Laboratories
Hartmarx
Johnson & Higgins
Mead Corporation
Monet Jewelry
Phillips-Van Heusen Corporation
Restaurant Associates
Sanyo Business Systems
Tissot, S.A.
Uniden Corporation of America
Wild Turkey Premium Spirits

MONET JEWELRY

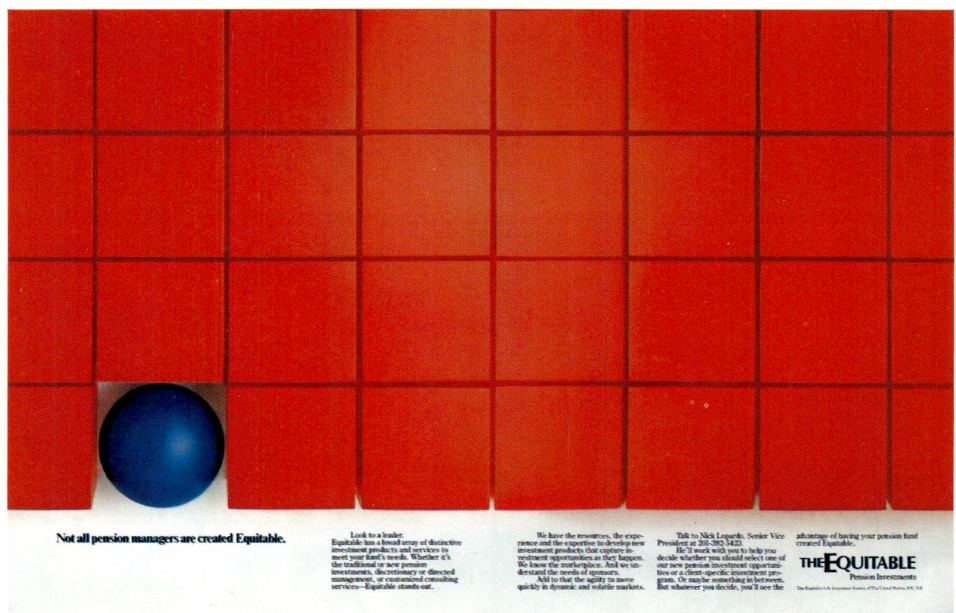
THE EQUITABLE

ADIDAS, U.S.A.

TISSOT, S.A.

The Agency Book **27**

Calvillo, Shevack & Partners, Inc.

1350 Avenue of the Americas
New York, New York 10019
212.245.7300

Contact: Ric Calvillo
Chairman

Employees: 75

Annual Billings: $52,000,000

Gross Billings by Media: NA

UNIDEN CORPORATION OF AMERICA

PHILLIPS-VAN HEUSEN CORPORATION

MEAD CORPORATION

ARGENTI

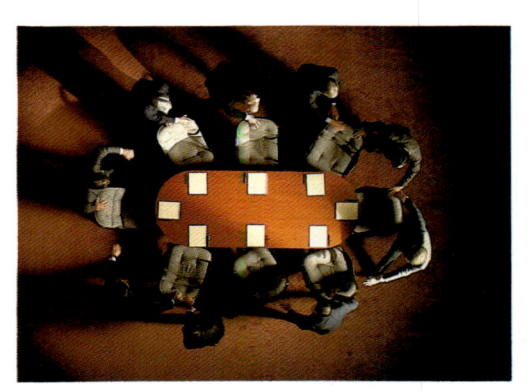

HARTMARX

Early on we saw the potential Chuck Yeager had as a spokesman. For three years now he's been building awareness and sales for AC-Delco parts.

Picking up nearly two full market share points was the result of these sharp substrategies for National Car Rental. Here, the award-winning Camaro promotion.

One of the great turnaround stories is Eastern Airlines in 1985, and this Frequent Traveler promotion—another award-winner—is one of the reasons.

In a difficult year for lodging chains, Howard Johnson has brought business travelers back with this campaign and an innovative early-morning media strategy.

While other mass after-shaves decline in sales, Mennen Skin Bracer continues to grow in sales and share, through a highly effective creative and media strategy.

GMAC competes with banks for car loans, and very successfully. One reason is this entertaining but aggressively competitive television campaign.

We seem to specialize in competitive campaigns: If ice-cream begins to lose ground to Tofutti, this award-winning commercial will be the reason.

Can powerful emotion power the sale of trucks? Chevrolet proves it can with this "Lean on Me" campaign, one of the outstanding automotive campaigns for 1985. And of course—Chevy trucks are #1 in sales.

Further proof that research guidance and great creative execution make an ideal combination: this image-building award-winning television campaign for Rockwell International.

IT WORKED FOR THEM.
IT WILL WORK FOR YOU.

Campbell-Ewald Company

ADVERTISING / WELL DIRECTED

30400 Van Dyke Avenue
Warren, Michigan 48093
313.574.3400

Contact: Richard D. O'Connor
Chairman

Employees: 766

Founded: 1911

Annual Billings: $450,000,000

Gross Billings by Media:

Newspaper	2%
Magazine	26%
DM	3%
Outdoor	2%
TV	56%
Radio	11%

The trouble with us is we're not very sophisticated. Take the term "creative philosophy." Do we have one? Well, yes—but it's not based upon anything complicated, like "psychographic segmentation" or "emotional involvement." No.

Our creative philosophy is based on money.

We think that advertising probably costs too much. So every time you do an ad, it ought to cost less than the ad before.

The media won't cost less. It never does. The only way for the cost of ads to go down is for their efficiency to go up.

This is a philosophy you will probably agree with. Everybody does. We haven't got it patented.

And while lots of people agree with our philosophy, not many can make it work.

We might be the only agency that does make it work.

If you were our client, here is what we would be saying to you:
A. Have a strategic plan and follow it.
B. Do research and respect it.
C. Always build on the past.
D. Stay simple. Be firm.
E. Have people who believe in A, B, C, D.

A. "Have a strategic plan and follow it."
We know how depressing it is when you've just had a brilliant idea and somebody says "Yes, but is it on strategy?" Be glad that stubborn person is in the meeting. If you don't take the trouble to design a strategy, and make certain that you stick to it, you'll never know how you got from X to Y. And if you don't know that, how will you do it the next time?

B. "Do research and respect it."
Some of our clients do more research than others. None of them does as much as we would like. We have a selfish reason for saying this: We think we *use* research better than most agencies.

Anybody can collect facts or process data. Not everybody can spot strategic implications in the data or pull an advertising strategy out of the numbers. We do it all the time.

But you can't use research well unless you respect it. You can't ignore it when it disagrees with you. You shouldn't pretend that a couple of focus groups substitute for really projectable data, especially when you're betting a lot of money on the strategy.

Our creative people live easily and work well with research. And we have both the marketing successes and the creative awards to prove it.

C. "Always build on the past."
It always surprises us when marketers forget what happened last year or two years ago. "Reinventing the wheel" is probably the most expensive (and ultimately the most wasteful) practice in planning advertising—starting from scratch every year, when there is no real need to do so.

If we were working with you, our presentations would begin with what went right and what went wrong last time: Nothing teaches like a mistake. Many of our clients maintain tracking studies and expect us to improve our performance every year. We like to play by such rules.

We follow the advice of two famous American philosophers, George Santayana and Bert Lance.

> "Those who cannot remember the past are condemned to repeat it."
> –G. Santayana
> *The Life of Reason*

> "If it ain't broke, don't fix it."
> –B. Lance
> Carter Administration, 1977

D. "Stay simple. Be firm."
These are really rules for creative. It goes without saying that the best creative work is simple. The hard part is holding off all the helpful people who want to improve the work. That's where the "Be firm" comes in.

You should expect disagreement from us from time to time, and leave room for it. Figuring out what a client wants and giving it to him is a lousy way to work. We know because we've done it when there was no other way. You can't change a client unless you keep him.

Tell you one thing, though. We will always be able to tell you *why* we think a particular ad or commercial will work. We don't expect acts of faith, not at first, anyway. And another thing: The idea will always be strong enough to work even if the production budget is small. Execution is very important, but it isn't everything.

Are you beginning to get some idea of what we'll be like to work with? We'll bring you strong and simple ideas. They will be presented forcefully, by people who believe in them. You will like this way of working.

E. "Have people who believe in A, B, C, D."
Now we come to the central issue: people.

Go back to those "principles" we listed. Our A-B-C-D. Notice the language: "stick," "respect," "build," "firm." These are qualities of character.

There seems to be no mention of *creativity* which, after all, is what an advertising agency is all about. We don't think we need to trumpet that concern: You know it and so do we. Our creative directors, writers, art directors and producers compete successfully with the best in our business: Last year we won 69 major creative awards in New York, Chicago, Los Angeles and Detroit.

Still, we put great emphasis on character. It is not enough to *have* a great idea. The difficult thing to do is execute it. Bring it to living effectiveness.

It takes *character* to do this.

Sticking to a plan. Respecting data. Using the past. Holding firm.

We've always done this in managing our own business. And having doubled our size in the past five years, we can say our way of working is unique to us. We developed it all by ourselves.

And *it works*. For us. For a blue-chip list of *very* successful clients. We know there are a few companies out there as well run as those who are already our clients.

We just have to find them.

We're at (313) 574-3400.

BECAUSE IT WORKS.

THE NEW AGE AT CAMPBELL·MI

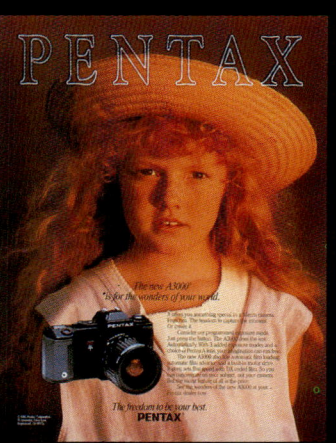

Pentax 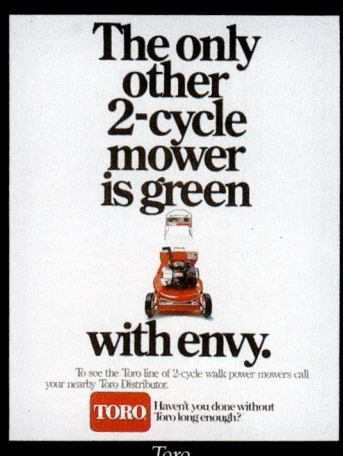   *Toro*    *Land O Lakes* 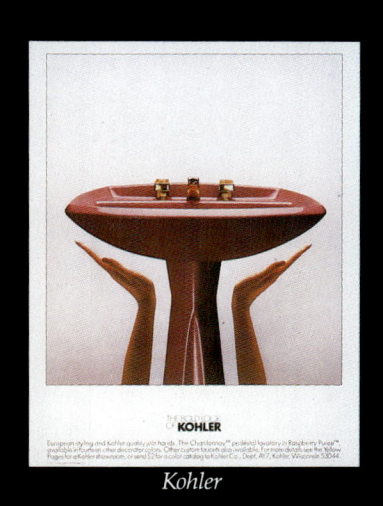   *Kohler*

Halo Lighting    *Kroger*     *Dairy Queen* 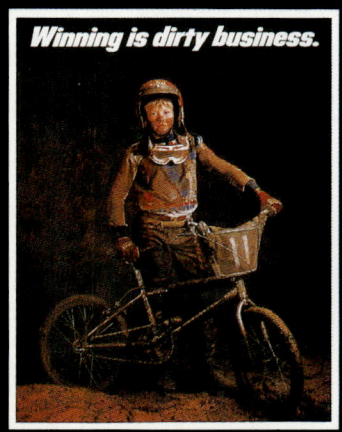   *Schwinn*

General Mills    *Andersen Windows* 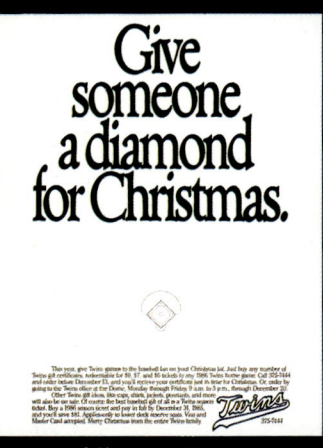   *Minnesota Twins*    *Chicago Sun Times*

Campbell-Mithun Advertising

222 South Ninth Street
Minneapolis, Minnesota 55402
612.347.1000

Contact: William Dunlap
Chairman of the Board & CEO

Employees: 726

Founded: 1933

Annual Billings: $360,000,000

Gross Billings by Media:

Newspaper	8%
Magazine	25%
Outdoor	2%
TV	54%
Radio	8%

CAMPBELL·MITHUN ADVERTISING

737 North Michigan Avenue
Chicago, Illinois 60611
312.565.3800

Contact: William Stein
President

New spirit. New energy. New talents. Producing new creative with compelling strategy, astonishing execution. Renewing the commitment to our clients' success and continuing growth. We're as proud of them as we are of the work.

Allis-Chalmers Corporation
American Egg Board
Andersen Corporation
Ashley's Outlet Stores
Automation Products Division, Eaton Corporation
Babson Bros. Co.
Barton Brands, Ltd.
Cargill, Inc.
Chicago and North Western Transportation Co.
Chicago SUN-TIMES
Chicago Symphony Orchestra
Computer Depot
Consul Restaurant Corporation
Control Data
Conway Import Company, Inc.
Cutler-Hammer Division, Eaton Corporation
Dynascan, Inc.
Eaton Corporation
General Mills, Inc.
Great Clips, Inc.
Halo Lighting, Cooper Industries
Heller Financial, Inc.
Honeywell, Inc.
International Dairy Queen, Inc.
International Multifoods
Interstate Brands
John Morrell & Company
S.C. Johnson & Son, Inc.
Kimberly-Clark Corporation
Kohler Co.
Kraft, Inc.

The Kroger Company
Kroger Manufacturing Group
Lamaur Inc.
Land O'Lakes, Inc.
The Larsen Company
Masonite Corporation
Mead Johnson & Company
Midway Airlines
Minnesota Twins Baseball Club
Mirro Corporation
Montgomery Ward
NBI, Inc.
National Alliance of Business
Nickerson American Plant Breeders
Norwest Corporation
Pentax Corporation
Pet, Inc
Poly-Tech
Preferred Meal Systems
The Quaker Oats Company
Ralston Purina Company
Schwinn Bicycle Company
Specialty Brands, Inc.
The St. Paul Companies, Inc.
3M
Tombstone Pizza Corporation
The Toro Company
The Trane Company
United HealthCare Corporation
Welch Foods, Inc.
Wilson Foods Corporation

"The client made us do it."

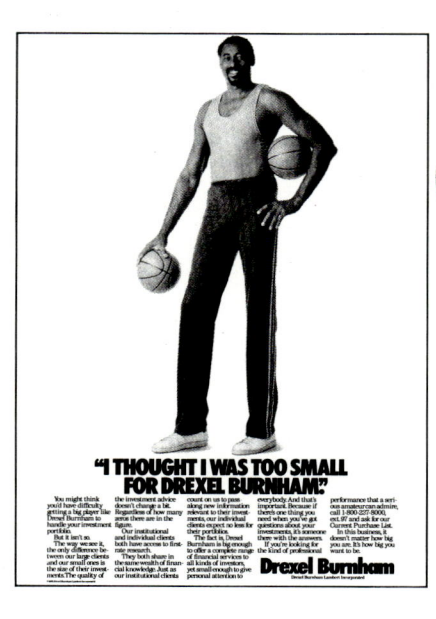

It's always there when you need it.

Apple

Pizza Hut

Yamaha

Bazooka

Make us do it for you.
Call Gene Cameron
(213) 622-7454

Chiat/Day inc. Advertising

517 South Olive Street
Los Angeles, California 90013
213.622.7454

Contact: Gene Cameron
Executive V.P.

Employees: 350

Founded: 1968

Annual Billings: $290,000,000

Gross Billings by Media: NA

Chiat/Day

79 Fifth Avenue
New York, New York 10003
212.807.4000

77 Maiden Lane
San Francisco, California 94109
415.465.3000

Client List

Apple Computer, Inc.
Ashton-Tate
Ask Computer Systems, Inc.
BusinessLand
California Cooler, Inc.
Christian Dior
Collagen Corporation
Drexel Burnham Lambert, Inc.
Gaines Foods, Inc.
Gillette Oral-B Laboratories
William Grant & Sons, Inc.
Intel Corporation
Libby, McNeil & Libby, Inc.
Maxicare Health Plan
Miles Laboratories, Inc.
Miller Brewing Company
Mitsubishi Electric Sales America, Inc.

Netair International Corp.
Nike, Inc.
Nikon Precision Incorporated
NYNEX Information Resources
Pizza Hut, Inc.
Plus Development Corp.
Porsche Cars North America
3M-Data Recording Products Division
Topps Chewing Gum, Inc.
Trump Casino Hotel
U.C. Berkeley Foundation
Whitney Museum of American Art
Worlds of Wonder, Inc.
Yamaha Motor Corp., USA

We Are The

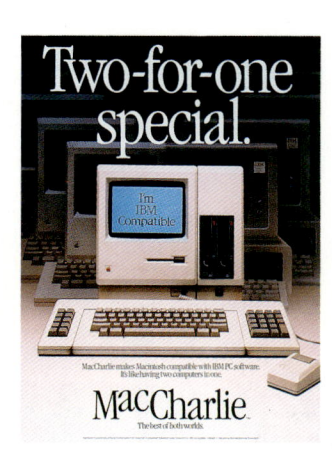

West.

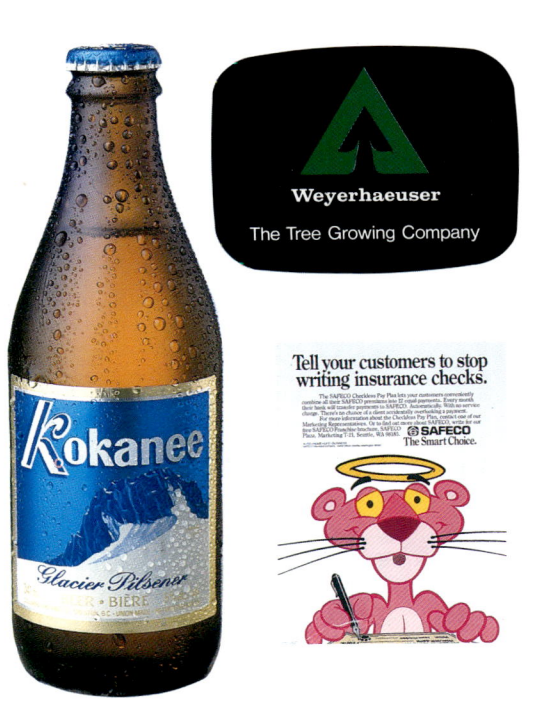

Cole & Weber, Inc.

16040 Christensen Rd. South
Seattle, Washington 98188
206.433.6200
Telex: 320121

Contacts: Hal Dixon, Chairman;
Hal Newsom, President

Employees: 262

Founded: 1931

Annual Billings: $135,000,000

Gross Billings by Media: NA

Cole & Weber

Cole & Weber is a uniquely western agency, with offices in major North American cities.

We work for international accounts like Boeing, Weyerhaeuser, Westin Hotels of Mexico, Kenworth, SAFECO, World Airways, and Pacific Western Airlines.

Creative excellence has helped build this seven-office complex into the nation's third largest, Western-based agency.

The operation is a full-service company, with public relations, marketing, collateral, and research capabilities in each office. Plus the world-wide resources of Ogilvy & Mather.

The agency has doubled in size every five years for the past twenty years. In 1986, we will exceed $150 million.

Offices

Seattle, Washington

San Francisco, California

Los Angeles, California

Portland, Oregon
Morton/Cole & Weber

Salt Lake City, Utah
TPC/Cole & Weber

Vancouver, BC, Canada
WestCan/Cole & Weber

Calgary, Alberta, Canada
WestCan/Cole & Weber

At DFS, our job is to create ambitious advertising as bright and shiny as the top of the Chrysler Building.

Ambitious Advertising is an idea that captures the essence of DFS. In action, it is the kind of advertising that can close the gap between where your business is and where it can be. It sets lofty goals, then employs a disciplined process to achieve them. It succeeds for these reasons:

OPTIMISM. Ambitious Advertising believes it can move people, deliver a bigger audience, sell more product. Our track record reaffirms that optimism. We handle 21 #1 brands including Toyota, the #1 Import Car and Truck; Sheer Energy, the #1 Pantyhose; Bounty, the #1 Paper Towel and Cheerios, the #1 Cereal.

INTELLIGENCE. Ambitious Advertising develops unique strategies grounded on a genuine understanding of people's needs—rational, emotional or both. It recognizes that uniqueness, inventiveness, imagination are critical—in copy, in strategy, in media, in promotion, in research.

DISCIPLINE. Ambitious Advertising disciplines itself to be imaginative and innovative every single time it executes an idea.

PRESSURE. Ambitious Advertising puts the pressure on and keeps it on. Pressure creates the leverage needed to produce advertising and marketing programs that generate response greater than the dollars spent.

SPIRIT. Ambitious Advertising brings good news to people. It is proud of its mission; so, it puts its best face forward and asks for the order.

These are the reasons why you're already familiar with so many of our campaigns. "Gentlemen Prefer Hanes." "Toyota—Who Could Ask For Anything More." "Bounty—The Quicker Picker Upper." "Nothing Beats A Great Pair of L'eggs." "Choose Fresh. Choose Wendy's."

The list goes on and on, filled with advertising as bright and shiny as the top of our home—the Chrysler Building. Ambitious Advertising. At DFS, we're dedicated to it because we want to close the gap between where you are and where you can be.

Dancer Fitzgerald Sample, Inc.

Chrysler Building
405 Lexington Avenue
New York, New York 10174
212.661.0800
Telex: 664905
Cable: DAFISAM

Contact: Gary M. Susnjara
Chairman, DFS/NY

Employees: 4,958

Founded: 1932

Annual Billings: $2,224,000,000

Gross Billings by Media:

Newspaper/Supps.	4%
Magazines	14%
Outdoor	1%
TV	75%
Radio	6%

DFS/NY Client List

Advertising Council, Inc.
American Automobile Association
American Cyanamid
Shulton, Inc.
Beneficial Management Corp.
Blue Bell, Inc.
Cadbury—U.S.A.
CPC International, Inc.
Best Foods Division
Consolidated Edison Co. of New York, Inc.
Donnelley Directory
Donnelley Information Publishing
Entre Computer Centers, Inc.
Fresh Air Fund
General Electric Co.
Big G Cereal Division
Fundimensions
Kenner Parker
New Business Division
Sperry Division
Yoplait USA, Inc.
Helene Curtis
Lorillard Division of Loews Theatres, Inc.
Martlet Importing Co. Inc.
The Masters Brewing Company
Mexican Tourism
Fonatur
Mexican National Tourist Council
Nabisco Brands, Inc.
Life Savers, Inc.
Biscuit Division
Procter & Gamble Co.
Procter & Gamble Co. of Canada, Ltd.
Republic Airlines, Inc.
Royal Crown Cola Company
Sara Lee Corporation
Bali Co.
Hanes Corporation
Popsicle Industries
State of Florida, Department of Citrus
Special Olympics
Toyota Canada, Inc.
Toyota Dealer Associations
Toyota Motor Sales U.S.A., Inc.
U.S. News & World Report
Wendy's International, Inc.

Jim	David	Rocco	Kevin	Don
President	Chairman	Vice	Media	Creative
Moo Shu	*Shrimp*	Chairman	Director	Director
Beef	*with*	*Ta-Chin*	*Ginger*	*Sweet*
	Lobster	*Beef*	*Chicken*	*and*
	Sauce			*Sour Pork*

Great advertising doesn't always happen 9 to 5.

David Deutsch Associates

655 Third Avenue
New York, New York 10017
212.867.0044
Telex: 225749 DDA UR

Contact: Jim Aucone
President

Founded: 1969

Annual Billings: $33,000,000

Gross Billings by Media:	
Newspaper	10%
Magazine	30%
DM/Collateral	6%
Outdoor	2%
TV	30%
Radio	15%
Business Publications	7%

Client List
Air Afrique
British Petroleum
CBS Publications
CommTek Publishing
Crouch & Fitzgerald
Damon
Frette Fine Linens
Glamour Magazine
P.H. Glatfelter Company
Gulf Air

National Securities & Research
Oneida Silversmiths
People's Bank of Connecticut
The Pontiac Dealers of NY/NJ/CT
RCA Global Communications
Reeves International
Samsung Electronics America
The Singer Company
Streets & Co.
Louis Vuitton

Chun Yung Lau
Delivery Boy
Wok 3rd Avenue

WE BUILD TRAFFIC

Davis, Johnson, Mogul & Colombatto, Inc. (DJMC)

3435 Wilshire Blvd.
Los Angeles, California 90010
213.383.3332

Contact: Brad A. Ball
President

Employees: 220

Founded: 1958

Annual Billings: $120,000,000

Gross Billings by Media:

Newspaper	17%
Magazine	3%
DM	2%
Outdoor	3%
TV	53%
Radio	22%

DJMC

731 Market Street, San Francisco, CA 94103 (415) 546-1100,
Dick Brennan, V.P. Operations

101 SW Main St., Suite 1200, Portland OR 97204, (503) 241-7781,
Jane Bassett, V.P. Operations

1615 York Rd., Suite 305, Lutherville, MD 21093, (301) 823-7500,
Henry Smith, Gen. Manager

Division:
Ad Latina (Hispanic Advertising & Marketing Specialists)
(213) 251-4400   3435 Wilshire Blvd., Suite 720, Los Angeles, Ca., 90010
Julio Castellanos, SR VP, Managing Director

Subsidiary:
Gelman & Gray Communications, Inc. (Public Relations)
(213) 251-4600
3435 Wilshire Blvd., Suite 908, Los Angeles, Ca., 90010   Chuck Gelman, President & CEO   Rosalind Gray, Executive VP

Bandini Fertilizer
California Sports, Inc. / The Forum
CasaBlanca Fan Company
Chief Auto Parts
Disney On Ice of Northern California
Flavorland Foods, Inc.
Glendale Federal Savings & Loan
Grace Home Centers West
Greater Los Angeles Visitors & Convention Bureau
KABC-TV
KGO-TV
Knott's Berry Farm
Knott's Food Products
Lamborghini West
Marine World/Africa U.S.A.
McDonald's Central Coast Operators Assn.
McDonald's Central Valley Operators Assn.
McDonald's Operators Assn. of Bakersfield, Calif.
McDonald's Operators Assn. of Southern Calif.
McDonald's Operators Assn. of San Francisco/Monterey Bay Area
McDonald's Operators Assn. of Sacramento Central Valley
McDonald's Operators Assn. of Medford, Oregon
McDonald's Operators Assn. of Portland, Oregon
Mid-Atlantic Toyota Dealers Assn. (Five State Region)
Mid-Atlantic Toyota Distributors, Inc.
Northern California Toyota Dealers Adv. Assn.
Northwest Toyota Dealers Adv. Assn. (Five State Region)
Ralphs Grocery Company
Ringling Bros. Circus of Northern California
Southern California Toyota Dealers Adv. Assn.
U.S. Borax

This is dedicated to the guys who grew up watching Jackie Robinson torturing a pitcher just by leading off third base.
He was beautiful to watch.
He would come roaring around second and slide into third base like he was going to carry any third baseman who dared get in his way right up into the Ebbets Field stands.
Then he would get up, dust himself off, stand on the base and ignore the pitcher for the first few seconds.
But the pitcher, the pitcher couldn't take his eyes off him. And if you were a young kid sitting in the bleachers, you couldn't take your eyes off him either.
Then Jackie took his lead, one step...two steps...three steps...four.
Now his eyes were fixed on the pitcher. Both his arms reaching out. Then the pitcher would go into his stretch and their eyes would meet and everyone in the ball park would hold their breath. And the pitcher would lose the battle of the eyes. His attention would go to the batter and he would make his pitch.
Suddenly there was number 42. Getting up to full speed in 3 strides. There would be a cloud of dust, an angry catcher, a frustrated pitcher, another run on the scoreboard for the Dodgers. And you coming out of your seat screaming with joy.
Jackie Robinson was a hero.
A hero who taught us more than baseball. He was the handsome, ebony giant of our youth who taught us determination, taught us perseverance and finally he taught us justice.
The new owners of the New York Mets feel that you and your kids should get as much out of baseball now as you did then. We feel that there is something very special about sharing a baseball game with your kids. With your family and friends.
The new Mets are a young team and that means they may not win every day. But they're a proud team and they'll be trying every day.
And baseball, when it's played by proud young people who try, is beautiful, win or lose.
Come see Steve Henderson, Lee Mazzilli, Doug Flynn, Elliott Maddox, Joel Youngblood, Craig Swan, Alex Trevino and all the Mets take on Dick Williams and his tough Montreal Expos with Larry Parrish, André Dawson, Ron LeFlore and Ellis Valentine this Tuesday and Wednesday.
Mets
The New Mets. The Magic is back.

Rolls-Royce. Simply the best motor car in the world.
For information, contact your local authorized dealer or the national Rolls-Royce office (1-800-851-8576). © Rolls-Royce Motors, Inc. 1985.
The names "Rolls-Royce" and "Corniche" and the mascot, badge, and radiator grille are registered trademarks, as are the Bentley name, mascot, and badge.

THE LARGEST AND HEALTHIEST FOUR-YEAR-OLD IN AMERICA.
HealthAmerica
We're making health care in America better.

COINTREAU
IMPORTED
LIQUEUR SPECIALITE
ANGERS
FRANCE
80 proof
750 ml
PRODUCT OF FRANCE

THE SHARPLY ETCHED LINES OF THE IMPULSE JUST BECAME A BLUR. INTRODUCING THE TURBO.
When Car and Driver first saw the sleek, sculptured, Giugiaro-designed Impulse, they wrote a review that in our minds simply couldn't be improved.
"The Impulse," they said "has already chiseled a place in the granite of automotive history."
Given a review like this, most manufacturers would be happy to leave well enough alone. At Isuzu, we set out to chisel an even larger place for ourselves.
We created an advanced new fuel-injected, overhead cam 2-liter engine powerplant fitted with an incredibly sophisticated intercooled turbocharger.
A powerplant that not only turns out an exhilarating 140 horsepower, it turns the Turbo Impulse into one of the world's fastest GT cars.
So what does Car and Driver have to say now?
"The Impulse is simply a brilliant design." — "Here is a car so polished in its manners and fashionable in its attire, that you don't notice the street-fighter muscles."
"Not only does it go . . . it goes with pleasure."
"Whooee! Next stop, Hall of Fame."
All we can say is, it looks like we were wrong. Apparently, the reviews could be improved.
THE FIRST CAR BUILDERS OF JAPAN.
ISUZU

Della Femina, Travisano & Partners Inc.

625 Madison Avenue
New York, New York 10022
212.421.7180
Telex: 428985

Contact: Jerry Della Femina
Chairman

Employees (U.S.): 315

Founded: 1967

Annual Billings: $250,000,000

Gross Billings by Media:

Newspaper	15%
Magazine	11%
DM	2%
Outdoor	2%
TV	58%
Radio	12%

Clients

Airborne Express; American Isuzu Motors; Beech-Nut Nutrition Corp.; Book-Of-The-Month Club: Quality Paperback Book Club, Fortune Book Club, Cooking & Crafts Book Club, Dolphin Book Club; Bulova Watch Company; WCBS-TV; Campus Sportswear; Carl's Jr. Restaurants; Chemical Bank; Seagram's Mixers; Cointreau America; The Commodity Exchange; CooperVision; Dow Chemical: Dow Bathroom Cleaner, Handi-Wrap, Saran Wrap, Tough Act, Ziploc Bags; Beck's Beer; Financial Guaranty Insurance Corp.; Fisher Office Furniture; Gold Kist; WBZ-TV; Hayes Microcomputer Products; HealthAmerica Corporation; WXRX-FM; Lloyds Bank of California; Merle Norman Cosmetics; Metromedia Telecommunications; Mr. Build; National Medical Enterprises; New York Mets; Ohrbach's; Pacific Southwest Airlines; KCET-TV; Ralston Purina Company; Rolls-Royce Motors; Coppertone Suntan Products; Six Flags Great Adventure Amusement Park; Six Flags Magic Mountain Amusement Park; Sunshine Biscuits; TransAmerica Corp.; USA Cable Network.

ZIPLOC, DOW CHEMICAL

MEOW MIX

SEAGRAM'S

AIRBORNE EXPRESS

CHEMICAL BANK

Doremus is a unique advertising and public relations agency, one of several autonomous subsidiaries of BBDO International. Our roots reach deep into the financial community (we were founded, along with Dow-Jones and the Wall Street Journal, by C.W. Barron). Today we serve clients in categories that range from investment banks to government tourist agencies to consumer electronics. Doremus is made up of the three segments, all roughly equal in size.

Advertising.
Doremus believes its job is to create advertising which helps its clients solve their marketing problems. We have developed a partnership with a select list of clients, working with them to identify their prime prospects' problems, then positioning clients' products or services as solutions to these problems. The solutions we create are not only sound strategically, but highly memorable as well (see the examples on these pages). Our BBDO connection is very helpful in giving us access to world-class TV production facilities, as well as Research and Broadcast Media Services.

Financial Notices.
"Tombstone" advertising, the print ads which record major financial transactions, has always been an important part of our business. We are today the undisputed leader in this field, placing more pages of advertising in the Wall Street Journal than any other agency. Our clients include the leading investment banking firms and many of the largest commercial banks and thrift institutions.

Public Relations.
We believe public relations is an important part of the marketing equation, and are specialists in financial and corporate communications. As such, we are the primary public relations resource in the BBDO Group, in many cases serving advertising clients not only of Doremus, but of other BBDO agencies as well.

Doremus & Company

120 Broadway
New York, New York 10271
212.964.0700
TWX: 710-581-3903,
or 710-581-3904

Contact: Curtis R. Troeger
Chairman & CEO

Employees: 325

Founded: 1903

Annual Billings: $170,000,000

Gross Billings by Media:

Newspaper	64.8%
Magazine	22.8%
DM	5.9%
Outdoor	.3%
TV	3.9%
Radio	2.3%

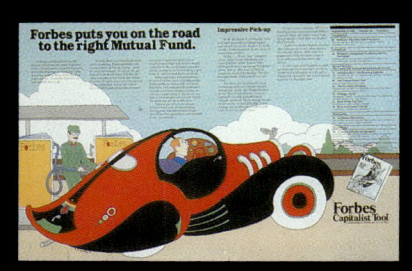

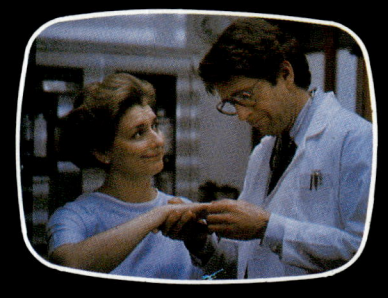

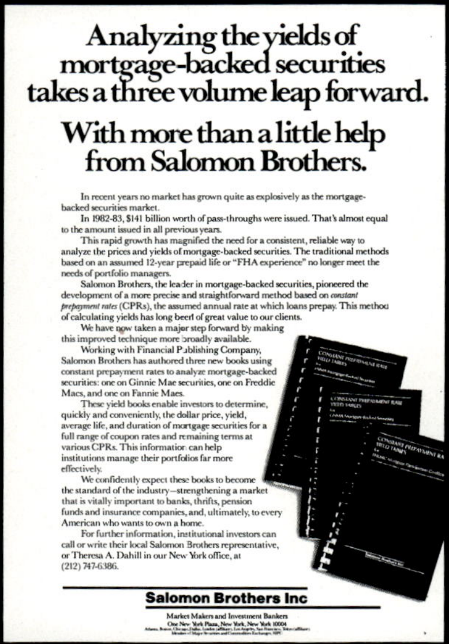

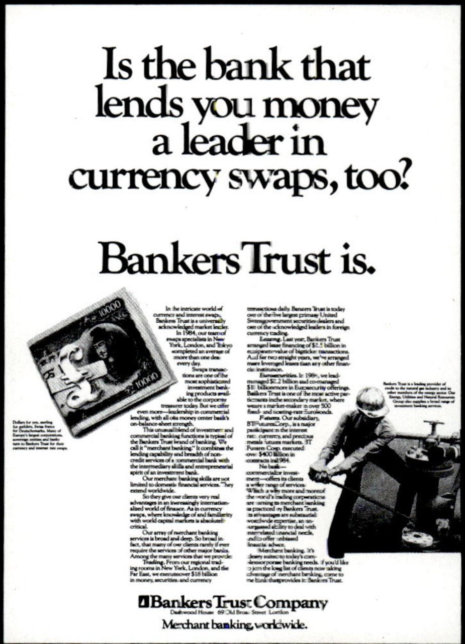

The Agency Book **45**

YEAR AFTER YEAR WE GIVE OUR CLIENTS THE SAME OLD THING.

The Agency Book **47**

Doyle Dane Bernbach Group Inc.

437 Madison Avenue
New York, New York 10022
212.415.2000
Telex: 62794
Cable: DOYDANBACH

Contact: Barry E. Loughrane
President & CEO

Employees: 3,508

Founded: 1949

Annual Billings: $1,580,000,000

Gross Billings by Media:

Newspaper	18%
Magazine	25%
DM	5%
Outdoor	3%
TV	45%
Radio	4%

All of those E's are Effie Awards. Awards that honor an advertising agency's marketing ability and the effectiveness of its work. Hence the E.

Since 1976, the year we started entering campaigns, Doyle Dane Bernbach has won 91 Effies. Which is more than twice as many (133% to be exact) Effie Awards as any other agency.

This is especially remarkable considering that DDB has built a reputation, not for its marketing ability, but for its creative ability. Another area in which we happen to lead the industry.

Since 1981, for example, DDB has won more creative awards than any other agency. Nearly a hundred major creative awards in all, at the One Show, Art Director's Club, Clio Awards, and Andy Awards.

These awards weren't dominated by one or two creative teams at DDB. Or by one or two accounts. The awards were won by dozens of copywriter/art director teams. And for dozens of clients.

What this all means to a current client or potential client is that DDB can be a pretty dull place. Because, one way or the other, year after year, you get the same old thing.

PROMISES PROMISES.

A great agency has a sense of purpose and a set of values that everyone shares in and is committed to. At EPB we want to be known for the strength of our client relationships and the quality of our people. And to be an organization where talented and dedicated people can do their best work and be rewarded for their performance. To reach these goals we are committed to the following principles:

1. <u>We succeed only when our clients succeed.</u> Their bottom-line is ultimately our bottom-line. So we must take the initiative and treat their business and money as if it were our own. This sense of ownership means we expect to be held accountable for results.

2. <u>Our focus must be on our client's customer.</u> Serving the customer is why both our clients and we exist. So we must make it a point to be in close touch with our client's customer. That's where most creative ideas really begin and where they must ultimately be tested.

3. <u>Effective communications programs must be well-orchestrated.</u> They are total symphonies more than medleys of specialty solos. So our goal is to create for each client a unique program that integrates Advertising, Public Relations, Direct Marketing, Sales Promotion, Design, or Research into a single comprehensive effort. Our capacity to integrate all these disciplines makes us unique. And our challenge is to make each individual specialty among the best in its own field, while we concentrate on merging the disciplines into each other.

4. <u>Excellence is a team concept.</u> This is a collaborative business, between client and agency and among ourselves. So we expect every member of our staff to be a team player, to be a contributor, and to be motivated by a sense of accomplishment. When we enable everyone to contribute, the client and the team will always win.

5. <u>No guts, no glory.</u> To do great work we must be willing to reject the expected, to trust our intuition, and to dare to reach for inspired solutions. If we don't have any failures, then we simply aren't trying hard enough.

6. <u>Successful relationships are built on trust.</u> Our goal is to have long-term clients and associates whom we respect and who let us contribute to their growth. We know that if we can't build and maintain a climate of trust, these relationships won't work and so ultimately won't last.

7. <u>Communications is 90% listening.</u> We are in the persuasion business; so everything we do depends upon how well we listen to and communicate with our clients, their customers, and each other.

8. <u>There are no shortcuts to quality.</u> Discipline is more fundamental to success than brilliance; so the true spirit of an organization lives in its sense of discipline and its attention to details. So we must do our homework and take pride in doing things right the first time.

9. <u>There is no finish line.</u> Progress is doing everything a little better each day. If we pay attention to how we can make ourselves and the company incrementally better everyday, then there will never be a limit to how good we can be.

10. <u>We have to feel good about what we do.</u> If we do all of the above we can take pride in our company, ourselves, and what we do for a living. We can look in the mirror and feel proud about how we got where we are—and good about where we are going.

The Agency Book 49

The Earle Palmer Brown Companies

6935 Arlington Road
Bethesda, Maryland 20814
301.657.6000

Contact: Mr. Jeremy Brown
President & CEO

Employees: 250

Founded: 1952

Annual Billings: $120,000,000

Gross Billings by Media:

Newspaper	15%
Magazine	12%
DM	18%
Outdoor	3%
TV	30%
Radio	22%

RESULTS RESULTS.

1. With 3 million dollars of advertising we generated over 9 million dollars worth of free publicity for Marriott's Big Boy Restaurants and our "Stay or Go" campaign.

2. In a dramatic strategic shift away from occasion-oriented purchase, we helped The American Floral Marketing Council target an audience with unlimited potential—convincing consumers to buy flowers for themselves.

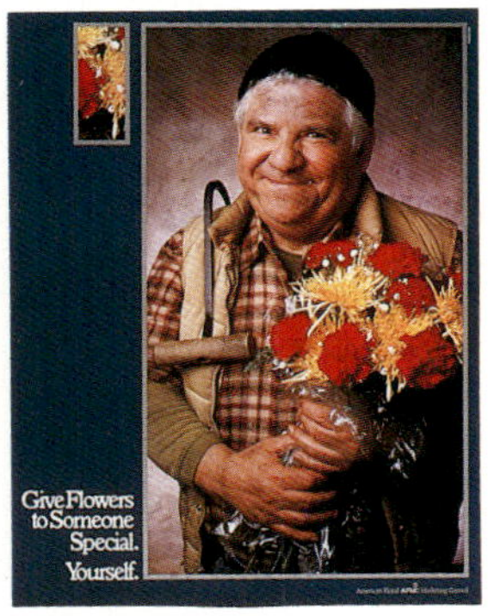

3. With breakthrough Advertising, Public Relations, and Direct Marketing, Airbus Industrie, a European consortium of aerospace manufacturers, broke into the American market with billion dollar sales.

4. We've helped Hechinger, a major East Coast Home Center chain, grow from a wonderful store with a high price perception and no television budget into a major broadcast presence with a reputation for the best prices in town.

5. Our aggressive Advertising and Direct Mail strategies helped AMF Head maintain leadership in a shrinking tennis market, dominate the squash world, and win a lot of creative awards along the way.

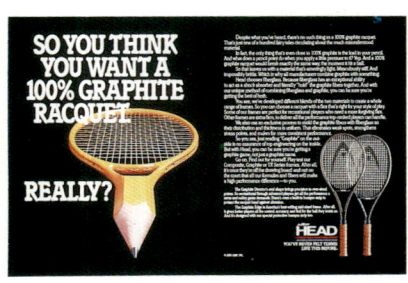

6. Circulation tells the story: while morning newspapers across the country are showing declines, we've helped The Baltimore Sun top its own circulation highs again and again.

7. Amtrak's Southwest Chief was new and improved, but until we redesigned materials and captured some major national media coverage, it lacked the riders it deserved.

8. When the convenience chain, WaWa, advertised with a dramatic new TV campaign, sales for their hoagie product went up 30%.

9. Within 72 hours of a national press conference, we were on "Good Morning America" and the front page of The New York Times with Blue Cross and Blue Shield's revolutionary LifeCard.

10. We've been recognized for creative excellence in every category from direct mail to logo design. In every medium from small space to national television. Proof that when it comes to designing the integrated campaigns that these times demand, we do it better than anyone else.

Client List

American Home Products
Corporation
Chesebrough-Pond's Inc.
Genesee Brewing Company, Inc.
MasterCard International Inc.
Minolta Corporation
Nabisco Brands, Inc.
Nissan Motor Corporation
In U.S.A.
Noxell Corporation
R. J. Reynolds Industries, Inc.
Tambrands, Inc.
Texaco Inc.
The Travelers Corporation
Union Carbide Corporation

Esty

William Esty Company, Inc.

100 East 42nd Street
New York, New York 10017
212.692.6200

Contact: Laurence Wassong
President

Employees: 597

Founded: 1932

Annual Billings: $520,000,000

Gross Billings by Media:	
Newspaper	3%
Magazine	15%
DM	2%
Outdoor	14%
TV	63%
Radio	3%

WITH OVER $500 MILLION IN BILLING AND ONLY 13 CLIENTS…

WE CAN SPREAD OURSELVES PRETTY THICK.

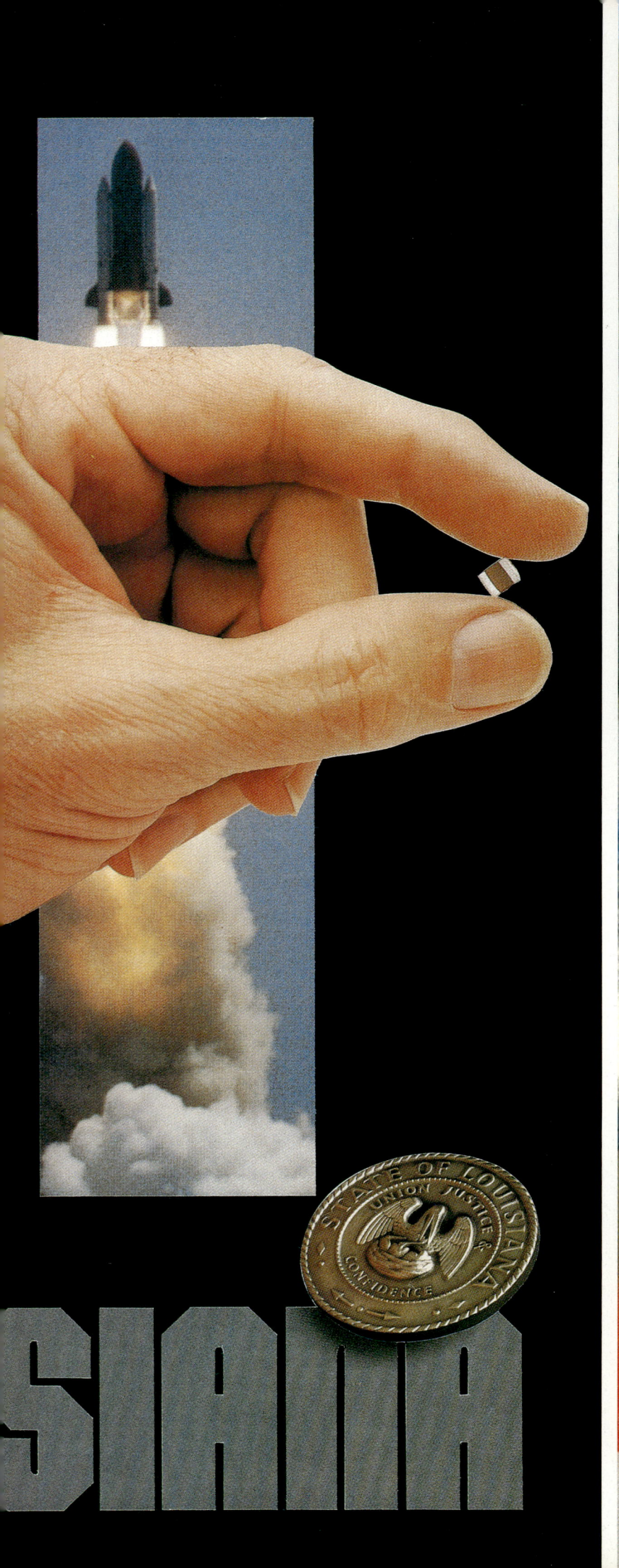

Kozy Kitten

Fitzgerald Advertising Inc.

1055 St. Charles Avenue
New Orleans, Louisiana 70130
504.529.3161
Telex: 81 951 5423

Contact: Joseph L. Killeen, Jr.
President

Employees (U.S.): 33

Founded: 1926

Annual Billings (U.S.): $15,200,000

Gross Billings by Media:

Newspaper	23%
Magazine	12%
Outdoor	2%
TV	47%
Radio	16%

fai

. . . to do a few things well.

Left: Coast to coast television and magazine campaign to lift Louisiana spirits, and attract new business.

Middle: First television spot for Kozy Kitten cat food products in national test markets.

Right: Best Read Ads (per Starch) in U.S.A. Food Service magazines.

In the words of Cervantes, "By a small sample, we may judge of the whole piece..."

"Whenever a client asks me to recommend someone who is truly wired into the Spanish market, I immediately reach for the phone and call Font & Vaamonde. I have never worked with a group of professionals who were as totally involved in a client's marketing program. They know how to talk to the Spanish-speaking consumer and, perhaps equally important, they have an on-going dialogue with the trade that ensures that your product will be there when that consumer comes looking for it."

Spencer Plavoukos
Chairman & CEO, SSC&B Lintas Worldwide

"To call Font & Vaamonde an 'advertising agency' is to only tell part of the story. This full service agency has a unique approach to Merchandising and Promotions, using shelf talkers, window banners, and P.O.P. materials to turn the store into another media. They don't stop at the preparation of the layout. They continue to work with us to achieve the best distribution for the product and the best way to reach the wholesalers and retailers, bodegas and supermarkets alike. Their information extends past the general and covers every detail of these Hispanic consumers including their ages, countries of origin, religions, consumption patterns, numbers of children...They'll even give you their shoe size."

Nick Marcalus
President, Marcal Paper Mills

"Font & Vaamonde has Merchandising and Promotions down to a science. They use stores like another media and reach the consumer with creative impact right at the point of purchase. Their Merchandising team is at home in-the-field throughout the U.S.—when they say they know every corner of every Hispanic neighborhood they mean it."

Robin D. Mills
President, Glenbrook Laboratories

"From my first meeting with Pedro Font I recognized him to be an executive of tremendous insight, creativity and energy—a true 'ad man'. His eye for expansion into the U.S. Hispanic market with new products has amounted to significant gains for InterAmerican Foods. Whatever doubts we had prior to the launching of Cafe Del Bueno were eclipsed by the dedication, perseverance and the sales results achieved by Pedro Font and his group. I am proud to say the result of our relationship has been an overwhelming success."

Barry Zook
President, InterAmerican Foods

"The creative strategy work that preceded copy development was extremely well done and resulted in superb creative executions that are dynamic and exciting. The television commercials developed indicate that your Agency knows what makes the U.S. Hispanic consumer tick and how to motivate them...I also want to add that Font & Vaamonde has earned the trust, confidence and respect we at Mennen have in your Agency."

Dominic J. LaRosa
VP Marketing, The Mennen Company

"FoVa has done an excellent job in the Knorr Bouillon media planning and buying. We are very pleased that we are working with FoVa in the Hispanic marketplace."

Richard Lamley
VP, Warwick Advertising

"Even before selecting Font & Vaamonde as our agency we were most impressed by the cohesive nature of the group of high caliber professionals who would be servicing our account. We are pleased to say that this team approach has proven tremendously valuable. We know that our account is being cared for not by one individual, but by a team that will dedicate all their talents and expertise to achieving results in the Hispanic marketplace."

Cheryl Suhr
Sr. Brand Manager, Glenmore Distilleries

"Font & Vaamonde has done in-depth research and analysis on the Hispanic market so that they can speak directly to the issues that concern marketing people today. They show with specifics that these consumers are a dynamic growth opportunity for packaged goods today."

Bruce D. Hillenbrand
Marketing Manager, CPC International Inc.

Font & Vaamonde Associates, Inc.

183 Madison Avenue
New York, New York 10016
212.679.9170

Contact: Pedro Font
President & Director of
Creative Services

Employees: 50

Founded: 1980

Annual Billings: $21,000,000

Gross Billings by Media:

Newspaper	3%
Magazine	15%
Outdoor	20%
TV	40%
Radio	22%

No more "¡mañana mañana!" Hoy—Today—Now is the moment to make a breakthrough in the U.S. Hispanic Market.

Five years ago, as the U.S. Hispanic market began to manifest itself as a "country within a country," Font & Vaamonde made the decision to demonstrate the value of this market to U.S. advertisers. When we opened our doors we foresaw the "Hispanic Boom." Now it's a reality.

We did not conform to standard advertising agencies' conventions. Instead, we specialized. We made an exclusive commitment to achieve creative excellence, to develop and implement trenchant Marketing and Merchandising strategies and to utilize customized Hispanic concepts as the basis for realizing our objectives.

Thorough research of the Hispanic market in its entirety was one of our primary objectives from the start. Over the past five years, numerous studies conducted by our own Marketing Department have accomplished successful results for each of our accounts. As strong believers in the necessity of research, we welcome the renowned studies of Yankelovich, Strategy Research and most recently SAMI. These sources have enabled the advertising and marketing industries to more effectively read the changing face of the U.S. Hispanic market.

Today this is one of the nation's fastest growing markets with trends depicting continuous growth. This fact, combined with an advantageous cost per thousand makes this one of the most profitable advertising investments to gain market shares.

Your company can avail itself of our full-service capabilities or work with any one of the fine specialized Hispanic Market advertising agencies in the United States.

Now is the time to surpass the competition...
To gain share and position...
To face the challenge and be creative...
Now is the time to break through!

CLIENTS:

Baby Magic	Knorr Bouillon
Bayer Aspirin	The Kroger Company
Cafe Del Bueno	Lady Speed Stick
CPC International	Malta Dukesa
Desmond & Duff Scotch	Malta El Sol
Diaparene	Marcal Paper Mills
d-CON Insecticides	The Mennen Company
Felipe II Brandy	Midol
Glenbrook Laboratories	Panadol
Glenmore Distilleries	Phillips' Milk of Magnesia
Heineken Beer	Skin Bracer
InterAmerican Foods	Speed Stick

Levi's®

Kimberly-Clark, Softique

Mazda

Clairol

WOULD YOU BET THE BRAND ON A DISEMBODIED NOSE?

Would you sing those gritty, streetsmart 501 Blues about your product?

Would you tell the world that "only a handful of people" can appreciate Mazda's RX-7?

For that matter, would you have approved "Does She Or Doesn't She?"

Maybe you would, maybe you wouldn't, but you can't *know* until you're working with an agency that gives you *risks worth taking*.

An agency that takes the relevant and makes it unexpected.

We're that agency. Foote, Cone & Belding.

Always relevant—but always reaching out for the pertinent quirk, the offbeat hit, the magic button that goes *click* in the mind.

Keep us in mind next time you find your advertising merely relevant.

The unexpected: FCB

Foote, Cone & Belding Communications, Inc.

401 N. Michigan Avenue
Chicago, Illinois 60611
312.467.9200
Telex: 910-221-5091

Contact: Norman W. Brown
Chairman

Employees: 6,000

Founded: 1873

Annual Billings: $1,875,000,000

Gross Billings by Media:

Newspaper	18.6%
Magazine	12.1%
DM	1.4%
Outdoor	2.5%
TV	57.5%
Radio	7.9%

FCB

FCB/New York
Manager: Burtch Drake

FCB/Chicago
Manager: Bruce Mason

FCB/Los Angeles
Manager: Hugh Duncan

FCB/San Francisco
Manager: Jack Balousek

Lewis, Gilman & Kynett/
Philadelphia
Chairman: Robert Wilder

re$ults

Grant/Jacoby, Inc.

500 North Michigan Avenue
Chicago, Illinois 60611
312.664.2055

Contact: Bruce I. Carlson
President

Employees: 87

Founded: 1938

Annual Billings: $50,200,000

Gross Billings by Media:

Newspaper	19%
Magazine	21%
DM	12%
Outdoor	2%
TV	44%
Radio	2%

A little history

In 1977, one of the premier promotion and graphic design houses in Chicago made a critical strategic business decision.

Grant/Jacoby decided to become a full service advertising agency. The company that had redesigned McDonald's Golden Arches and invented Ronald McDonald, the in-flight magazine, and some of P&G's biggest promotions decided to redesign and reinvent itself. Billings were $7 million.

Today, Grant/Jacoby is a full service advertising agency in the $50 million billings neighborhood. And still growing.

Our idea is to serve a limited list of blue-chip clients with an almost unlimited list of services.

Including, of course, uncommon advertising.

Advertising that makes something happen

Over the years, we have noticed that lengthy, lofty advertising agency philosophies about the creative product get pinned up on copywriters' walls, but don't necessarily stick in their hearts and heads.

That's why our philosophy is based not on *why* and *how*. But rather on *what*.

Our what is the kind of advertising that makes something happen.

We want very much to create superb advertising. But we want that advertising to move attitudes, or move people to action and, in the end, move companies, products, services and even P/E ratios forward.

It's called results.

Grant/Jacoby full service versus full service

Compared to other advertising agencies, there is one thing different about Grant/Jacoby full service.

It's our upbringing.

Having started as a design and sales promotion agency, we grew up focusing on how to sell products and services. On helping sales managers make quotas and brand managers make bottom lines. On street fighting.

We bring this viewpoint to our advertising clients in the form of a wide range of services.

Beyond advertising, some of our capabilities are marketing counsel, sales promotion, public relations, packaging/labeling, direct marketing, point-of-sale, sales presentations, catalogs/brochures, and corporate identity. All on staff.

A final 30-second commercial

In summary, Grant/Jacoby has managed to fit large-agency talent and services in a medium-size package.

This combination of experience and size lets us focus our energy on creating a superb creative product. And it enables us to pay the right kind of personal attention to a limited list of blue-chip clients.

However, as a company that has doubled in the last four years, Grant/Jacoby will not be exactly the right size forever.

Talk to us soon.

Some advertising agencies feel they must adopt a single philosophy in order to fix themselves in what is a relentlessly diverse environment. Which seems to us a contradiction.

At Greenstone & Rabasca, we choose to address different problems in different ways. And to let the resulting solutions speak for themselves—and for us.

Greenstone & Rabasca Advertising Inc.

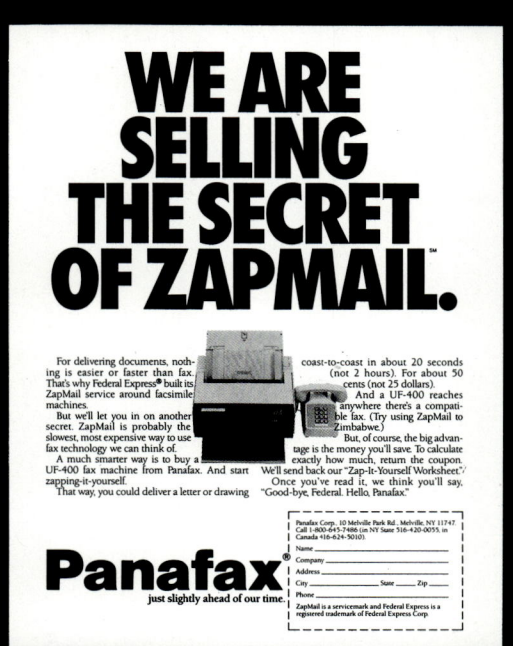

Greenstone & Rabasca Advertising, Inc.

One Huntington Quadrangle
Suite 1N05
Melville, New York 11747
516.249.2121
Facsimile: 516.249.2179

Contact: Kenneth Rabasca
President

Employees: 46

Founded: 1972

Annual Billings: $18,000,000

Gross Billings by Media:	
Newspaper	30%
Magazine	44%
DM	5%
Outdoor	1%
TV	10%
Radio	10%

PRINT

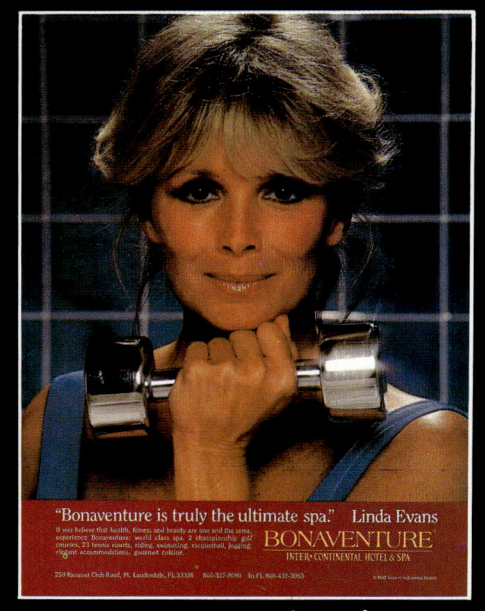

Bonaventure Inter-Continental Hotel & Spa

CIRRUS Systems, Inc.

Murdoch & Coll, Inc.

TELEVISION

Cash Station Inc.

Stein & Company

Continental Can Company

DIRECT RESPONSE

The First National Bank of Chicago

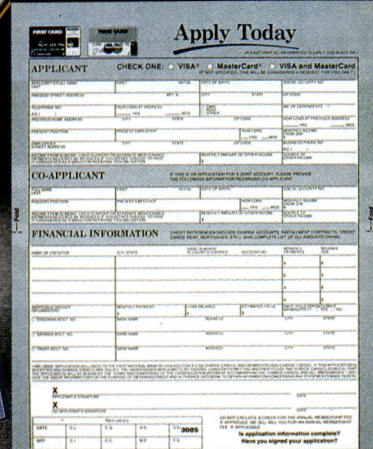

The First National Bank of Chicago

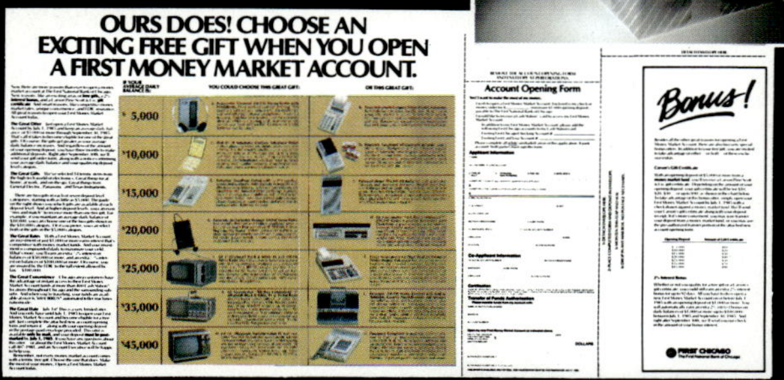

The Agency Book **63**

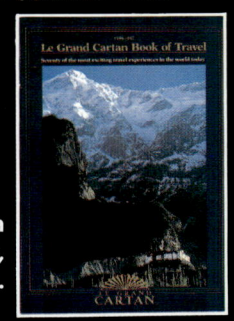

Haddon Advertising, Inc.

919 North Michigan Avenue
Chicago, Illinois 60611
312.943.6266
Facsimile: 312.787.7586

Contact: Harvey L. Haddon
President

Employees: 52

Founded: 1965

Annual Billings: $30,000,000

Gross Billings by Media:

Newspaper	15%
Magazine	23%
DM	26%
TV	11%
Radio	25%

Haddon

Subsidiary:
Haddon, Lynch and Baughman, Inc.
Public Relations
919 North Michigan Avenue
Chicago, Illinois 60611
312.649.0371

Contact: Kevin G. Lynch
Senior Partner

Safety Harbor Spa & Fitness Center

*Market makers.
Share takers.
Record breakers.*

Aggressive, market-driven clients.
A creative, strategic-thinking agency.
The results? Results.

The Carlton Club

The Ritz-Carlton Chicago
A Four Seasons Hotel

Cartan Tours, Inc.

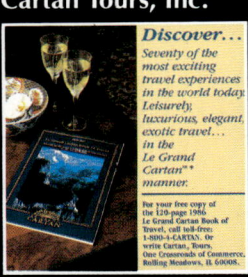

We're HBM/CREAMER. One agency with a two-word philosophy. Be Somebody. To stand out in a world of advertising clutter, each client, each product, must have personality. Without it, no one will remember you. And if you have the wrong personality, no one will believe you. HBM/CREAMER advertising makes our clients Be Somebody. And because it does, our advertising sells.

It's helped make Titleist the Number One Ball in Golf; Stanley, America's Do-It-Yourself Company; A&W, America's Number One Root Beer. And it's helped put Stouffer's at the top of the frozen food category.

The list goes on, but if our approach to advertising intrigues you and you'd like to know more, call or write our President, Ed Eskandarian.

STANLEY POWERLOCK®

BE SOMEBODY.

We're HBM/CREAMER. One agency with a two-word philosophy. Be Somebody. Like Stanley. It's America's Do-It-Yourself Company. And they got there with the help of advertising that made them an important somebody to the people they want to reach. That's HBM/CREAMER advertising.

The kind of advertising that helped make Titleist the Number One Ball in Golf. A&W, America's Number One Root Beer. And helped put Stouffer's at the top of the frozen food category. The list goes on, but if this approach to advertising makes sense to you and you'd like to know more, call or write our president, Ed Eskandarian, at 1633 Broadway, New York, N.Y. 10019, 212-887-8000.

HBM/CREAMER

New York/Boston/Chicago/Hartford/Pittsburgh/Providence/Washington, D.C.

A&W

BE SOMEBODY.

We're HBM/CREAMER. One agency with a two-word philosophy. Be Somebody. Like A&W. They're America's Number One Root Beer. And they got there with the help of advertising that made them an important somebody to the people they want to reach. That's HBM/CREAMER advertising.

The kind of advertising that helped make Titleist the Number One Ball in Golf. Stanley, America's Do-It-Yourself Company. And helped put Stouffer's at the top of the frozen food category. The list goes on, but if this approach to advertising makes sense to you and you'd like to know more, call or write our president, Ed Eskandarian, 1633 Broadway, New York, N.Y. 10019, 212-887-8000.

HBM/CREAMER

New York/Boston/Chicago/Hartford/Pittsburgh/Providence/Washington, D.C.

HBM/CREAMER, Inc.

Paramount Plaza, 1633 Broadway
New York, New York 10019
212.887.8000
Telex: 960806 - HBM/CRMR/NY

Contact: Edward Eskandarian
President & CEO

Employees: 726

Founded: 1916

Annual Billings: $350,000,000

Gross Billings by Media:	
Newspaper	6%
Magazine	32%
Outdoor	1%
TV	56%
Radio	5%

BE SOMEBODY.

We're HBM/CREAMER. One agency with a two-word philosophy. Be Somebody. Like Stouffer's. Now at the top of the frozen food category. They got there with the help of advertising that made them an important somebody to the people they want to reach. That's HBM/CREAMER advertising.

The kind of advertising that helped make Titleist the Number One Ball in Golf. A&W, America's Number One Root Beer. And Stanley, America's Do-It-Yourself Company. The list goes on, but if this approach to advertising makes sense to you and you'd like to know more, call or write our president, Ed Eskandarian, at 1633 Broadway, New York, N.Y. 10019. 212-887-8000.

HBM/CREAMER
New York/Boston/Chicago/Hartford/Pittsburgh/Providence/Washington, D.C.

BE SOMEBODY.

We're HBM/CREAMER. One agency with a two-word philosophy. Be Somebody. Like Titleist, the Number One Ball in Golf. They got there with the help of advertising that made them an important somebody to the people they want to reach. That's HBM/CREAMER advertising.

The kind of advertising that helped make Stanley America's Do-It-Yourself Company. A&W, America's Number One Root Beer. And helped put Stouffer's at the top of the frozen food category.

The list goes on, but if this approach to advertising makes sense to you and you'd like to know more, call or write our president, Ed Eskandarian, at 1633 Broadway, New York, N.Y. 10019, 212-887-8000.

HBM/CREAMER
New York/Boston/Chicago/Hartford/Pittsburgh/Providence/Washington, D.C.

Response Selling System
Breakthrough advertising. These days, a message has to break through a lot more than media clutter. It has to break down barriers erected by contemporary consumers who have conditioned themselves not to respond. At Healy-Schutte & Company, we break through those barriers with distinctive selling ideas developed by following a unique, disciplined approach we call, appropriately, RESPONSE. Response is an acronym for the eight marketing and creative principles described here... basics sadly missing from much of today's advertising. It's an operational system exclusive to our agency, and it has proven its effectiveness time after time with exciting advertising and even more exciting results for our clients.

R E S P

Our "We'll Show You How" program positioned M&T Bank as a major regional entity in the highly competitive retail financial marketplace. Research revealed that bank responsiveness was the *Relevant* key issue with M&T's business customers. We used intriguing case histories citing the bank's unusual eagerness to tailor its services to the needs of its clients.

With new names and benefit offerings heating up the already competitive health insurance arena, our client Health Care Plan needed a high-impact message to register its primary claim to fame. HS&C's research singled out Health Care's complete coverage as the key consumer motivator. It became our client's *Exclusive* benefit.

To be successful, advertising must isolate a product or service virtue and state it in a *Succinct* way. We packaged Health Care Plan's most meaningful consumer benefit in an arresting manner, focusing attention on the one insurance plan that finally plugs up the holes in health care coverage.

The *Promise* is service. The message is that Prolab delivers. But these ads for Prolab Laboratory Animal Diets from Agway increase the selling impact by stating the promise in a way that demands attention. All HS&C ads convey a visual or verbal promise right up front.

©1985 Healy-Schutte & Company

The Agency Book **67**

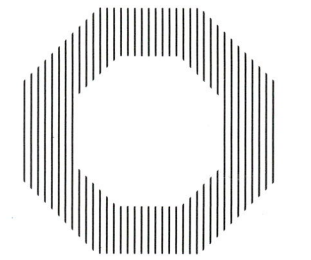

Healy-Schutte & Company

1207 Delaware Avenue
Buffalo, New York 14209
716.884.2120

Contact: Alden F. Schutte
President & CEO

Employees: 96

Founded: 1974

Annual Billings: $30,000,000

Gross Billings by Media:

Newspaper	14%
Magazine	25%
DM	1%
TV	47%
Radio	13%

O N S E

For Prolab, we added a charming element of humanity to the lab animal diet problem, using a humorous focus on the poor beleaguered lab technician to cut through typical trade book clutter. *Original* in approach and impact.

For more than five years now, A.M.&A.'s department stores have been Western New York's leader in fashion advertising. Consistency of theme (the *Notable* factor) throughout a variety of TV commercials has made "A.M.&A.'s of course" number one in retail ad message recall.

We packaged Rich's expertise in the in-store bakery industry under the banner "The Bakery Profits System." And we developed an advertising *Style* as bold and aggressive as the program itself, with a 3-page spread ad promising increased profits via this grabber headline: "This is the last red ink you'll ever see in your bakery."

It doesn't always take big four-color production to make a big impression. For Rich's, we extended "The Bakery Profits System" in an *Efficient* way across a series of easily updated support materials that were produced inexpensively in two colors, yet present the unified, professional image Rich's wanted for its field sales representatives.

iMi
The Search Is Over.
Styrofoam
On-Site Sales Tools from Dow
Show home buyers you build with the best.
Dow Styrofoam Brand
Our homes make energy affordable.
Wherever. Whenever.
Preformed Line Products
True to the core.
Get Truck Happy
Bedford
The Ultimate Security Force
ASSA
Diebold is Security.
Wherever it's needed.
Diebold
12 Months or 24,000 Meals without an Oil Change
FryLight
Ask a Roadranger.
Eaton
Tiger Grip Adhesives & Sealants

We have the same solution for every product.

That solution is creativity. Creativity based on solid research that breaks barriers, generates immediate interest, provokes action, gets sales moving.

We do it for all our clients — business-to-business, professional, consumer and retail. Because at Jayme we think the best ideas come from out-thinking rather than out-spending the competition.

That means developing the unique, memorable idea that will differentiate our client in the marketplace. Then utilizing it in a strategic, cost-effective mix of advertising, public relations, sales promotion and marketing support.

Our balance of strong marketing savvy and big idea creativity has been good for our clients. And good for us. Over the past three years, we've moved up among the top 250 out of 7,000 U.S. ad agencies.

So if you have to go up against some stiff competition, get an agency that can help you out-think the other guys. Call Mike Cargile, President of The Jayme Organization, Advertising/Marketing/Public Relations/Sales Promotion/Direct Response, at 216-831-0110.

HELPING YOU OUT-THINK YOUR COMPETITION.

JAYME

The Jayme Organization, Inc.

23200 Chagrin Boulevard
One Commerce Park Square
Cleveland, Ohio 44122
216.831.0110
Facsimile: 216.464.2308

Contact: Michael E. Cargile
President

Employees (U.S.): 70

Founded: 1947

Annual Billings (U.S.): $27,000,000

Gross Billings by Media:

Newspaper	12%
Publications	62%
DM	10%
TV	5%
Radio	10%

JAYME

NO PURCHASE NECESSARY.

Now, the best cellular mobile telephone money can buy is the best cellular mobile telephone money can lease.

Through Oki's new $49.95-A-Month Leasing Program.*

A program that gives you everything that made Oki the best selling cellular telephone in America.

All the features.
Performance.
Quality.
Reliability.
Even the Oki warranty, for the life of your lease.

All at a very affordable monthly rate.
Just $49.95.
And you can get the name of the Oki dealer nearest you by calling Oki at 1-800-228-2028, ext. 65. (In Nebraska, 1-800-642-8300, ext. 65.)

At this price, the cellular telephone you couldn't afford to buy has become the cellular telephone you can't afford to be without.

Oki. America's first cellular telephone.

Where do waves begin?

Somewhere between Friday and Monday.

For it's the weekend when America's movers and shakers make a dash for the nearest newsstand.

With one goal in mind. To grab their copies of next week's Barron's.

More than one third of our circulation comes from newsstand sales. And 17 out of every 20 newsstand copies are sold on Saturday and Sunday.

They're purchased by those who are clearly the wavemakers of American business and finance.

The affluent influentials who set trends instead of following them; the forward-looking who live on the edge of tomorrow; the significant few who set the pace for everyone else.

So their decisions are far more than ripples. They're waves. Growing. Surging. And sweeping across the broad landscape of the business world.

Why Barron's?

Because they know we focus on what's most important to the most important people.

Money.
Markets.
Investments.
And the price the world puts on the companies they own or manage.
What better audience for your advertising?
What better environment for your company?
Barron's.
Where you can make your own waves every business week.
**Barron's.
How the smart money gets that way.**

Ma's Choice

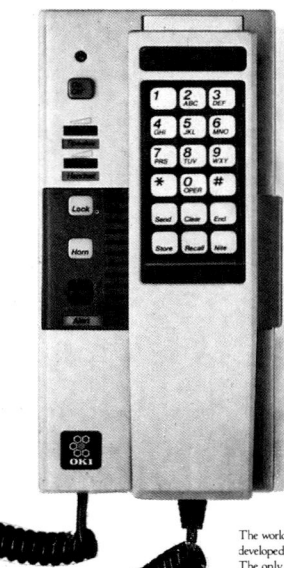

The world's first cellular mobile transceiver developed for Bell Laboratories.
The only telephone selected by AT&T subsidiary, Advanced Mobile Phone Service, Inc.

OKI
OKI ADVANCED COMMUNICATIONS
One University Plaza, Hackensack, NJ 07601

Yesbutters don't just kill ideas.

They kill companies, even entire industries.

Take the issue of factory automation. The yesbutters have all the answers.

Yesbut we're different. Yesbut we can't afford it. Yesbut our business doesn't need it. Yesbut we're too small. Yesbut we couldn't sell it to our work force. Yesbut we can't explain it to the shareholders. Yesbut let's wait and see.

All the answers. All the *wrong* answers.

The issue isn't factory automation. It's staying in business in a complex and competitive world.

We ought to know. For General Electric has invested *billions* in factory automation and other technologies.

Call the GE Business Information Center at (518) 438-6500, and we'll tell you what we've learned. And tell you about programs, seminars and plant tours that will give you the chance to see what we've done.

For now, here are three points to ponder.

Automation isn't evolution but revolution. It can help you design, test, manufacture—faster, better, more economically than ever before.

Automation is leverage. Payback isn't always the issue. What is important is how you will gain the efficiency you need to survive and succeed in a competitive world.

Automation is a journey, not a step. You can go as far and as fast as you'd like, and still reap the benefits.

We use automation. We provide automation. So between our experience and the products and systems we sell, there's something to be gained by calling (518) 438-6500.

Before the yesbutters yesbut you right out of business.

GE
(518) 438-6500

… The Agency Book **71**

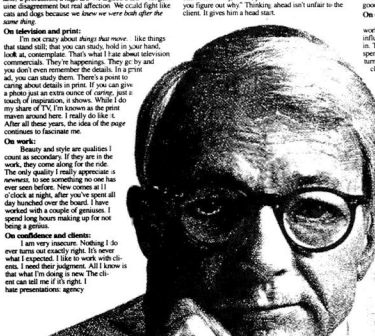

The Johnston & Johnston Group

551 Fifth Avenue
New York, New York 10176
212.490.2121

Contact: J.J. Johnston
Chairman

Employees: 38

Founded: 1974

Annual Billings: $26,500,000

Gross Billings by Media:

Newspaper	35%
Magazine	45%
DM	2%
Outdoor	6%
TV/film	9%
Radio	3%

More work, faster work, better work.
The Johnston & Johnston Group is a radically different advertising agency with a philosophy that's meaningful and measurable: more work, faster work, better work.

More work, because there's quality in quantity.

Faster work, because today's marketing windows can open and shut faster than most ad agencies can open a job.

Better work, because creative is the ultimate lever, increasing reach by as much as 19× — and increasing impact by an even greater margin.

We underpromise—and overperform
While advertising tradition dictates that agencies overpromise and under-perform, we underpromise—and overperform. The heart of our business: a literate, intelligent creative product that respects the good sense of the reader or viewer—and advertising that doesn't look, read, sound, or smell like advertising.

The world's first electronic agency.
We are the world's first electronic advertising agency, with talent in three locations working together via computer links and high-speed facsimile. The advantages of this unique organization are important to any marketer who'd like to get more leverage from each advertising dollar: a true "national" communications organization with a real sense of regional differences; a longer "working window" so that impossible deadlines can be met; the ability to tap the best production, art and design talent in the world.

The Johnston & Johnston Group.

The one communications organization that offers new answers to the perplexing new problems that confront today's marketers.

An invitation.
Invest thirty minutes in a conversation, and you'll have a better idea of why some of the world's most sophisticated marketers have called us the most intriguing advertising agency in America—and why our work has helped companies like yours achieve quantum leaps in advertising efficiency and effectiveness.

This is what KS&J did for AT&T.

AT&T is a registered trademark of AT&T, Inc., the American Telephone & Telegraph Corporation.

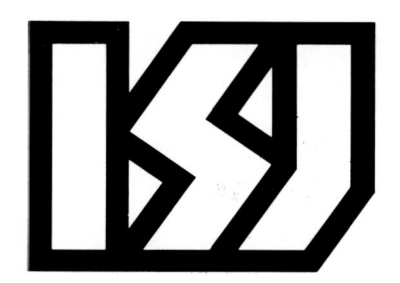

Kerlick, Switzer & Johnson Advertising, Inc.

727 North First Street
St. Louis, Missouri 63102
314.241.4656

Contact: Michael G. Switzer
President

Employees: 35

Founded: 1980

Annual Billings: $14,000,000

Gross Billings by Media:	
Newspaper	25%
Magazine	12%
DM	5%
Outdoor	3%
TV	30%
Radio	25%

This television commercial scene sent shockwaves through AT&T. Because in the few months that we've handled the account of this rival, Illinois-based long distance company, our client has nearly doubled its revenues. Stealing market share from AT&T among others, in an industry where smaller companies are quickly dispatched.

Make no mistake, this result was achieved only through the efforts of an agency committed to producing bold-stroke advertising. The kind of advertising that's rocketed several of our other clients to national prominence within their industries, each time at the expense of stronger, more formidable competition.

You may not have heard of Kerlick, Switzer & Johnson. We're certainly not the biggest or the best known. We do, however, have a history of creating success. So when it comes time to review your account, please make sure we're one of the agencies you talk with. You'll find we can do something surprising for your company. And your company's competition.

What can we do for your competition?

Consumers don't read focus group results.
They don't review positioning statements
and copy platforms. Don't analyze marketing
strategies or media plans.

Consumers just see advertising. And they
either tune in or tune out.

So, after all this work that goes into the work,
the ads are still the thing.

keye/donna/pearlstein

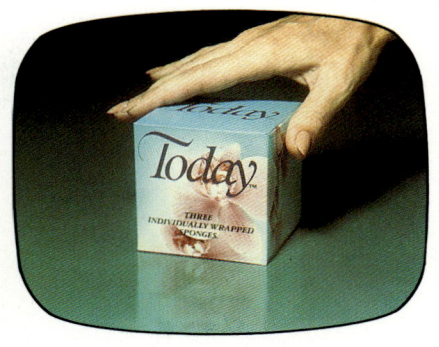

TODAY® CONTRACEPTIVE SPONGE  LAURA SCUDDER'S POTATO CHIPS  TOMY TOYS

The Agency Book 75

keye/donna/pearlstein

11080 Olympic Boulevard
Los Angeles, California 90064
213.477.0061

Contact: Leonard Pearlstein
President & CEO

Employees: 110

Founded: 1969

Annual Billings: $70,000,000

Gross Billings by Media:

Newspaper	6%
Magazine	34%
Outdoor	5%
TV	45%
Radio	10%

STATE OF CALIFORNIA TOURISM

ROLM BUSINESS SYSTEMS

VIVITAR CAMERAS AND ACCESSORIES

AMERICAN HAWAII CRUISES

KAEPA ATHLETIC SHOES

DEL TACO FAST FOODS

SUZUKI AUTOMOBILES

We have doubled our billings in just two years.
Because we show clients how to make their business grow. We have the management, the people and the credentials to do just that. We've done it before. Our track record proves it. Now we'd like to prove it to you.

Our unique "Matrix for Advertising and Positioning."
—M.A.P., for short—gives you a fresh look at your marketing options, your consumers, your competition and how your product or service can best live up to its potential. What's more, M.A.P. works regardless of the size of your business or your budget, whether you're launching a new product or reviving an old one.

Great creative work thrives on M.A.P.!
Crisp, clear strategic direction gives creative people solid ideas to chew on. Result: your ads and commercials are original, fresh and built to make a compelling point. Not just glittering superficiality. Come see us. We'll show you what we mean.

Thank you

Ted Bates • SSC&B • Compton • Y&R • B&B • Esty • JWT • K&E
N.W. Ayer • Geers Gross • D'Arcy • HBM Creamer • McCann Erickson
Wells Rich Greene • Leo Burnett • Mike Sloan.

Colgate • General Foods • J&J • Lincoln-Mercury • Northwest Airlines
Pitney Bowes Credit Corp.* • Seagrams • P&G • American Express • Gillette
Hunt Wesson • Lufthansa • Heublein • McDonald's • Economics Laboratory*
Jarlsberg® Cheese* • RJR • Sunoco • Lever Brothers • Hush Puppies • Kodak
Revlon • Coca-Cola • General Motors • Exxon • Wella • Ryder • Texaco
Chesebrough-Ponds • Miles Laboratories • Air France • Nestle • Tampax
Standard Brands • S.C. Johnson • Levi Strauss • Goodyear • Princess Cruises
Kentucky Fried Chicken • Christian Brothers • Mobil • Bermuda • Eveready®
American Can • Sterling Drug • L&M • Pillsbury • United Airlines • Falstaff Beer
Wilkinson Sword • Nabisco • Carnation • Frigidaire • First Claims Group
General Electric • Royal Caribbean Cruise Line, Inc. • Roure Dupont
American Home • Connecticut Savings Bank*

You trained us well. If it weren't for you we wouldn't be the agency we are.

Indicates current clients of KMS. The rest are our staff's composite resume. Some list!

The Agency Book **77**

KMS
Knudsen Moore Schropfer, Inc.

666 Glenbrook Road
Stamford, Connecticut 06906
203.967.7200
Facsimile: 203.967.7241

Contact: Joseph DelGaldo
Executive V.P.

Employees: 30

Founded: 1964

Annual Billings (U.S.): $14,800,000

Gross Billings by Media:

Newspaper	10%
Magazine	15%
DM	10%
Outdoor	5%
TV	50%
Radio	10%

If you smoke

please try Carlton

SURGEON GENERAL'S WARNING: Quitting Smoking Now Greatly Reduces Serious Risks to Your Health.

Box and 100's Box Menthol: Less than 0.5 mg. "tar", 0.05 mg. nicotine; Soft Pack, Menthol and 100's Box: 1 mg. "tar", 0.1 mg. nicotine; 100's Soft Pack and 100's Menthol: 5 mg. "tar", 0.4 mg. nicotine; 120's: 7 mg. "tar", 0.6 mg. nicotine av. per cigarette, FTC Report Jan. '85. Slims: 6 mg. "tar", 0.6 mg. nicotine av. per cigarette by FTC method.

We make you laugh.
We make you cry.

We inform you, excite you, entertain you, involve you.
News reports that are vital.
New recipes that are delightful.
A tragedy that's almost too painful to hear.
A comic strip that's really too funny for words.
Fashions for the eye.
Music to your ears.
A spy story that's a figment of someone's imagination.
A spy story that's just happened in real life.
Communicating the serious.
Documenting the frivolous.
Facts. Fiction. Fantasy. Reality.
Information about the world that enriches and expands our minds while it changes and shapes our lives.
In homes across the country, where there's a television, a book, a newspaper, a radio, a magazine.
Millions upon millions of people everyday are watching us, hearing us, reading us.
It's a responsibility we don't take lightly.

THE HEARST CORPORATION

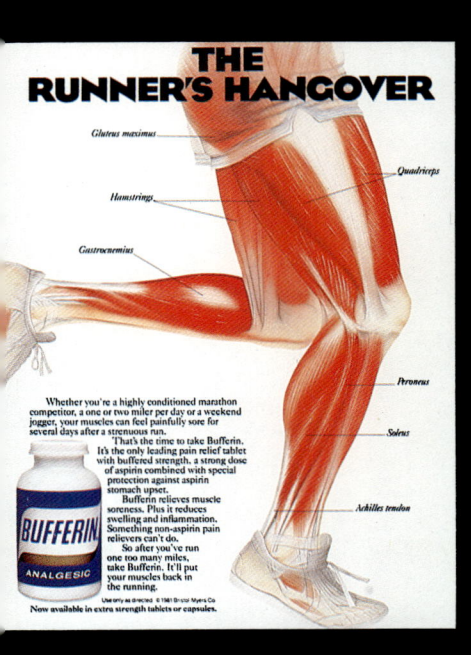

Laurence, Charles, Free & Lawson, Inc.

261 Madison Avenue
New York, New York 10016
212.661.0200

Contact: Thomas E. Lawson
President

Employees: 229

Founded: 1952

Annual Billings: $240,000,000

Gross Billings by Media:

Newspaper	18%
Magazine	22%
Outdoor	11%
TV	40%
Radio	7%
Other	2%

History

Laurence, Charles, Free & Lawson bills in excess of $240 million with a client list which includes many of America's top consumer companies. The agency ranks among the top 20 in New York.

Founded on the commitment of top management involvement in day-by-day activities of its clients' programs, the agency has an enviable record in retention of, and growth with, its key clients. In fact, the average tenure for its top clients is over fifteen years, and over sixty percent of the agency's growth in the past five years has been with its existing client base. More assignments from existing clients is surely the true *proof of performance*.

FRESH.
FROZEN.
BREADED.
LIVE.
SMOKED.
CANNED.
The FULTON LOBSTER COMPANY
If you don't know fulton, you don't know fish.

Your Best Friends Deserve...
Carr's Table Water Crackers
Carr's
America's favorite imported cracker.
15¢ off any box of Carr's crackers

What a light idea!
Marielle Foods
40¢
Save 40¢
Marielle Foods® Quiche

Apollinaris
The water with essential minerals for those who are serious about health and fitness.
20¢
Save 20¢ on Apollinaris Mineral Water

DIAL-A-MUPPET
976-4444

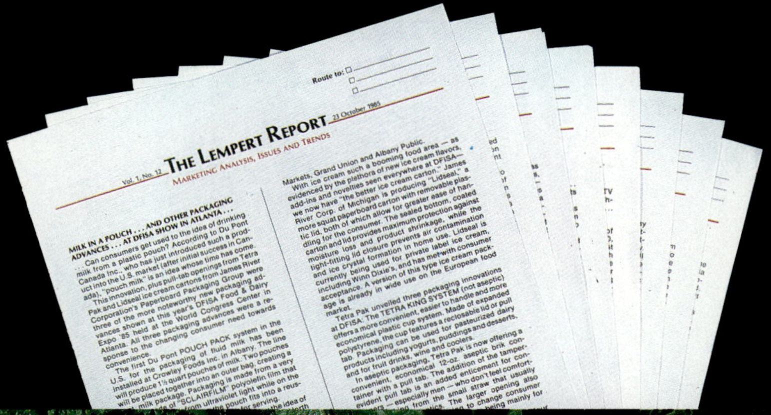
The Lempert Report
Marketing Analysis, Issues and Trends
Route to:
Milk in a pouch . . . and other packaging advances . . . at DFISA show in Atlanta . . .

APPLE
Ssips
A Refreshing Drink
FULL DAY SUPPLY OF VITAMIN C

alouette

The Lempert Company, Inc.

202 Belleville Avenue
Belleville, New Jersey 07109
201.759.2927

Contact: Philip Lempert
President

Employees: 34

Founded: 1974

Annual Billings: $16,250,000

Gross Billings by Media:	
Newspaper	10%
Magazine	30%
DM	8%
Outdoor	2%
TV	35%
Radio	15%

What's The Lempert Company doing in Belleville, New Jersey?

Producing results that count.
Our objective is to build a loyal following for a client and the client's products. To increase market share. To score breakthroughs in the marketplace for new products by pinpointing additional opportunities. And even to reverse a decline in product sales or consumer base.

Specializing in food advertising.
Our expertise is in the food industry — foodservice as well as retail. We keep up with the latest in nutrition, cooking, handling, distribution and retailing. We talk food with brokers, editors, retailers, technologists, manufacturers and, most of all, consumers.

Developing creative strategies.
We create and execute whatever strategy it takes to increase a client's business. We think. Investigate. Analyze. We study every aspect of a client's business — and the effect of emerging trends on it. Only then do we create a strategy.

Keeping the industry informed.
The Lempert Report, our biweekly marketing, advertising and issues newsletter, is the first to point out developing trends as they relate to the food industry. Currently read by over 2,500 business and media leaders, The Lempert Report has provoked comment in Forbes, Fortune, and publications from coast to coast.

Having fun.
We're new enough to be full of enthusiasm. Old enough to have an excellent track record. Big enough to service any client. And we're in Belleville, New Jersey. No distractions. No big-city hang-ups. No middle layers. Our clients talk directly to department heads.

Why should you come to The Lempert Company?
For insightful marketing, unforgettable advertising and effective public relations. We'll make your message clear. Every effort will deliver high impact, simplicity, strength and quality.

As Phil Dougherty said in The New York Times of July 23, 1985, "Watch The Lempert Company."

The advertising we create for our clients is a lot more famous than our name. But we prefer it that way.

Ten years ago, nobody knew what a Subaru was. Today, Subaru of America is the fifth ranked imported car in the United States.

Three years ago, Citizen Watch Company had very little brand recognition in this country. In the two years they have been a client of ours, their sales have more than doubled.

And in less than one year, we helped change McCall's image from "old fashioned" to fashionable.

What makes all three of these case studies interesting, is that each client was enormously outspent in the marketplace.

Proof positive that an advertiser doesn't have to outspend the competition, if he outthinks them.

So if you're unfamiliar with the kind of results our clients have been experiencing, perhaps it's time you become familiar with Levine, Huntley, Schmidt and Beaver.

Levine, Huntley, Schmidt and Beaver is an independently operated, majority-owned subsidiary of Grey Advertising.

ONE OF THE BORING HOUSEWIVES WHO READS McCALL'S.
McCall's MORE THAN THE EXPECTED.

ONE OF THE DRAB HOMEBODIES WHO READS McCALL'S.
McCall's MORE THAN THE EXPECTED.

IF YOU'RE NOT FAMILIAR WITH PERHAPS YOU'LL RECOGNIZE CARLY, TINA

Client List
Alvin Ailey
Australia & New Zealand Banking Group
Citizen Watch
International Information Network
Knoll International
Kronenbourg U.S.A.
Management Science America
McCall's
New York Air
Seagram's Distillers
Subaru of America
Subaru Regional Distributors
Tel-Plus Communications

Levine, Huntley, Schmidt and Beaver, Inc.

250 Park Avenue
New York, New York 10177
212.557.0900
Telex: 12-6363 LHSB-NYK

Contact: Bob Schmidt
President

Employees: 125

Founded: 1972

Annual Billings: $85,000,000

Gross Billings by Media:	
Newspaper	10%
Magazine	10%
Outdoor	10%
TV	50%
Radio	20%

ONE OF THE OLD-FASHIONED GIRLS WHO READS McCALL'S.
McCall's
MORE THAN THE EXPECTED.

ONE OF THE DULL CONFORMISTS WHO READS McCALL'S.
McCall's
MORE THAN THE EXPECTED.

LEVINE, HUNTLEY, SCHMIDT AND BEAVER. BETTE AND YOKO.

Okay. We admit it. On occasion, it's been known to snow in Buffalo.

But that's not the real blizzard in town. At Levy, King & White, there's a blizzard of creative ideas in advertising, sales promotion, public relations and market research. And it's taking the world by storm.

Our recent "Stop DWI" campaign won first place in a prestigious international public affairs and consumer education awards competition.

Our film for the National Committee for Prevention of Child Abuse won a bronze medal at the New York International Film Festival.

Our proven expertise in sales promotion has attracted major national clients from coast to coast.

Once they discover Buffalo, they're stuck here. Not in snow. But on Levy, King & White. Give us a call and you'll be stuck, too.

THEY FOUND A BLIZZARD OF IN BUFFALO

LK&W

Levy, King & White

620 Main Street
Buffalo, New York 14202
716.853.6755

Contact: Peter King
Chairman & CEO

Employees (U.S.): 105

Annual Billings (U.S.): $29,000,000

Gross Billings by Media: NA

The Agency Book **85**

When we go to work for you, it's with you.

Our clients' success is our success. We pride ourselves on longstanding marketing partnerships. We like to grow brands from the seed of an idea to the full bloom of a full blown line extension.

The first thing our clients notice is "us". We operate as a task force. There are no departmental barriers. The free flow of copy and research and art and merchandising and media ideas brings out our creative best and our best creative. And the us includes "them".

We put more creativity into the development of solid strategies than a lot of agencies put into their creative. Because if it isn't right up front, it won't get better later on.

Only then are we ready to take a leap into the wild blue yonder of imagination that sells. The thing we're looking for is provocative truth. It satisfies the eye and ear. It passes all the requisite tests, including time. It turns marketing plans into marketing realities.

And when it all comes together, it's not just advertising.

Together we create Brilliant Persuasion.

The great marketing minds you've been looking for in New York, Chicago, Atlanta and L.A. are right here. In Winston-Salem. Between the ocean and the mountains. So are the victories.

Packaging breakthrough. Adapt the elegance and femininity of perfume and make-up graphics to pantyhose. Women love this pearl.

People don't read furniture ads, they "feel" them. We made this one feel distinctive.

This award-winning corporate identity campaign is aimed at financial movers and shakers. Go ahead and make your move.

Hanes

She's tough but for a good cause – Hanes underwear. Everybody loves Inspector 12. Campaign recall is in the top 15% of all commercials ever tested.

The Agency Book 87

Blue Bell, Wrangler Div; Century Furniture Co; Fairchild Industrial Products Co; Gravely Int'l., Inc; Hanes Hosiery; Hanes Knitwear; Jefferson-Pilot Corp; Jefferson Standard Life Ins Co; L'eggs Products, Inc; McDonald's, Mac Central Co-op; McLean Trucking Co; Oakwood Homes Corp; Peanut Shack of America, Inc; Pilot Life Ins Co; RJ Reynolds Tobacco Co; Sealy of the Carolinas, Inc; Stanback Co; Wachovia Bank & Trust Co; WIX Div, Dana Corp.

LONG HAYMES CARR

Long, Haymes & Carr Incorporated

P.O. Box 5627
140 Charlois Blvd.
Winston-Salem, North Carolina
27113
919.765.3630

Contact: Joseph A. Haymes, Jr.
President & CEO

Employees: 120

Founded: 1949

Annual Billings: $43,000,000

Gross Billings by Media:

Newspaper	23.3%
Magazine	25.0%
DM	13.9%
Outdoor	1.1%
TV	46.9%
Radio	3.7%

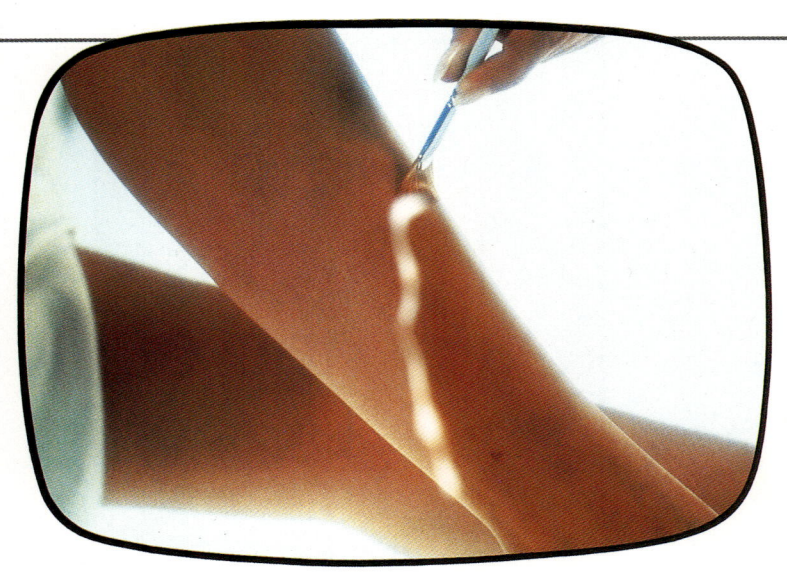

The right simile sells like gangbusters. New Isotoner Pantyhose "fit like you painted them on."

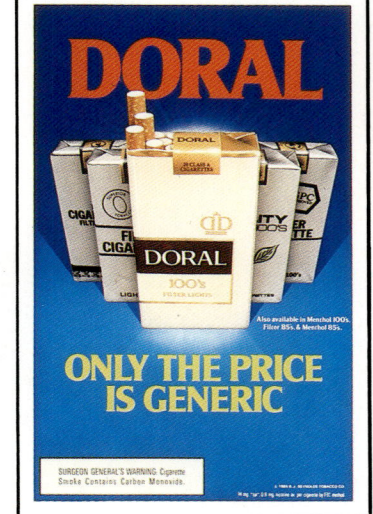

Brilliant Persuasion

How do you stay on top in a world full of high-priced designer jeans and low-priced imitations? Stay authentic.

We helped the client read the consumer smoke signals and introduce the first branded "generic" cigarette.

Aspirin advertising doesn't have to cause headaches. *(Target: blue collar people who don't believe white coats.)*

Storyteller/gospel singer Wendy Bagwell: "One time me and Geraldine and little Jan sang in a church where they believed in the handling of rattlesnakes. We didn't know that till we got there, and they offered me one. I told the girls, 'Don't panic. Look around. Find out where the back door is.' Geraldine said, 'I already looked and there ain't one.' I said, 'Reckon where do they want one?' It was enough to give you a headache that only a Stanback could handle. And that's a fact with my hand up." Anncr (VO): Snap back (SFX: finger snaps) with Stanback.

© 1986 Long, Haymes and Carr Inc.

The toughest taskmaster of a good advertising agency is the agency itself.

It asks more of itself than its clients do.

It measures its own performance every day, not just in terms of awards won, but in terms of sales gained.

We're happy with our record on both counts.

But what pleases us most is that over the years we've managed to help win sales and kudos for clients, regardless of how big or small their budget.

The radio commercial below is one example. The "little tramp" you've seen on television is another.

So, the person who tells you that the size of the budget isn't nearly as important as the size of the idea is worth listening to.

But what pleases us most is that over the years we've managed help to win sales and kudos for clients, regardless of how big or small their budget.

(John Cleese): "Hallo, have you heard about this rather unusual English candy which has a more **sophisticated** kind of taste than regular candy, not quite as sweet but a very fine classy sort of taste, and it's made by an English firm called Callard and Bowser and it really is **jolly good.** In fact, the truth is it's jolly, jolly good, and I know you'll like it, and as I say it is English **so please buy it** because we need the money in England at the moment. I mean we're all as poor as church mice. **Servants** are unbelievably expensive and our industry's practically disappeared. About all we make now is **muffins and** cricket bats

Lord, Geller, Federico, Einstein, Inc.

655 Madison Avenue
New York, New York 10021
212.421.6050
Telex: 237699 WWBUS UR
ATTN: LGFE

Contact: Richard J. Lord
Chairman & CEO

Employees: 284

Founded: 1967

Annual Billings: $220,000,000

Gross Billings by Media:	
Newspaper	11%
Magazine	23%
DM	1%
Outdoor	2%
TV	60%
Radio	3%

and really good candy and half the cricket bats come from Hong Kong. So please, do us a favor and just try this Callard and Bowser candy. It's a rather sophisticated taste and I'm sure you'll approve of it and after all I mean we did fight on your side in the War and we always let you beat us at golf. And incidentally, let's not forget you pinched our language. If we hadn't forgotten to copyright that you'd be paying us the most amazing royalties every week. So instead please buy Callard and Bowser's rather sophisticated English candy and help England back on its feet. Frankly, I think it's the least you can do."

Luckie & Forney, Inc. is the largest advertising agency in Alabama and one of the Southeast's top ten. Known for an outstanding creative product, it's won virtually every creative award regionally as well as nationally. Being one of the Southeast's largest advertising agencies, it also offers its clients fully staffed PR, Marketing, and Direct Marketing services. To many clients an advertising agency's credit rating is important. Luckie & Forney's record of financial responsibility is as good as any agency's in the country, better than most on Madison Avenue. Its growth has been substantial, tripling in just five years.

Clients

- Alabama Gas Corporation
- American Cast Iron Pipe Company
- Avondale Mills
- BellSouth Advanced Systems
- BellSouth Advertising & Publishing
- Blount International, Ltd.
- Blue Cross and Blue Shield of Alabama
- Carter Investments, Inc.
- Coca-Cola Bottlers
- Ernst & Whinney
- GameTime, Inc.
- Hardwick Clothes, Inc.
- Inverness Properties
- Kinder-Care, Inc.
- Liberty National Life Insurance
- McKee Baking Company
- QMS, Inc.
- Rust International Corporation
- South Central Bell
- SouthTrust Corporation
- Torchmark Corporation
- University of Alabama Hospitals
- Vulcan Materials Company
- Western Supermarkets
- WTTO-TV

YOU CAN TELL AN AGENCY'S CREATIVE PHILOSOPHY JUST BY LOOKING AT IT.

A creative philosophy shouldn't take a lot of words to express. If you like what you see here, you'll like our creative philosophy.

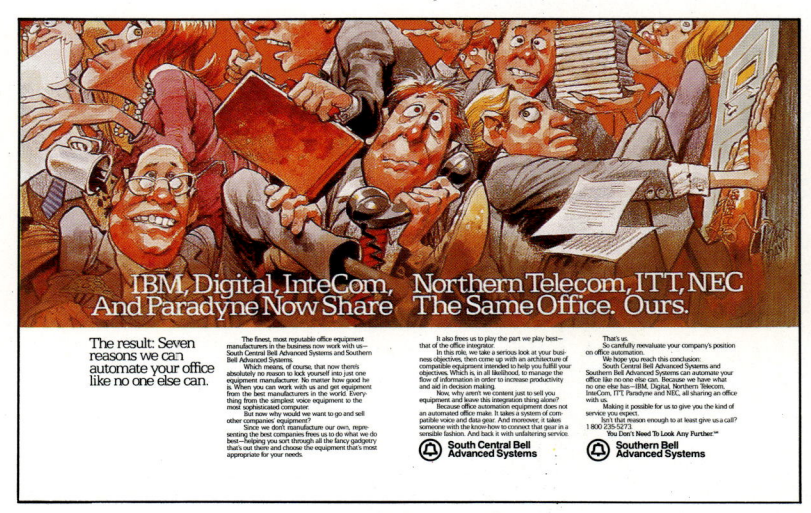

BellSouth Advanced Systems

South Central Bell

BellSouth Advanced Systems

South Central Bell Yellow Pages

The Agency Book **91**

Luckie & Forney, Inc.

120 Office Park Drive
P.O. Box 7484A
Birmingham, Alabama 35253
205.879.2121

Contact: Frank Lee
President

Employees: 100

Founded: 1953

Annual Billings: $50,000,000

Gross Billings by Media:

Newspaper	23%
Magazine	25%
DM	1%
Outdoor	2%
TV	40%
Radio	9%

Little Debbie Snack Cakes

Blue Cross & Blue Shield of Alabama

South Central Bell

Alabama Gas Corporation

South Central Bell

Liberty National Insurance

Inverness. A MetLife Planned Community

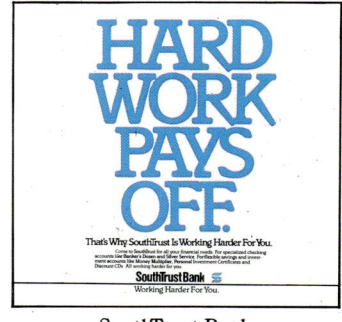

SouthTrust Bank

GameTime, Inc.

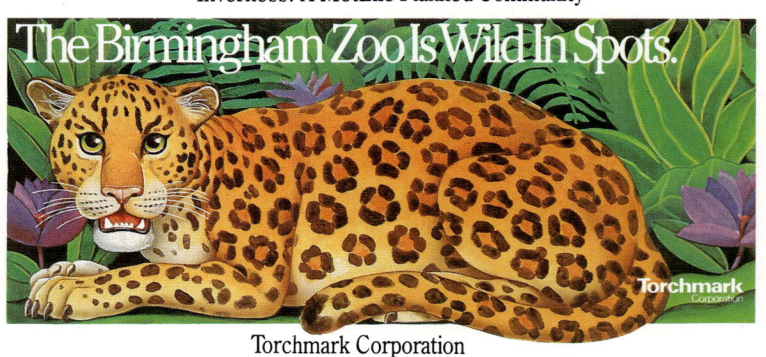

Torchmark Corporation

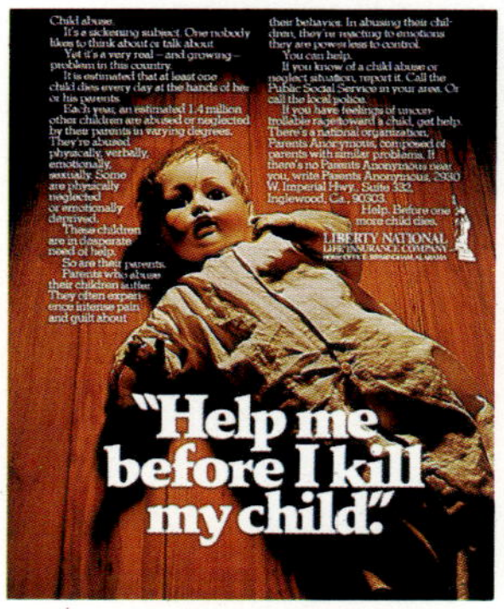

Liberty National Insurance

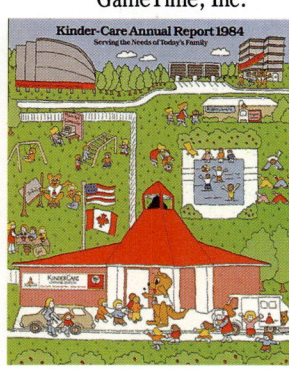

Kinder-Care Learning Centers

SEARS
The Amazement Park
CEDAR POINT
MARC
ADVERTISING
Pizza
Hut
SERVISTAR
SERVISTAR

Find out why some of America's largest consumer/retail advertisers shop at MARC

They come from Wichita, Kansas; Sandusky, Ohio; Butler, Pennsylvania; Chicago, Illinois. They come from all over America to MARC Advertising in Pittsburgh, because we've got something to sell that brings customers in to buy. What are these smart clients buying? MARC's unique approach to consumer/retail advertising.

Image building while traffic building

There are thousands of advertising agencies in America. MARC is one of the select few that has specialized in consumer/retail advertising for more than 30 years. The first thing we learned was that you must create traffic every day, not just during special sales and events. This realization was the springboard to our retail advertising philosophy: image building while traffic building.

Today, merely running price/item advertising without a positioning concept is about as effective as selling ice cubes to eskimos. That's why MARC specializes in the development of advertising programs that do two jobs for the price of one: we generate immediate sales and create a lasting identity. So when customers think of buying, they think of our clients first.

The art of retail positioning

In the over-saturated marketplace of the 80's, consumer/retail has become a harder sell than ever—and only retailers with a strong position are going to cash in. At MARC we realize that great advertising is only a small part of the sale. What's even more critical is establishing a distinct and clearly defined retail position, so that everything from the store design, product mix, site selection, merchandising and promotion can be unified into one cohesive marketing program that sharply differentiates your store from the competition's in the customer's mind.

Retail advertising vs. creativity

At MARC we create advertising that runs tonight and works tomorrow. But does this inescapable retail reality preclude creativity? Not at MARC it doesn't. Our work has won over 20 major national and international awards for creative excellence. In the past two years alone we've been honored by Advertising Age Magazine, The New York Art Directors' Club, The New York International Film Festival, and the Clios... just to name a few.

A few of our satisfied customers

Pizza Hut shops at MARC for development and testing of national sales promotion programs for television. ServiStar® Hardware, with 1700 stores nationally, shops at MARC for its advertising and marketing. Sears, the world's largest retailer, shops at MARC for regional advertising in over 35 markets. And Cedar Point, the Midwest's finest amusement park, has shopped at MARC for the past 13 years for marketing and advertising programs. MARC is where America's smartest consumer/retail advertisers shop for a precious commodity they haven't found any place else—advertising that builds traffic and image at the same time. If that's what you're in the market for, come to Pittsburgh and go on a shopping spree at MARC Advertising. Everything you buy is guaranteed to sell.

MARC Advertising
It runs tonight and works tomorrow.

MARC Advertising

Four Station Square
Pittsburgh, Pennsylvania 15219
412.562.2000

Contact: Anthony L. Bucci
Senior Vice President &
Director of Client Services

Employees: 110

Founded: 1955

Annual Billings: $45,000,000

Gross Billings by Media:

Newspaper	20%
Magazine	2%
DM	7%
Outdoor	1%
TV	60%
Radio	10%

MARC

GUEST QUARTERS

WHEN YOU'RE BUILDING A NAME NOBODY WORKS HARDER FOR YOU THAN McCAFFREY AND McCALL.

An open letter to David McCall and his cohorts.

Dear David,

Here's one ad we sneaked past you when you weren't looking. We created it all by ourselves to surprise you with a public display of gratitude.

We recently opened new hotels in Tampa, Fl. and Charlotte, N.C., with advertising support from McCaffrey and McCall. Within just a couple of months, both were well on their way to profitability—a remarkable achievement by the standards of our industry. Your counsel and the creative execution contributed greatly to our success. You even gave us a considerable amount of change back from our budget.

I particularly want to thank Peter Manley, Richard Feiss, Charlie Brown, Carolyn Foley, Carl Christie, Camille McMennamin, Murdo MacLeod, Peter Spacek, Judy Hultquist, Marvin Fried, Lin Davis, Stan Forman, Angela Castro, Bill Bildersee and Barbara Kunen. And that's really just the beginning of a long list of people there whose efforts made a difference for us.

If the time ever comes for the satisfied clients of McCaffrey and McCall to stand up and be counted, please note that we're already standing.

Sincerely,

Michael M. Dickens

Michael M. Dickens
President, Guest Quarters Hotels

GUEST QUARTERS
THE ALL SUITE HOTELS
(800) 424-2900

Reprinted with permission of Adweek.

"The client wrote it!"

The first time we saw this ad was in the April 22, 1985 issue of Adweek. Our Guest Quarters client created and placed it without our knowing a thing about it.

Most agencies have clients who appreciate them. But to our knowledge, no other agency ever had a client who told the world.

If you're interested in the same standard of commitment that impressed our client Guest Quarters, give McCaffrey and McCall a call.

McCaffrey and McCall, Inc.

575 Lexington Avenue
New York, New York 10022
212.421.7500
Telex: 654029

Contact: William R. Haldane
Senior Vice President
Director of Business Development

Employees: 370

Founded: 1962

Annual Billings: $200,000,000

Gross Billings by Media:	
Newspaper	14%
Magazine	30%
DM	*
Outdoor	1%
TV	48%
Radio	2%
Other	5%

*Direct Marketing accounts for approximately 16% of total billings across selected media.

McCaffrey and McCall, Inc.

Client (Year Assigned to Agency)

Air Canada (1979)
American Broadcasting Companies, Inc. (1964)
Citibank, N.A. (1984)
Exxon Corporation (1966)
Falcon Jet Corporation (1982)
Guest Quarters (1982)
The Hartford Insurance Group (1967)
Hiram Walker Incorporated (1934)
Mercedes-Benz of North America, Inc. (1979)
National Coffee Association (1984)
New York Stock Exchange (1984)
North American Philips Corporation/Norelco (1954)
Pfizer Inc. (1965)
Puerto Rico Tourism Company (1985)
T. Rowe Price Associates, Inc. (1982)
Westvaco (1967)

Contact:
William R. Haldane
Senior Vice President
Director of Business Development
(212) 421-7500

McCaffrey and McCall Direct Marketing

Client (Year Assigned to Agency)

Air Canada (1982)
Educational Products Inc. (1984)
Electronic Mall (1985)
Exxon Corporation (1985)
Falcon Jet Corporation (1982)
The Hartford Insurance Group (1983)
Mercedes-Benz of North America, Inc. (1981)
New York Stock Exchange (1984)
North American Philips Corporation (1985)
T. Rowe Price Associates, Inc. (1982)
Westvaco (1985)

Contact:
Robert Cherins
President of Direct Marketing
(212) 303-6000

HOW TO MAKE A JADED NEW YORKER BECOME A NATIVE NEW YORKER AGAIN

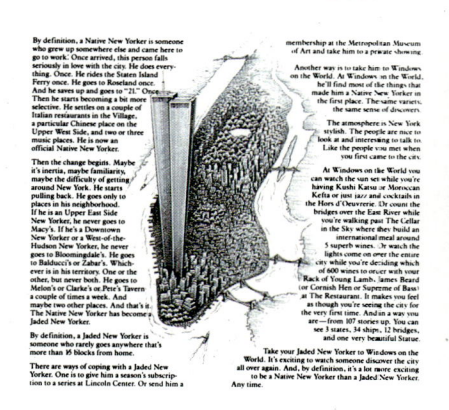

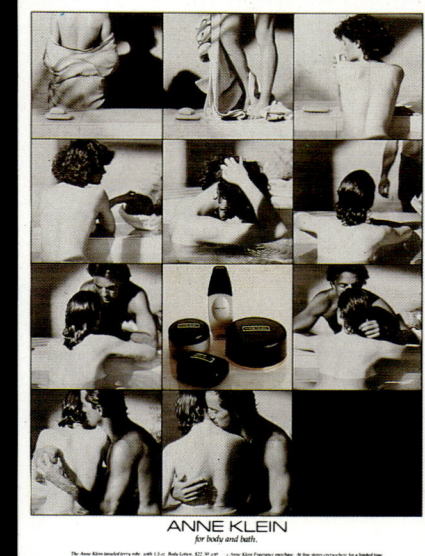

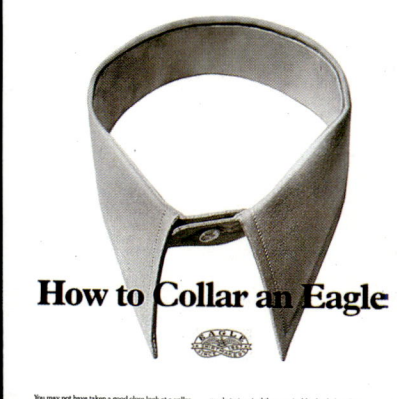

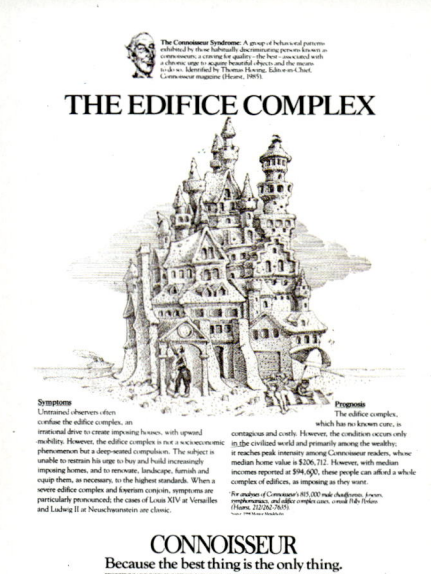

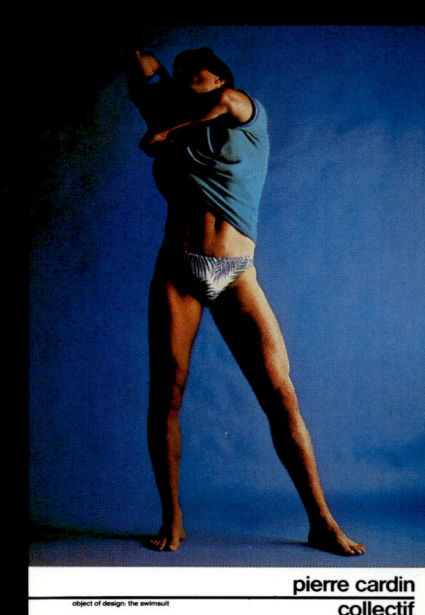

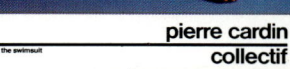

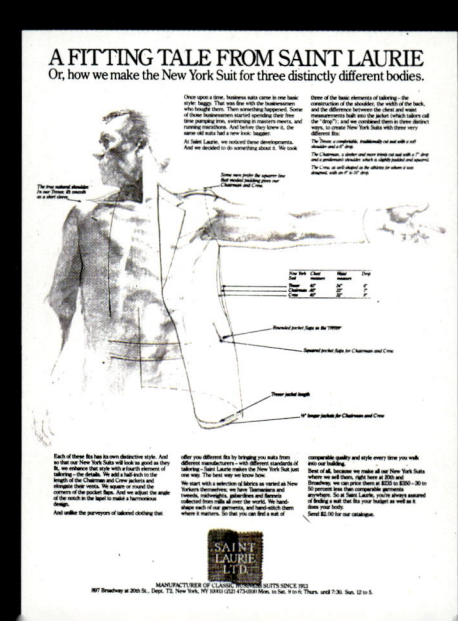

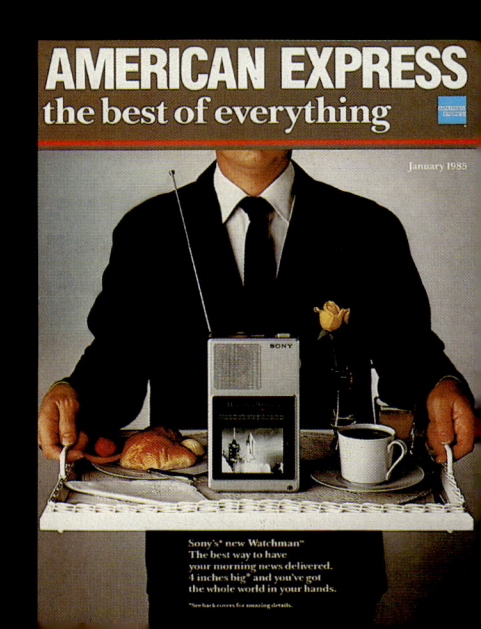

How to Collar an Eagle

ANNE KLEIN
for body and bath

THE EDIFICE COMPLEX

CONNOISSEUR
Because the best thing is the only thing.

Sophia Loren Eyewear
by Zyloware

pierre cardin
collectif
object of design: the swimsuit

ALONE IN THE FIELD

HOUSE BEAUTIFUL

A FITTING TALE FROM SAINT LAURIE
Or, how we make the New York Suit for three distinctly different bodies.

SAINT LAURIE LTD.

AMERICAN EXPRESS
the best of everything

January 1985

Sony's new Watchman.
The best way to have your morning news delivered.
4 inches big* and you've got the whole world in your hands.

The Agency Book **97**

McCaffery & Ratner, Inc.

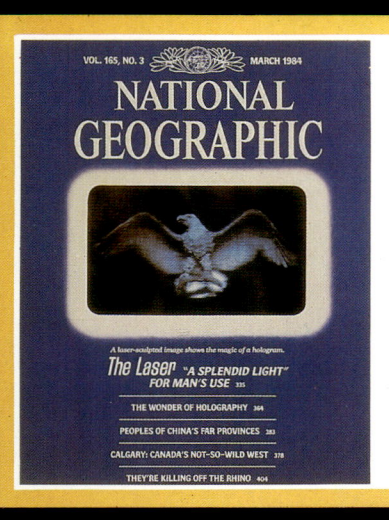

370 Lexington Avenue
New York, New York 10017
212.661.8940

Contacts: William McCaffery
President & Creative Director;
Samuel I. Ratner
Chairman

Employees: 36

Founded: 1983

Annual Billings: $23,800,000

Gross Billings by Media:

Newspaper	23%
Magazine	35%
DM	3%
Outdoor	5%
TV	20%
Radio	14%

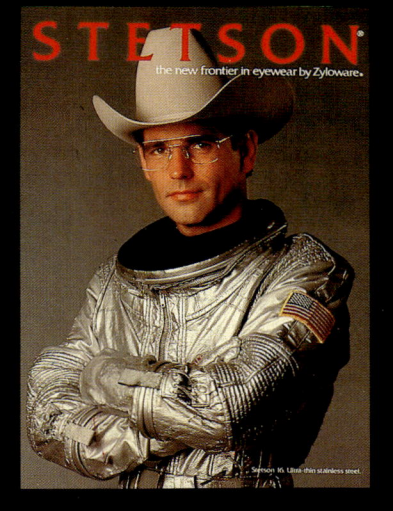

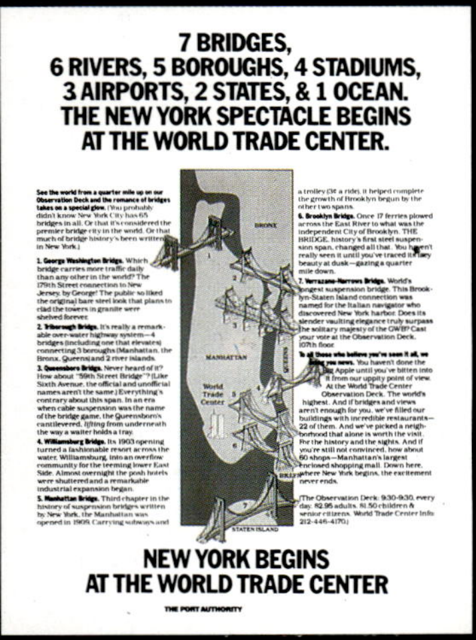

Creative Philosophy

Our creative philosophy is that the best advertising is advertising that grows directly out of the inherent individual attributes of each singular product or service—attributes that no other product has or is perceived to have. There are those inherent attributes in almost every product. There *is* a difference between a Mercury and an Oldsmobile, between a Winston and a Marlboro, between Bayer and Bufferin. And the good creative agency digs until they find this difference. In those rare circumstances where no difference exists, the job is to create one based on the product performance or its history or the consumer's perceptions or a gap in the market place that this product or service could suitably fill pre-emptively.

Because we practice this philosophy in everything we do, we have no "look" or "style" or "format". Everything we do is informative, intriguing and believable, but the way we do it is totally dependent on the individual story of the product itself.

The result of practicing this philosophy is that we can advertise three different magazines and develop three totally different product stories for them—all equally effective. Connoisseur Magazine "Because the best thing is the only thing", House Beautiful because it's "Alone in the Field" and National Geographic becomes "The National Holographic, Photographic, Cartographic, Oceanographic, Topographic, Psychographic, Demographic." We position and advertise Saint Laurie in a much different way than we positioned our advertising for Paul Stuart. For Inhilco, we represent nine different restaurants and do different work for each one of them. For Anne Klein our singular positioning is accomplished through the use of pictures alone. Our introductory television for Viadent Toothpaste creates an entire new category in the field. And if we had Rolls-Royce we would create a campaign that in no way resembled a Mercedes campaign. And if we had Mercedes we would create a campaign that in no way resembled Peugeot. We would do three vastly different campaigns for the three of them because each car has its own story and deserves its own campaign.

Not surprisingly, an agency that works and has worked this way for accounts of all descriptions is better equipped to find the singular attributes of any specific product or service than an agency which specializes in one basic style. Specialization can be binding and mind-shutting: the tendency is to sameness. Broad experience teaches an agency that there is something individual to say about *every* product in *every* category. That is the most basic of our beliefs.

Coke
DRISTAN® LONG LASTING NASAL SPRAY
Häagen-Dazs BUTTER PECAN ICE CREAM
Speed Stick DEODORANT
352 TRÈS BERRIE
274 GERANIUM
L'ORÉAL
20 FILTER CIGARETTES
CAMEL LIGHTS
LOW TAR CAMEL TASTE
Kodak
AMERICAN EXPRESS
3728 423456
J N NELSON
Lufthansa
Alka-Seltzer
NET WT. 3 OZ.
PURVEYORS TO THE IMPERIAL RUSSIAN COURT
Ste Pierre Smirnoff
VODKA
80 PROOF
DISTILLED FROM
HARTFORD, U.S.A.
TRUTH WELL TOLD
L O R E A L
Ragamuffin.
L'OREAL
Presenting the pinstripe that's a little out of line.
swatch
On six continents, one word is synonymous with punctuality.
Lufthansa
AMERICAN EXPRESS
For those who control their finances, rather than the other way around.
THE GOLD CARD
20 CIGARETTES
KING SIZE
Winston
FILTERS
RICH TASTE
MARTINI & ROSSI IN A GLASS BY ITSELF
Only sunflower oil could make this Promise
Promise
Save 40¢

McCann-Erickson New York

485 Lexington Avenue
New York, New York 10017
212.697.6000
Telex: 620514

Contact: John Dooner
Executive VP & General Manager

Employees: 700

Founded: 1911

Annual Billings: $400,000,000

Gross Billings by Media:	
Newspaper	6%
Magazine	22%
Outdoor	1%
TV	62%
Radio	9%

McCANN-ERICKSON
Truth Well Told

Tell me, you muse as you flip through the pages quickly, exactly what kind of advertising agency *is* McCann-Erickson, anyway?

A "strategic" agency?

A "creative" agency?

Yes, we answer back.

Seventy-four years ago, when the agency was only a year old and really rather small, a significant conclusion was reached.

"Truth Well Told" would be our motto.

We would not divide "strategy" and "creative" into separate camps. We would let each serve the other. We would find the essential truth of a client's product or service—not only the *objective* truth but also the *subjective* truth as perceived by the consumer—then communicate it very, very well.

Over the years, we haven't strayed from the motto.

"Truth Well Told" it was, and "Truth Well Told" it is.

"Strategy" without "creative" is worthless. "Creative" without "strategy" is even more so.

Remember who we are if anyone tells you otherwise.

American Home Products
American Express Company
AT&T Communications
Beatrice Foods
Coca-Cola USA
Cosmair, Inc. (L'Oreal)
Eastman Kodak Company
Gillette Company
Haagen-Dazs
Heublein, Inc.
Johnson & Johnson Advanced Care Products
Baby Products Company
Lever Brothers Company

Lufthansa German Airlines
Mennen Company
Nestle Company
Pace University
R.J. Reynolds Tobacco Co.
Renfield Importers Ltd. Martini & Rossi Vermouths and Aste Spumante
Shearson Lehman Brothers
Simac Appliances Corp.
Sony Corporation of America
Swatch
Trinidad & Tobago Tourist Board
U.S. Department of Treasury

Offices throughout the U.S.A. and Canada
Albuquerque • Atlanta • Baltimore • Boston • Chicago • Cincinnati •
Cleveland • Columbus • Dallas • Denver • Detroit • Edmonton •
Ft. Lauderdale • Houston • Kansas City • Los Angeles • Minneapolis •
Montreal • New York • Ottawa • Philadelphia • Phoenix • Pittsburgh •
Raleigh • Rochester • St. Louis • San Diego • San Francisco •
Santa Ana • Tampa • Toronto • Vancouver • Washington DC • Wichita

Clients
Leading corporations in every business & industry, including a significant representation of Fortune 500 firms

Member
American Association of Advertising Agencies

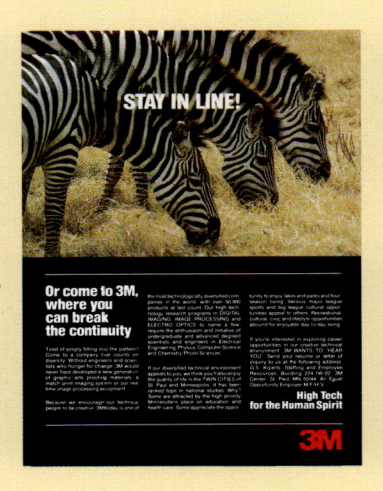

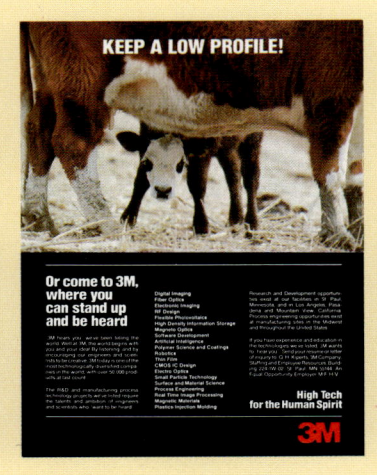

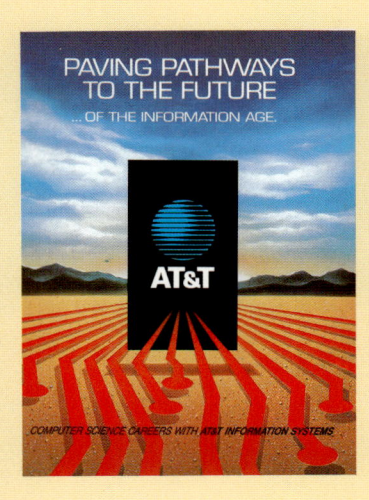

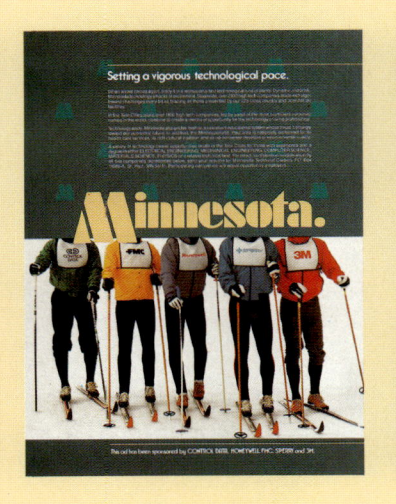

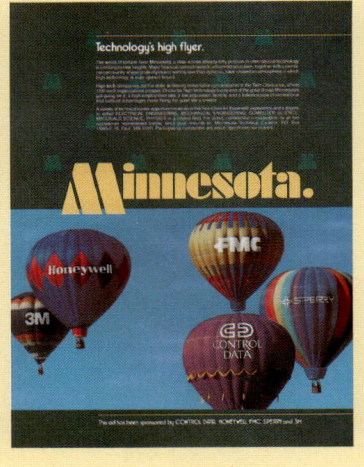

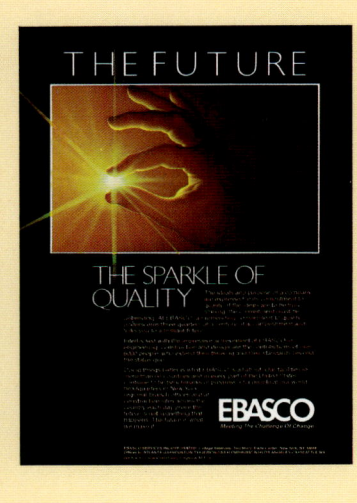

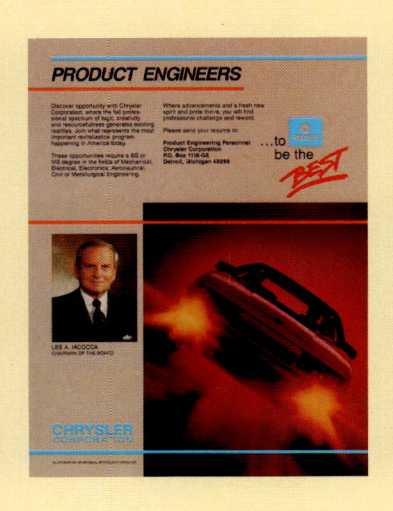

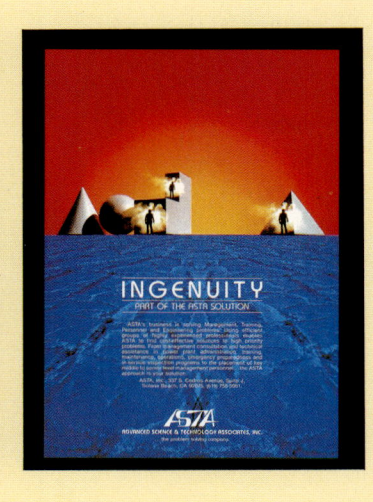

Nationwide Advertising Service Inc.

The Penthouse
Statler Office Tower
Cleveland, Ohio 44115
216.579.0300

Contact: Thomas A. Richey
President

Employees: 300

Founded: 1947

Annual Billings: $110,000,000

Gross Billings by Media: NA

We've got a lot of nerve being in this book

After all, this is a book of product ads. And here we are showing you ads strictly for careers. But the same way great product advertising pays off in sales, great recruitment advertising pays off in topnotch personnel. Your company's image as an employer comes out a winner, too. If you want the best people available — for technical, managerial, sales or professional positions — you need recruitment advertising that hits the market hard.

You need Nationwide Advertising. The leader in recruitment.

Needham Harper Worldwide Clients

American Honda Motor Company, Inc.	Dorsey Laboratories, Inc.	McDonald's Advertising Associations	G.D. Searle & Co.
Amtrak	Embassy Pictures, Inc.	Morton Salt	Sears, Roebuck and Co.
Amurol Products Co.	Fortune Magazine	Mrs. Paul's Kitchens, Inc.	Sharp Health Systems
Anheuser-Busch Cos., Inc.	Frigidaire Co.	The Nashville Network	Source Telecomputing Corp.
Armour-Dial, Inc.	Frito-Lay, Inc.	The National Guard Bureau	Southern Living Magazine
Associated Press Broadcast Services	General Mills, Inc.	One Magnificent Mile	State Farm Insurance Co.
Bayless Markets	Home Federal	Q-107 FM	Surburban Bank
Binney & Smith, Inc.	Honda Dealer Advertising Associations	Quasar Co.	Union Carbide Corp.
California State Lottery	Household Finance Corp.	Ramada Inns, Inc.	The Washington Post
Campbell Soup Co.	Kraft, Inc.	RCA Corp.	Wm. Wrigley Jr. Co.
Carter-Wallace, Inc.	Kubota Tractor Corp.	Rubbermaid Inc.	WJLA-TV
Cellular One	La Petite Boulangerie	San Diego Union/Tribune	Wolverine World Wide, Inc.
The Clorox Co.	Manor HealthCare Corp.	Sandoz Nutrition Corp.	Xerox Corp.
		Sandoz U.S.A.	

When you have only 30 seconds to live, it's amazing what you can do.

Honda "It's a Rocket"

Bud Light "Call for Bud Light"

Amtrak "Comforts"

The Agency Book **103**

Needham Harper Worldwide, Inc.

909 Third Avenue
New York, New York 10022
212.758.7600

Contact: Keith Reinhard
CEO

Employees: 2,600

Founded: 1925

Annual Billings: $842,100,000

Gross Billings by Media:

Newspaper	6%
Magazine	19%
Outdoor	2%
TV	66%
Radio	7%

Wheaties "What the Big Boys Eat"

Xerox "Monk"

Bud Light "Olympic Tribute"

Sears "Cheryl Tiegs"

BASIS SOAP

NIVEA

How to make $24 million look like $240 million.

YELLOW PAGES

AXELROD

LINX CELLULAR PHONE SERVICE

NIVEA SUN

HUGHES LABORATORIES

SOUTHERN NEW ENGLAND TELEPHONE
Bronze Lion, Cannes Film Festival; Clio Finalist; Silver Award, International Film and TV Festival; First Place, International Broadcasting Awards; 2 First Place Telly Awards; First Place, New England Broadcasting Awards.

CROWLEY FOODS
Bronze Telly Award.

YELLOW PAGES
Finalist, International Film and TV Festival.

MURPHY'S OIL SOAP
One of Adweek's 10 Best Packaged Goods Commercials, 1985.

The Agency Book **105**

Posey & Quest, Inc.

6 Glenville Street
Greenwich, Connecticut 06831
203.531.4900

Contact: James H. Quest
President & CEO

Employees: 32

Founded: 1977

Annual Billings: $24,000,000

Gross Billings by Media:

Newspaper	20%
Magazine	35%
TV	35%
Radio	10%

At Posey and Quest, we don't believe that the size of an advertising budget should dictate the quality of advertising.

You can always make a budget go further, work harder and appear bigger than first seems possible.

And you can always do good work for good clients.

For more proof, call Jim Quest.

Clients.
Beiersdorf: All consumer products: Nivea Hand & Body Lotion, Creme, Oil; Nivea Sun Care; Basis Soaps; Aquaphor Ointment; New Products.
Conoco/DuPont: Corporate Advertising.
Crowley Foods: All products: Crowley Dairy Products; Axelrod Dairy & Cheese Products; Netherlander Cheese.
Economics Laboratory: New Products.
Gulf + Western: Corporate Advertising.
Hughes Laboratories: Replex Medication; Corporate Adv.
The Murphy-Phoenix Company: Murphy's Oil Soap.
Pastabilities Restaurants: All Advertising.
Penta Hotels: New York Penta Hotel.
Southern New England Telephone: Cellular Mobile Division; Yellow Pages/Directory Services Division.

Subsidiaries.
New York Office:
307 East 56th Street
New York, New York 10022.
(212) 750-5566.

We're hot in both towns. With $12-million of our 1985 year-end billings secured through new business acquisitions that year. Our philosophy is simple. Provide clients with great work, good vibes, and the most responsive service in the business. If that sounds good to you, check us out. Contact Hal Donofrio in Baltimore, or Philly.

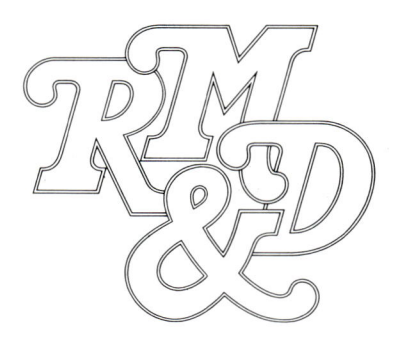

Richardson, Myers & Donofrio, Inc.

120 West Fayette Street
Baltimore, Maryland 21201
301.576.9000
Telex: 254 7113

Contact: Hal Donofrio
President & CEO

Employees: 130

Founded: 1964

Annual Billings: $53,500,000

Gross Billings by Media:

Newspaper	16%
Magazine	36%
DM	2%
Outdoor	2%
TV	31%
Radio	13%

"RM&D? Isn't that the hot shop in Baltimore... or is it Philly?"

OUR CREATIVE ONE-TWO PUNCH

Ron Rosenfeld
Inducted into the
Copywriters
Hall of Fame–1971

Len Sirowitz
Inducted into the
Art Directors
Hall of Fame–1985

Rosenfeld, Sirowitz & Humphrey, Inc.

111 Fifth Avenue
New York, New York 10003
212.505.0200

Contact: Stephen E. Humphrey
President

Employees: 180

Founded: 1971

Annual Billings: $140,000,000

Gross Billings by Media:	
Newspaper	14%
Magazine	14%
TV	70%
Radio	2%

There are 9,089 advertising agencies in America. Only two have two principals who have been honored with Hall of Fame recognition. To discover how an agency with that kind of creative potency can make things happen for your company call:

Rosenfeld, Sirowitz & Humphrey

STOP!

Rumrill-Hoyt Advertising

635 Madison Avenue
New York, New York 10022
212.872.4000
Telex: 422293

Contact: Paul Goldsmith
President

Employees: 100

Founded: 1933

Annual Billings: $135,000,000

Gross Billings by Media:

Media	
Newspaper	6%
Magazine	39%
Outdoor	9%
TV	41%
Radio	5%

IT'S EASIER TO CALL RUMRILL HOYT NEW YORK 212 872 4000

And ask Paul Goldsmith about Actifed, America's No. 1 Cold Tablet. And Bacardi rum, America's No. 1 Spirit. And Unisa, America's No. 1 Sandal. And New York's Lottery. And Ladies' Home Journal. And Papillon Wines. And New York City Opera. And all our other clients who are happily laughing their way to the bank.

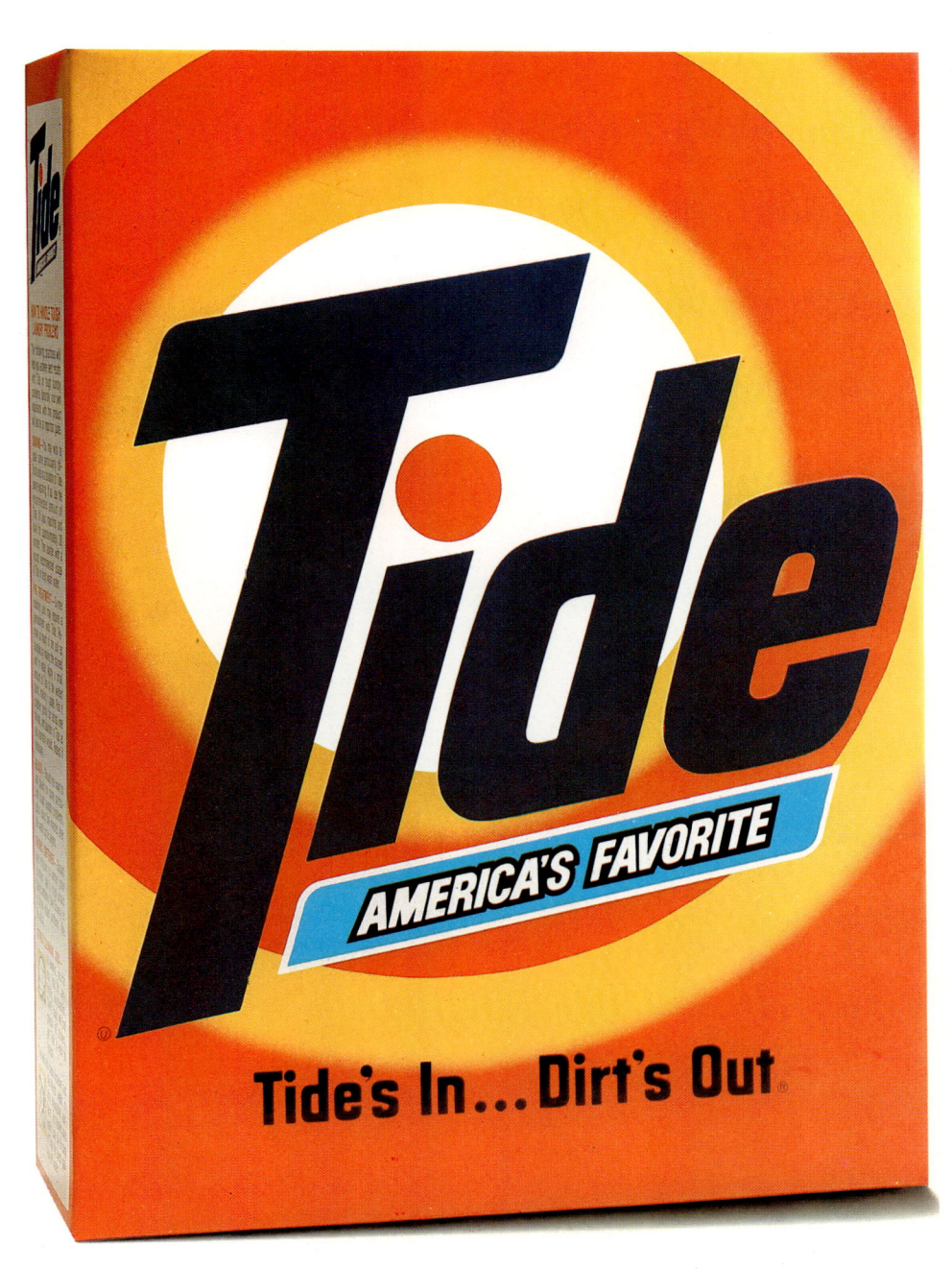

We know how to fight clean.

The Agency Book **113**

Saatchi & Saatchi Compton Inc.

625 Madison Avenue
New York, New York 10022
212.350.1000
Telex: 422293 SSCI

Contact: Ed Wax

Employees (U.S.): 1,325

Annual Billings (U.S.): $825,000,000

Gross Billings by Media: NA

We know how to fight dirty.

Clients and Products

Bojangles of America, Inc.: Chicken and Biscuit Fast Food.
Burmah-Castrol, Inc.: Motor Oil, Lubricants.
Chase Manhattan Bank: Corporate, Consumer, Wholesale (Business to Business), International.
Columbia Pictures: Motion Picture.
Continental Airlines: Passenger and Cargo Service.
Duffy-Mott Company Inc.: Juices, Sauces, New Products.
The Equitable Life Assurance Company of The United States: EVLICO.
Hertz Corporation: Rent-A-Car, Buy-A-Car, Rent-A-Truck, Car Leasing.
James River Corporation: Bolt Paper Towels, Aurora Bathroom Tissue, Brawny Paper Towels & Tissues, Gala Paper Towels and Tissues, Northern Bathroom Tissue, New Products.

Marriott Corporation: Courtyard by Marriott, Marriott Lifecare Residences.
Maxell Corporation: Recording Tapes.
Nikon Inc.: 35mm Cameras and Accessories.
Perdue Farms, Inc.: Fresh Chickens, Chicken Parts, Chicken Franks, Shenandoah Turkeys, Fresh Prepared Chicken Dishes.
Ralston-Purina Company: Pet Foods, Breakfast Products.
A.H. Robins: Robitussin Cough Remedies, Dimetapp Allergy Relief, Albee C-800 Vitamins, Z-Bec Vitamins.
Sharp Electronics: Consumer and Industrial Divisions.
Volvo of America Corp.: Automobiles.
Western Union: Mailgram, Electronic Cash Transfer.

THEY TAKE TOO BUT, BOY, DO

19 years and still running.

15 years and still running.

Some clients evaluate agencies on how quickly they come up with fresh new ideas. These clients invariably choose sprinters and end up changing their advertising every year.

Scali, McCabe, Sloves' 19 year history is marked with a succession of fresh new ideas. Name an award for creative excellence. We've won it. Twice. But the greatness of our ideas is best demonstrated by noting how many of them become fresh old ones.

Our campaign based on Volvo's longevity, safety and durability has been going strong for 19 years. Virtually unchanged.

Our Perdue Chicken campaign, featuring Frank Perdue, has been running for 15 years with much-heralded success.

The Agency Book **115**

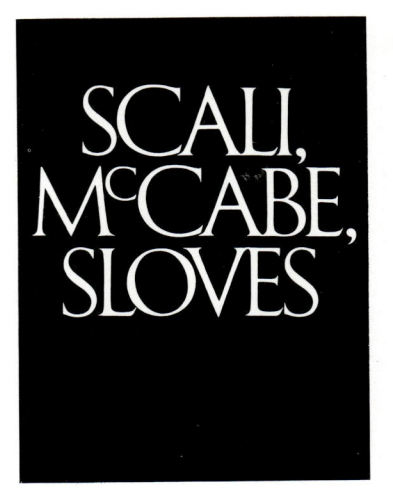

Scali, McCabe, Sloves, Inc.

SCALI, McCABE, SLOVES

800 Third Avenue
New York, New York 10022
212.735.8000
TWX: 7105814574 SMS Inc NYK

Contact: Marvin Sloves
Chairman & CEO

Employees: 405

Founded: 1967

Annual Billings: $250,000,000

Gross Billings by Media:	
Newspaper	10%
Magazine	21%
DM	9%
Outdoor	3%
TV	51%
Radio	6%

LONG TO GET THEY LAST.

10 years and still running.

5 years and still running.

For Castrol Motor Oil we formulated a campaign that's been building their business for 10 years. For Nikon, our campaign is going into its fifth year.

If you're ready for a campaign you can live with, call Marvin Sloves at 212-735-8000. Why wait any longer than you have to?

SCALI, McCABE, SLOVES, INC.
800 Third Avenue, New York, New York 10022 (212) 735-8000.

Offices in New York, Houston, Atlanta, Santa Monica, Toronto, Montreal, Mexico, London, Germany, Australia, France, Brazil.

Clients: Bojangles of America, Inc., Burmah-Castrol, Inc., Chase Manhattan Bank, Columbia Pictures, Continental Airlines, Duffy-Mott Company, Inc., The Equitable Life Assurance Society of The United States, Hertz Corporation, James River Corporation, Marriott Corporation, Maxell Corporation, Nikon, Inc., Perdue Farms, Inc., Ralston-Purina Company, Revlon, Inc., A.H. Robins, Sharp Electronics, Volvo of America Corporation, Western Union.

© 1986, Scali, McCabe, Sloves, Inc.

Client List

Child World
Avon Massachusetts.
America's second largest discount toy supermarket.

Digital Equipment Corporation
Maynard, Massachusetts.
Manufacturers of computer systems.

GenRad, Inc.
Waltham, Massachusetts.
Quality-management products and systems.

Leggat McCall & Werner, Inc.
Boston, Massachusetts.
Commercial and industrial real estate.

MEMTEC Incorporated
Salem, New Hampshire.
Reel-to-reel memory technology.

Sinclair Research Limited
Boston, Massachusetts.
Personal electronic products.

Vixen Yachts
Vineyard Haven, Massachusetts.
Custom builders of sailing yachts.

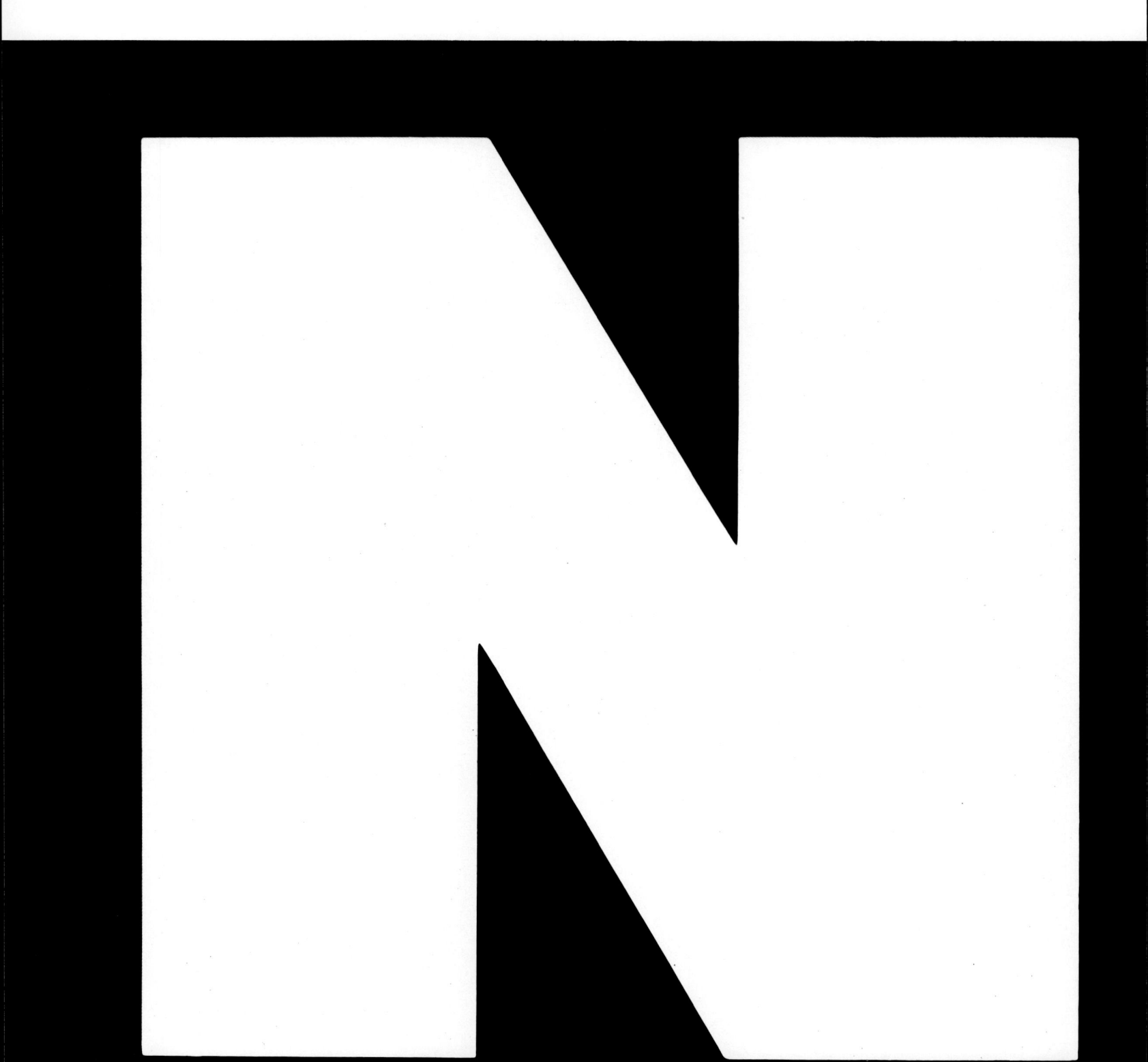

SPJ Schneider Parker Jakuc

31 St. James Avenue
Boston, Massachusetts 02116
617.542.3444

Contact: Robert Schneider
President

Employees: 31

Founded: 1963

Annual Billings: $20,000,000

Gross Billings by Media:	
Newspaper	20%
Magazine	50%
DM	5%
Outdoor	5%
TV	10%
Radio	10%

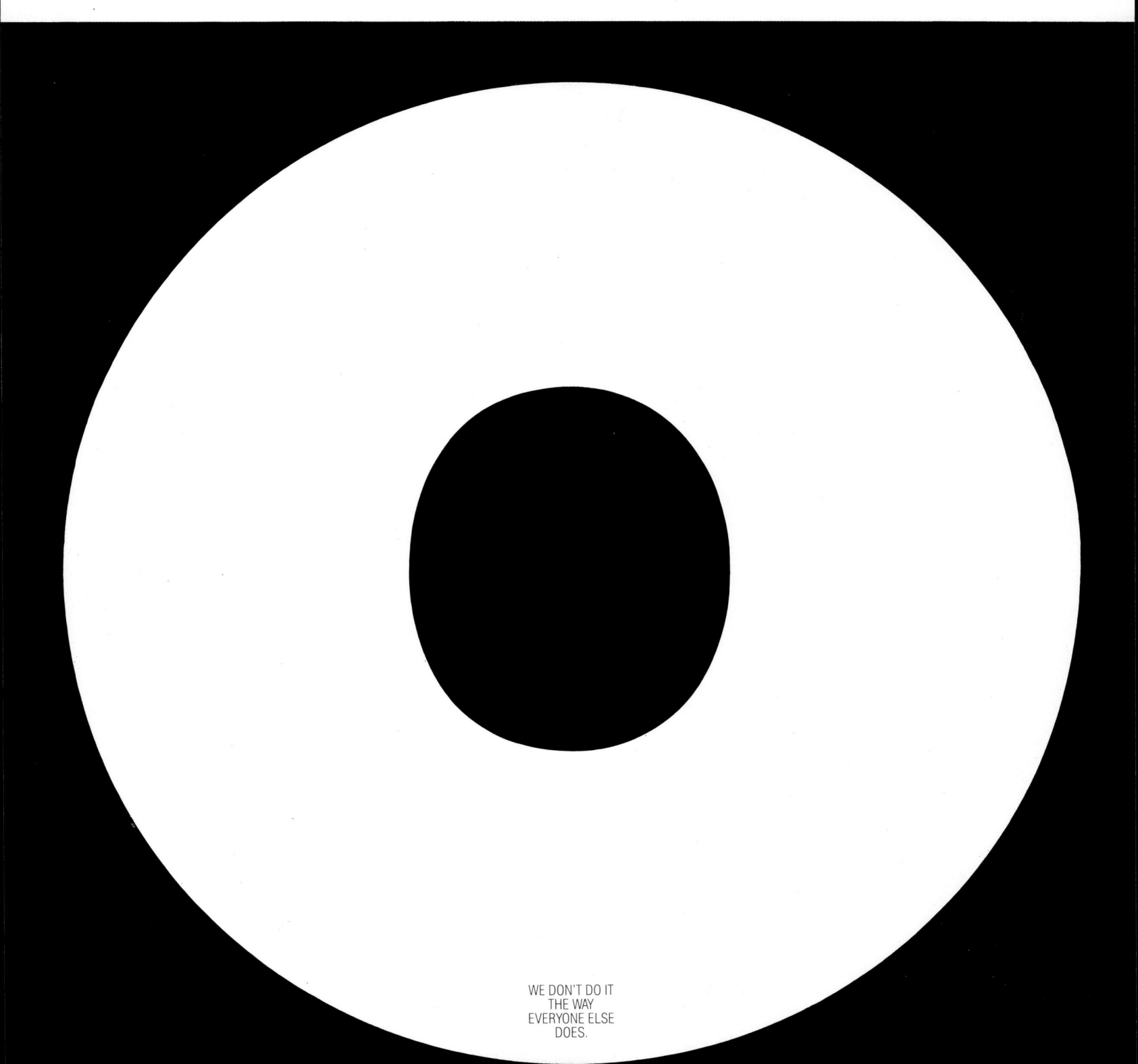

WE DON'T DO IT
THE WAY
EVERYONE ELSE
DOES.

Principal Officers

Stephen C. Scott: President and Chief Executive Officer.

Peggy Lancaster: Creative Director.

David W. Mills: Director of Client Services.

David S. Atha: Media Director/Treasurer.

Clifford M. Scott: Vice President/Account Supervisor.

Lynn Hockin: Vice President/Associate Media Director.

David Gordon: Vice President/Marketing.

Steve Jarvis: Vice President/Associate Creative Director.

Current Clients

Avalon Industries; Brooklyn, New York. Crayons, crafts, coloring books, and other activity toys.

Beatrice/Hunt-Wesson Foods; Fullerton, California. Special projects.

Gund, Inc.; Edison, New Jersey. America's premier line of stuffed toys.

Leisure Dynamics/Lakeside Games; Westport, Connecticut. Tubtown pre-school toys; boys' action toys; games for all age groups.

Seafood Broiler Restaurants; Lakewood, California. Chain of seafood restaurants in Los Angeles, San Diego and Northern California.

Jewel T Discount Grocery Stores; Grand Prairie, Texas. Chain of discount grocery stores.

Tomy Corp; Carson, California. Aurora AFX racing sets and hobby products.

SEAFOOD BROILER

LAKESIDE/Crossbows & Catapults

JEWEL T/Discount Grocery Stores

THE MONTEREY VINEYARD

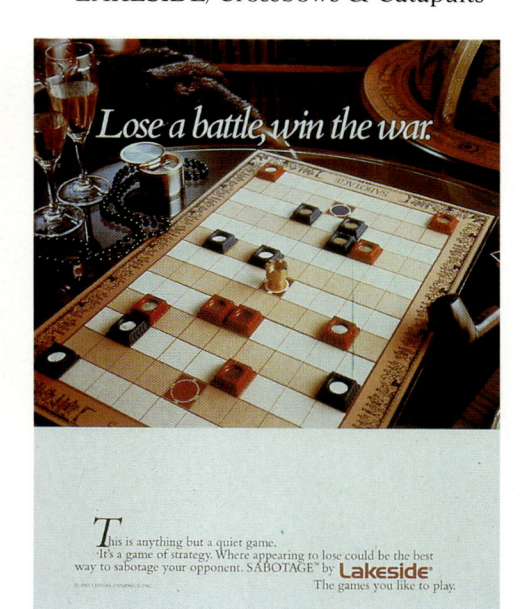

LAKESIDE/Sabotage

DEP/Cornucopia Valley

SEARS PLUMBER

GUND

SCOTT LANCASTER MILLS ATHA

Scott Lancaster Mills Atha

2049 Century Park East, Suite 860
Los Angeles, California 90067
213.552.6050

Contact: Stephen C. Scott
President

Employees: 26

Founded: 1976

Annual Billings: $22,000,000

Gross Billings by Media:

Newspaper	8%
Magazine	25%
DM	2%
Outdoor	5%
TV	40%
Radio	20%

Break a leg.

Seafood Broiler
SEAFOOD BROILER/Restaurant Chain

Finding the right advertising agency is really as simple as finding people you like who do advertising that you think is terrific. If you like the work shown here – really like it – then you're halfway home.

Now all you have to do is find out if you like us. And if we like you.

VAN LUIT

GUND

AAPRI

DEP/Paba Plus

GIORGIO

Health care.
Professionals.
Consumers.
Ethical drugs.
OTC drugs.
Diagnostics.
Medical services & technologies.
Marketing.
Leadership.
Creativity.
Worldwide.

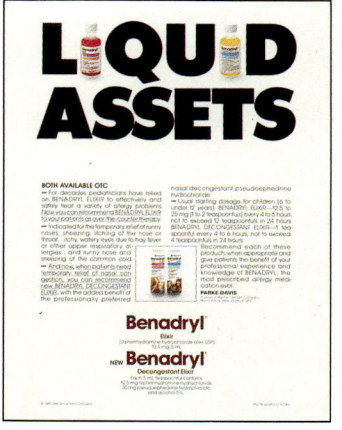

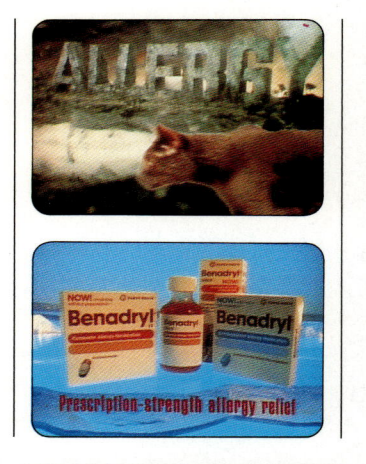

Sudler & Hennessey.

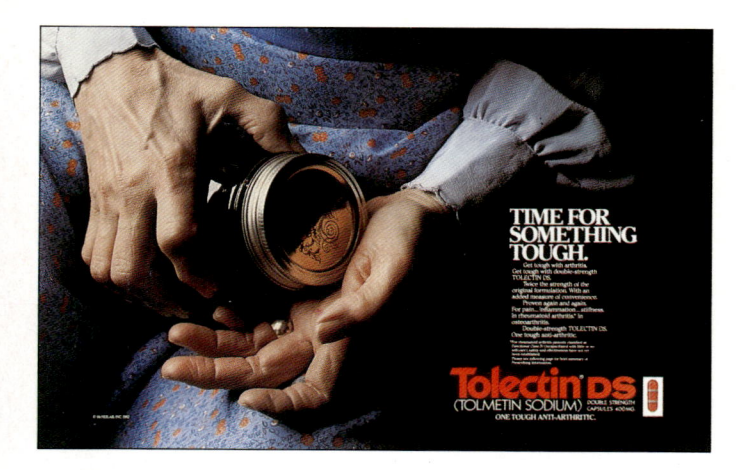

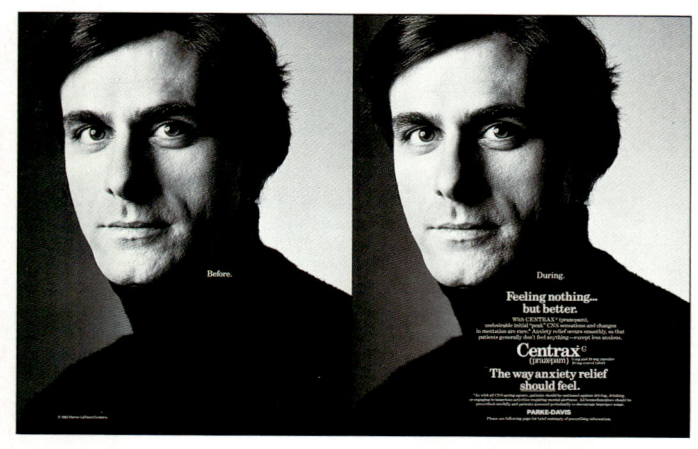

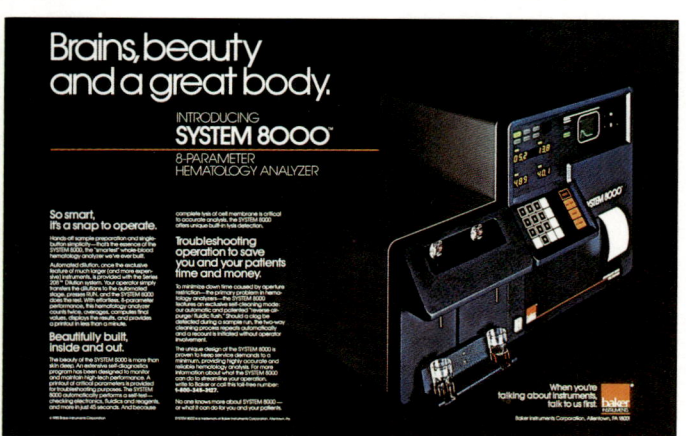

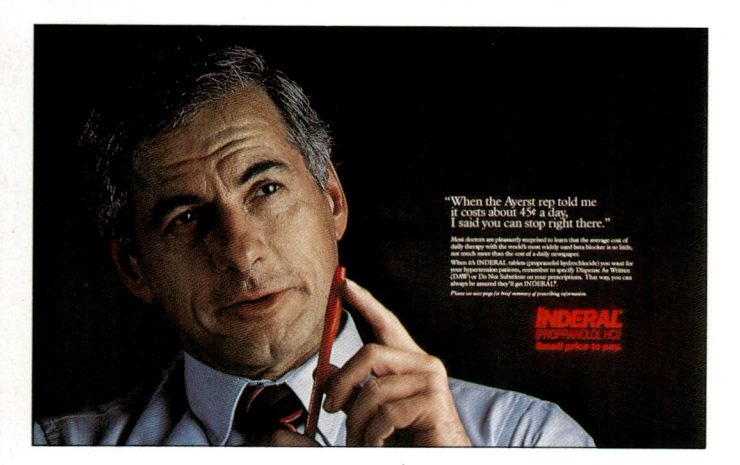

Sudler & Hennessey Incorporated

1633 Broadway
New York, New York 10019
212.265.8000

Annual Billing: $158,000,000

Gross Billings by Media: NA

Contacts: William B. Gibson
Chairman, President & CEO;
Arthur M. Rosen
Exec. V.P, Director Consumer Group

Employees: 264

Founded: 1936

Sudler & Hennessey Inc. U.S. Clients

Ayerst Laboratories
Baker Instruments Corporation
BASF Wyandotte Corporation
Beech-Nut Nutrition Corporation
Du Pont Pharmaceuticals
General Foods Corporation
Johnson & Johnson Health Care Division
Lever Brothers Household Products Division
Lever Brothers Personal Products Division
McNeil Pharmaceutical
Olin Chemical Corporation
Ortho Pharmaceutical
Parke-Davis
Roche Laboratories
Stuart Pharmaceuticals
Whitehall Laboratories

Sudler & Hennessey Consumer Group

Advanced Care Products
BASF Wyandotte Corporation
Cos Medica
Du Pont Pharmaceuticals
Jeffrey Martin Inc.
Olin Chemical Corporation
Parke-Davis
Stuart Pharmaceuticals

Sudler & Hennessey International

Colgate-Palmolive International
Merck Sharp & Dohme International
Warner-Lambert International

Intramed Communications Incorporated

Ayerst Laboratories
Barnes-Hind Inc.
BASF Wyandotte Corporation
Berlex Laboratories Inc.
Du Pont Pharmaceuticals
Johnson & Johnson
Lever Brothers
McNeil Pharmaceutical
Ortho Pharmaceutical
Parke-Davis
Roche Laboratories
Squibb International
Stuart Pharmaceuticals
Whitehall Laboratories

The agencies creating
America's best-remembered,
best-liked TV campaigns:

Backer & Spielvogel	Foote, Cone & Belding	Ally & Gargano	NW Ayer	McCann-Erickson	Needham Harper Worldwide	BBDO	Young & Rubicam	Doyle Dane Bernbach	J. Walter Thompson USA
4	4	5	6	6	7	7	7	7	21

Source: Video Storyboard Tests, Inc.

J. Walter Thompson U.S.A., Inc.

466 Lexington Avenue
New York, New York 10017
212.210.7000

Contact: Burton J. Manning
Chairman Bd. & CEO

Employees: 2,544

Founded: 1864

Annual Billings: NA

Gross Billings by Media:	
Newspaper	6%
Magazine	13.2%
DM	0.8%
Outdoor	1.10%
TV	57%
Radio	4.3%

Zap Proof.

Zap. Zap. Zap.

All across America impatient TV viewers are electronically avoiding commercials they don't like. Attention spans are growing shorter.

So are the chances of uninspired ad campaigns.

The solution is easy to see, but not so easy to achieve. Get creative work consumers would rather watch than zap.

Where can you find work like that?

Each year an independent research company, Video Storyboard Tests, Inc., interviews 20,000 consumers to find America's 25 most outstanding TV campaigns. Results are reported in the news media—from *The Wall Street Journal* to *CBS News*.

The agency with the most winners in 1984 (latest available figures) was J. Walter Thompson USA. Same for '83. And '82. And '81.

The four-year totals are in the chart.

How is your campaign doing?

Want to discuss ways to do better?

Let's talk.

Maybe together, we can create advertising with more zip.

And less zap.

J. WALTER USA

J. WALTER THOMPSON USA, INC.
Los Angeles • New York • Atlanta • Chicago • Detroit
San Francisco • Washington

Client List

AMF Ben Hogan Company
Best Products Co., Inc.
Borden, Inc.
Colorado Tourism Board
CompuShop Incorporated
The Dallas Morning News
Dillard Department Stores
Frito-Lay, Inc.
Frontier Airlines
Haggar Apparel Company
Health Care United
Imperial Sugar Company
Information Handling Services
InterFirst Corporation
Jones Intercable, Inc.
Labatt Importers, Inc.
La Quinta Motor Inns
Marion Laboratories, Inc.
Mountain Bell Telephone
Mrs Baird's Bakeries, Inc.
National Demographics and Lifestyles
PACE Membership Warehouse
PepsiCo Foods International
Pepsi-Cola Bottling Group
Pepsi-Cola Company
Pepsi-Cola U.S.A. Food Service Division
Phillips Chemical Company
Phillips Petroleum Company
Princess Cruises
Public Service Company of Colorado
Republic Health Corporation
Taco Bell Corporation
Texas Monthly
United Banks of Colorado

Tracy-Locke

P.O. Box 50129
Dallas, Texas 75250
214.969.9000
TWX: 910-861-4174

Contact: Howard Davis
President

Employees: 550

Founded: 1913

Annual Billings: $300,000,000

Gross Billings by Media:	
Newspaper	4%
Magazine	5%
DM	2%
Outdoor	1%
TV	70%
Radio	18%

To cut through the clutter, we used a Cleaver.

To tell the world about Tostitos® brand tortilla chips, we used a Cleaver named Beaver. He got Tostitos the attention it deserved. That got Frito-Lay the sales they expected. To see more of our hard-working advertising, call Howard Davis at (214) 969-9000.

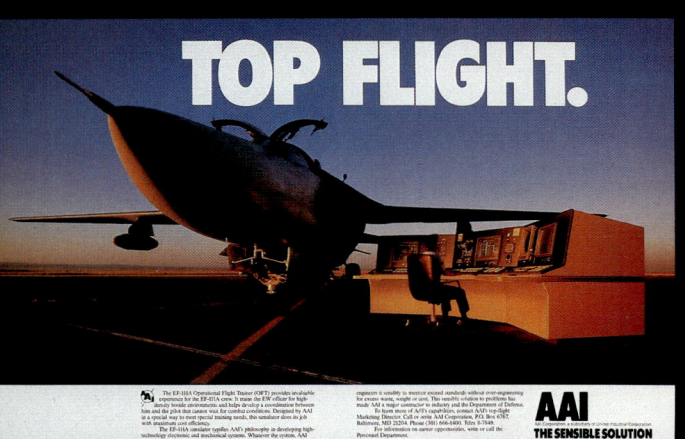

ARTIFICIAL INTELLIGENCE IS GIVING ONE OF THESE TWO DUMMIES A BRAIN

AND MARTIN MARIETTA IS MASTERMINDING IT.

HOW LONDON TRANSPORT KEEPS 5,800 BUSES IN HIGH GEAR.

MARTIN MARIETTA IS MASTERMINDING IT.

TOP FLIGHT.

AAI — THE SENSIBLE SOLUTION

THREE UNACCEPTABLE RESPONSES TO THE UNCOMPENSATED CARE CRISIS.

"Invisible dangers are the most terrifying."

You're on thin ice without it.

Now the coverage of choice gives you coverage with choices.

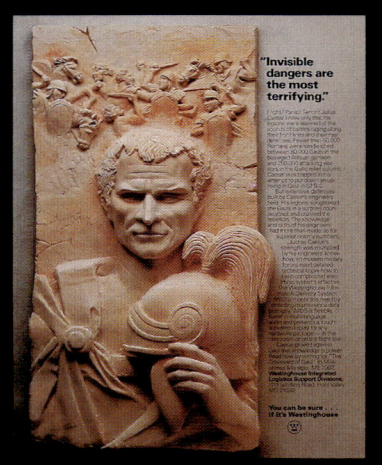

WON'T NEW YORK EVER STOP CALLING US CHEAP?

PORT BALTIMORE
It's where we are that counts.

Hersheypark
What screams and dreams are made of.

American Cancer Society
Fry now. Pay later.

The Agency Book **127**

VanSant, Dugdale & Co., Inc.

The World Trade Center
Baltimore, Maryland 21202
301.539.5400
Telex: 5106000692
(Answer back: VANSANT BALT)

Contact: Kenneth E. Mayhorne
President

Employees: 75

Founded: 1912

Annual Billings: $35,000,000

Gross Billings by Media:	
Newspaper	12%
Magazine	34%
DM	5%
Outdoor	1%
TV	41%
Radio	7%

How a $35-million agency headquartered in Baltimore is helping reap over $40-billion in sales for its clients.

It would be foolhardy, incredible and a lie to tell you we have a formula for helping to spur producing those results.

We don't have a formula.

We do have a mission. To apply the most brains and guts we can to every assignment to make our clients famous and successful.

In 75 years we've done a pretty good job.

For proof, we offer the statistic above and the advertisements to the left. If they entice you, we urge you to call Ken Mayhorne whose number is above.

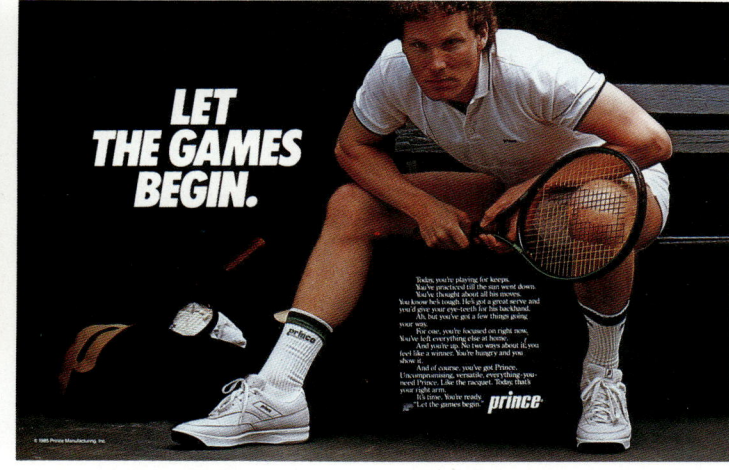

MOTHER: Fisher-Price
just re-invented the wheels.

Roller skates that grow with your
kids as they learn to skate.

BOY: ...she's skating!
Look!....she's skating!

MOTHER: Fisher-Price Roller Skates.
It's about time.

WOMAN: Aziza has revolutionized
nail polish! They got rid of the brush.

Then they streamlined the shape
and added a new kind of applicator..

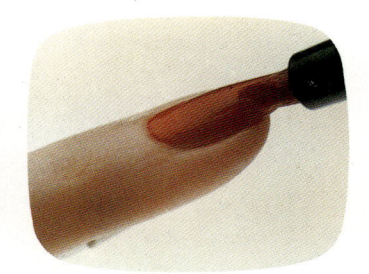

So it goes on in a matter of seconds!
The Aziza Polishing Pen...

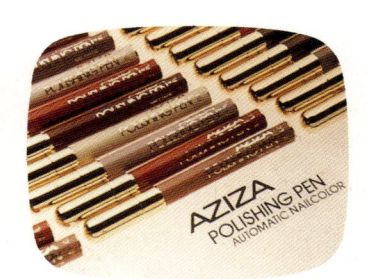

It's the most exciting thing that
ever happened to nail polish.

GRANDSON: Grandpa, the spaghetti's
ready. GRANDPA: Ready?

GRANDPA: These vegetables didn't
come from my garden.

GRANDPA: Mmmm...Whose garden is
this from? GRANDSON: It's from Ragu.

ANNCR (VO): Ragu Chunky
Gardenstyle.

# Waring & LaRosa, Inc.

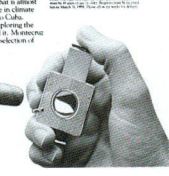

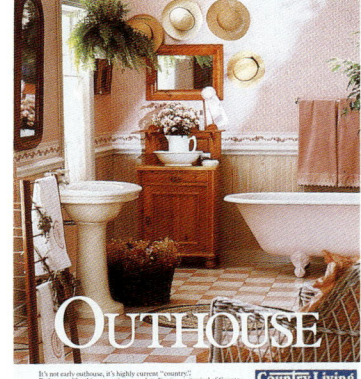

555 Madison Avenue
New York, New York 10022
212.755.0700

Contacts: Joe LaRosa
Chairman;
Saul Waring
President

Employees: 140

Founded: 1968

Annual Billings: $90,000,000	
Gross Billings by Media:	
Newspaper	3%·
Magazine	30%
Outdoor	.5%
TV	60.5%
Radio	6%

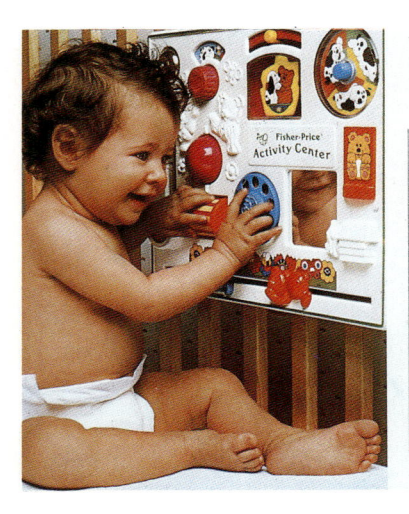

The non-formula ad formula and how it works.

The right solution for your advertising problem lies somewhere within the dynamics of your own marketing situation. If we start there, the outcome must be advertising that is such a special fit, no other brand could shoehorn its way into your campaign idea.

In the light of this, consider this sampling of our work. You'll see that whether it's for marinara or mascara or mineral water, what distinguishes our advertising is a unique presence. It is this presence that sets each of these products or services apart from everyone else in the marketplace. When executed with imagination, and appearing with consistency, the result is a consumer franchise that grows faster than the competition.

If you would like to see what our non-formula formula can do for your company, call Waring & LaRosa.

Hollister, Inc. You may not have a deep appreciation for catheters, but if you're looking for a new agency you might appreciate this: any client that lets us do good work will get good work from us. *Any* client. **Augsburger Beer** Maybe people haven't got our slogan down pat yet, but they are putting their lips on 600% more Auggies than when we started. **Lowrey** We absolutely refuse to sell cigarettes. Pianos are O.K. **Chicago Tourism** We put a lot more stock in our instincts, than in numbers. But when somebody tells you your campaign has increased awareness 163% its first year, it's hard not to repeat it. **Donahue** It's not mandatory that our clients lead their industry, be unique, fascinating and vastly superior to anything else in the marketplace. But it's nice. **Midland Hotel** It occurred to us that most people who stay at business hotels spend a lot more time staring at their plate than looking out the window. **Illinois Tourism** In the great civil war over tourism dollars Illinois had not exactly been on the winning side until we fired these opening salvos. **Multimedia** When a client comes to you with a product whose basic premise is already a great headline, all you do is get out of the way. **Amdek** If our work for these guys shows anything, it's that even without the media weight of an IBM or the production budget of Apple, you can still sell more of your product than your competitors do. **Dovebar** Truth is, almost anyone could sell Dove-Bars. But our work certainly hasn't hurt. **Gingiss Formalwear** Our first client and we still have a formal agreement with them. One of the great advertising tails of our times. **Beatrice Meats** We told one of the world's biggest packaged goods conglomerates to "say it with salami". And they did. **Exchange National Bank** We're proud to say we did an entire campaign for this bank without once mentioning free toasters. **WJKB-TV** We didn't think the world needed another "puff-piece" news promotion. With Detroit's Channel 2 now in first place, we're prepared to admit we may have been right. **Tenex** We don't know if sex sells, but we do know underwear jokes can move chairmats. **Old Chicago Beer** As everyone knows, the only way to sell beer is with smiling young people singing and greeting each other in bright, cheery fern bars. Sure it is.

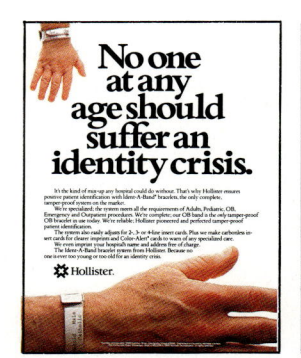

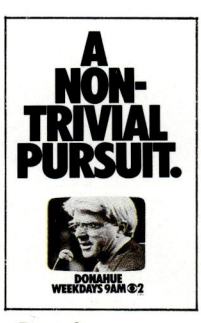

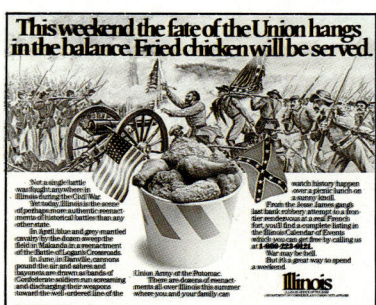

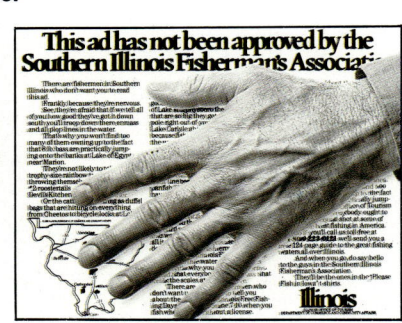

Zechman and Associates

333 N. Michigan Avenue
Chicago, Illinois 60601
312.346.0551

Contact: Jan Zechman
President

Employees (U.S.): 31

Annual Billings (U.S.): $23,000,000

Gross Billings by Media: NA

Multimedia Entertainment

Gingiss Formalwear

Exchange National Bank

Amdek Corporation

Beatrice Meats

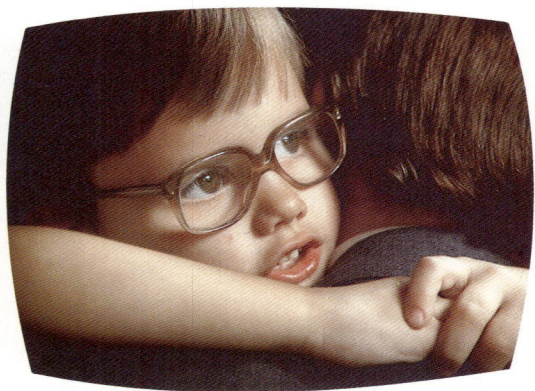

WJBK-TV

DoveBar

DoveBar

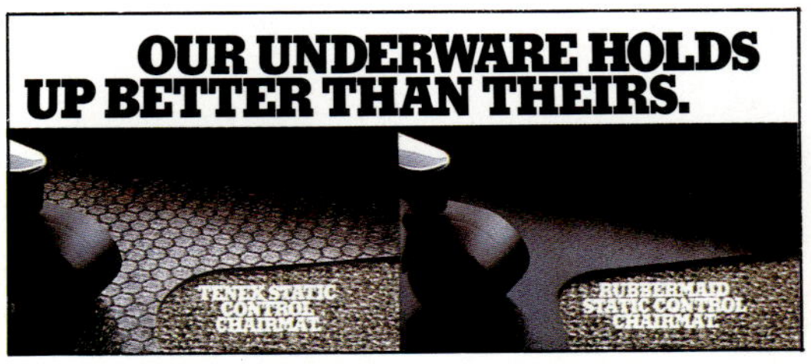

Tenex Corporation

Old Chicago Beer

Your Money™

Entertaining Encounters with Personal Finance by Gavin Brackenridge & Co., Inc.

Your Money is a trademark owned by Time Inc. Used with permission.

Gavin Brackenridge & Co., Inc. Creates Impact.

Ask W.R. Grace, or WANG, or Life of Virginia, or Alcoa.

We create promotional games that are remembered. Long after sales calls, direct mailings, press parties, and other promotional efforts are over, games continue to be played.

And games are far less costly than other promotional efforts.

We create high-quality, educational, entertaining, and enduring games that are fully integrated with your company goals. Each step in our creation of a game is planned to allow for minute refinements necessary to meet your goals. Then, we play-test…a lot. After all, a game that plays well, stays well.

Call or write for more information to Gavin Brackenridge, President, Gavin Brackenridge & Co., Inc., 540 Madison Avenue, New York, NY 10022, (212) 935-5470.

We report on the lively world of advertising.

ADWEEK

Experience in Everything You Need for State-of-the-Art Public Relations and Public Affairs, Everywhere.

UNITED STATES: New York (212) 697-5600; **Atlanta** (404) 688-7820; **Austin** (512) 476-9887; **Chicago** (312) 565-1200; **Dallas** (214) 979-0090; **Denver** (303) 623-7772; **Detroit** (313) 644-9150; **Fort Worth** (214) 263-7017; **Houston** (713) 961-3334; **Los Angeles** (213) 937-7460; **Minneapolis** (612) 332-8900; **Pittsburgh** (412) 391-5480; **St. Louis** (314) 241-1146; **San Antonio** (512) 299-1322; **San Francisco** (415) 781-2430; **San Jose** (408) 246-2181; **Seattle** (206) 682-6944; **Stamford** (203) 348-8800; **Tampa** (813) 221-7830; **Washington** (202) 638-2800; **CANADA: Toronto, Ontario:** (416) 926-7400; **Vancouver, B.C.** (204) 684-5891; **SOUTH AMERICA: Rio de Janeiro, Brazil** (021) 295-1182; **São Paulo, Brazil** (011) 211-2942; **EUROPE: Geneva, Switzerland** (41-22) 21.59.11; **Amsterdam, the Netherlands** (31-20) 97.20.21; **Bonn, West Germany** (*contact through Frankfurt office*); **Brussels, Belgium** (32-2) 640.04.95; **Dublin, Ireland** (353-1) 60.50.77; **Düsseldorf, West Germany** (49-211) 578021; **Frankfurt, West Germany** (49-69) 75603-0; **The Hague, the Netherlands** (31-70) 54.23.02; **London, United Kingdom** (44-1) 486.90.21; **London (Corporate), United Kingdom** (44-1) 405.8755; **Madrid, Spain** (34-1) 435.08.23/435.10/98/435.11.22; **Milan, Italy** (39-2) 70.22.76/70.23.56/70.86.50/79.93.74/79.87.26; **Paris, France** (33-1) 256.41.97; **Rome, Italy** (39-6) 67.95.128/67.91.854; **Zurich, Switzerland** (41-21) 252-76-40; **MIDDLE EAST: Manama, Bahrain** (0973) 250014; **FAR EAST: Hong Kong** (852-5) 779025; **Beijing, People's Republic of China** 50-2266, Ext. 3045; **Kuala Lumpur, Malaysia** (60-3) 287163/224544/224545; **Penang, Malaysia** (60-4892) 364330/364829; **Singapore** (65) 3385344; **Tokyo, Japan** (81-3) 212-2461; **AUSTRALIA: Adelaide** (61-8) 212-3900; **Brisbane** (61-7) 229-4233; **Canberra** (61-62) 95-3543; **Melbourne** (61-3) 690-4799; **Perth** (61-9) 322-4533; **Sydney** (61-2) 231-3300; **NEW ZEALAND: Auckland** (64-9) 794-211; **Christchurch** (64-3) 66040; **Wellington** (64-4) 724-453; **Whangarei** (*contact through Wellington office*); plus 65 associates in 25 countries.

That's Hill and Knowlton.

For a complimentary copy of our latest annual review and capabilities brochure, contact the office nearest you or send in the coupon below.

For more information, call (212) 697-5600.

HILL AND **KNOWLTON**
International Public Relations Counsel
420 Lexington Avenue
New York, NY 10017
Attn: Information Request

Name: _____

Organization: _____ Title: _____

Address: _____

In addition to the Hill and Knowlton services brochure and annual review, please send me specific information on:
_____

Hill and Knowlton

Getting Results Through Strategy and Action

Index Contents

Brand Index 138
Client Index 158
Location Index by Agency 172
Location Index by State 184

Brand Index

AA–Af

AAA Automobile Club of Missouri **73**
AAA Membership Solicitation **37**
AAA Midwest Conference Group **73**
AAA National Headquarters **37**
ABC Corporate Advertising **11**
AC-DELCO **29**
ACEMESA Olives From Spain **123**
A.E. Group Engine Components **69**
AMC Eagle Fleet **113**
AMC Eagle 4x4 **113**
AMC Jeep Fleet **113**
AMC Renault Fleet **113**
AMF Union Machine Division Apparel Equipment **49**
AMF Union Machine Division Bakery Equipment **49**
AMP Electrical Connectors **57**
AMP Electronic Components **57**
AMP Soderless Terminals **57**
AT&T Business to Business Advertising **99**
AT&T Communications **11**
AT&T Components & Electronics Systems **57**
AT&T Consumer Products **11**
AT&T Corporate Advertising **11**
AT&T Federal Systems **57**
AT&T Informative Advertising **11**
AT&T International Advertising **11**
AT&T Network Systems **57**
AT&T Technologies New Ventures **57**
AT&T Technology Campaign **57**
A&W Root Beer **65**
Aapri Apricot Facial Scrub **11**
Abbotts **81**
Acme Markets **21**
Actifed **111**
Acushnet Rubber **65**
Adensco Eyewear **7**
adidas **27**
Adolph's Meat Tenderizer **129**
Adorn Hair Spray **11**
Advance Pregnancy Test Kit **99**
Advanced Micro Integrated Circuits **75**
Afro Sheen **25**
After Eight Dinner Mints **123**

Ag–Al

Agree Shampoo & Conditioner **123**
Agri-Diagnostics Plant Diagnostic Tests **37**
AgriPro Corn **31**
AgriPro Forage Seeds **31**
AgriPro Soybean **31**
AgriPro Wheat **31**
Air Afrique **39**
Air Canada International Air Travel **97**
Air Products & Chemicals Industrial Gas Products **57**
Airborne Express **43**
Alabama Gas Corporation **91**
Alaska Tourism **57**
Albee C-800 Vitamins **115**
Alberto European Styling Mousse **21**
Alberto VO5 Hairdressing **21**
Alberto VO5 Shampoo **21**
Albertsons Grocery Stores **57**
ALCOA **65**
ALDI Food Stores **59**
Alexandra de Markoff **89**
Alfa Romeo Eyewear **7**
Alive Support Hosiery **37**
Alka-Mints **99**
Alka-Seltzer **99**
All American Sports Direct Marketing **37**
All Bran w/Extra Fiber **123**
All-Bran **123**
Allegheny Commuter Airline **123**
Allied Corp. A-C Polyethylene **111**
Allied Corp. Home Furnishings **111**
Allied Signal Corporate Advertising **47**
Allis-Chalmers Industrial Lift Trucks **31**
Allsorts **47**
Allstate Auto, Property, Life, Commercial & Health Insurance **23**
Almay Toiletries **113**
Almond Joy **37**
Almost Home Cookies **37**
Alouette **81**
Alpenrose Dairy Products **35**
Alpha Beta Markets **21**
Alpha Keri **79**

Al–Am

Alpha Microsystems Business Computers **75**
AlpWater Natural Mineral Water **37**
Alupent **15**
Amana Central Air Conditioning **57**
Amana Dishwashers **57**
Amana Furnaces **57**
Amana Microwave Ovens **57**
Amana Ranges, Cooktops & Ovens **57**
Amana Refrigerators **57**
Amana Room Air Conditioners **57**
Amana Washers & Dryers **57**
Amchem Metalworking Chemicals **57**
Amdahl Mainframe Computers **37**
American Airlines **21**
American Broadcasting Company Children's Programming **97**
American Broadcasting Company Daytime Programming **97**
American Broadcasting Company Movies/Theatricals **97**
American Broadcasting Company Network News Programming **11**
American Broadcasting Company Prime Time Programming **97**
American Broadcasting Company Special Assignments **11**
American Broadcasting Company Specials **97**
American Broadcasting Company Sports **97**
American Can Container Division **57**
American Cast Iron Pipes, Fittings & Valves **91**
American Cyanamid Animal Health Division **107**
American Express Direct Marketing **95**
American Express Gold Card **99**
American Express Platinum Card **99**
American Express Travel Services **99**
American Floral Marketing Council **49**
American Greetings Cards **47**
American Hawaii Cruise Line **75**
American Isuzu Motors **43**
American Lamb Council Market Development **11**

Am–Ar

American Photographer Magazine **39**
American Red Cross PenJer Chapter **107**
American Safety Razor Products **79**
American Satellite Communications **127**
American Thread Sewing Projects **77**
American Tourister Luggage **29**
Ameritech Corporate Advertising **123**
Ames Laboratories Blood Glucose Monitoring **123**
Amore **23**
AMPAD Clingers **5**
AMPAD Yellow Pad **5**
Amphora Pipe Tobacco **57**
Amtoy Toys & Dolls **47**
AMTRAK **49**
AMTRAK Auto Train **103**
AMTRAK Metroliner **103**
Analog & Digital Audio Equipment **89**
Anancin Analgesic Tablets & Capsules **51**
ANCO Windshield Wiper Products **123**
Andersen Corporation New Products **31**
Andersen Gliding Doors **31**
Andersen Window Units **31**
Animed Veterinarian Services & Supplies **37**
Anne Klein Fragrances & Bath Products **95**
Anne Klein II Women's Fashions **89**
Answer Pregnancy Test Kit **103**
Anusol **123**
Apollinaris **81**
Apple Commission, Washington **35**
Apple Jacks **23**
Apple Products **59**
Apple Raisin Crisp **123**
Aqua Net Mousse **21**
Aqual-Ban **113**
Aquaphor Ointment **105**
Aramis **3**
Arby's **93**
ARCO Chemicals **57**
Argenti **27**

Brand Index

Ar–Av

Arizona Lottery 57
Armour-Dial New Products 57
Armour Processed Meats 21
Arnold Bakers Dry Products 57
Arnold Bakers Grocery Products 57
Arnold Bran'nola 57
Arnold Brick Oven Premium Wheat Breads 57
Arnold Brick Oven Premium White Breads 57
Arnold Diet Thin 57
Arnold Foods New Products 57
Arnold Milk & Honey Bread 57
Arnold Rye & Pumpernickel Breads 57
Arnold Soft Rolls 57
Arnold Specialty Breads 57
Arnold Whole Grain Breads 57
Arrow CCSG Microcomputer Distribution Services 73
Arrow Company 3
Arrowhead Bottled Sparkling Water 123
Ashley's Outlet Stores 31
Assa Locks, Keys & Hinges 69
Associated Press Broadcast Services 103
Associates Commercial Financing 59
Asti Spumante 99
Astor Tobacco 107
Atune Hair Care Products & New Products 37
Audi Coupe GT 47
Audi 4000 47
Audi 4000 Quattro 47
Audi 5000 Sedan 47
Audi 5000 Turbo 47
Audi 5000 Turbo Quattro 47
Audi 5000 Wagon 47
Audi Quattro 47
Audiotel Cellular Telephones 61
Audiovox Car Stereo 61
Audiovox Cellular Telephones 61
Augsburger Beer 131
Aunt Jemima Easy Mixes 123
Aunt Jemima Frozen French Toast 123
Aunt Jemima Frozen Pancake Batter 123
Aunt Jemima Frozen Waffles 123

Av–Ba

Aunt Jemima Lite Syrup 123
Aunt Jemima Pancake Mixes 123
Aunt Jemima Syrup 123
Aunt Nellie's Canned Meat Sauce 123
Aunt Nellie's Canned Vegetables 123
Aunt Nellie's Liberty Cherries 123
Aurora AFX Racing 119
Aurora Bathroom Tissue 115
Aurora Products 119
Austin Hill 65
Australia & New Zealand Banking Group 83
Australian Tourism 11
Australian Trade Commission Economic Development 11
Automated Packaging Materials & Machinery 69
Automobile Club of California Insurance Services 11
Automobile Club of California Travel Agency 11
Automobile Club of Southern California Emergency Road Service 11
Avalon Industries 119
Aviance Line 51
Avis Car Leasing Division 27
Avon Corporate Advertising 11
Avon Product Advertising 11
Avon Representative Recruitment Advertising 11
AWACS Cellular Phone System 127
Axelrod Dairy & Cheese Products 105
Aziza Cosmetics 129
BASF 65
BDP Heating & Air Conditioning Equipment 11
BP Chemicals 39
BSS Bendover 57
B&M Baked Beans 31
BVD Underwear 113
Babe 21
Baby Fresh Baby Wipes 123
Baby Magic Products 55
Baby Ruth 21
Baby Wipes 123
Bac*O's 103
Bacardi Rum 111
Bachman Quality Snacks 107

Ba–Be

Backwoods Chewing Tobacco 21
Bahamas Express 7
Bahamas Ministry of Tourism 11
Bahamasair 7
Baileys Original Irish Cream Liqueur 13
Bain de Soleil 109
Baken-ets Brand Fried Pork Rinds 125
Balance Blend Spread 99
Baldwin Pianos 35
Bali Brassieres 37
Bali Micro Blinds 123
Bali Mini-Blinds 123
Bali New Products 37
Bali Pleated Shades 123
Bali Vertical Blinds 123
Baltimore Federal Financial 107
Baltimore Gas & Electric Company 107
Bama Jams & Jellies 47
Bama Peanut Butter 47
Bandini Fertilizer 41
Bank of Boston 65
Bank of Pennsylvania 107
Bank of Virginia 49
Banquet Frozen Foods New Products 57
Bantu 25
Barclays Bank of California Banking Services 37
Barron's Advertising Promotion 71
Barton & Guestier French Wines 47
Basis Soaps 105
Baskin-Robbins Corporate Advertising 35
Baskin-Robbins Ice Cream Products 123
Bayer Aspirin 55
Bayless Markets 103
Beatrice U.S. Food 25
Beatrice/Hunt-Wesson Special Project 119
Beck's Beer 43
Beech-Nut Nutrition Corp. 43
Beechnut Chewing Tobacco 37
Beefeater Gin 3
Beefeater Gin & Tonic 3
Bell & Howell Document & Mail Handling Systems 37

Be–Be

Bell & Howell Education & Training 37
Bell & Howell Micro-Imaging Systems 37
Bell & Howell Publishing 37
Bell & Howell Visual Communications Systems 37
Bell Atlantic Mobile Telecommmunications Products & Services 57
Bell Atlantic Telecommunications Products & Services 57
Bell Atlantic Yellow Pages Directories 57
Bell Laboratories Communications Research & Development 57
Bell of Pennsylvania Telecommunications Services 57
BellSouth Mobile Telephone Services 123
BellSouth Telecommunications Equipment 91
BellSouth Yellow Pages 91
Ben Franklin Cigars 21
Ben Hogan Golf Balls 125
Ben Hogan Golf Clubs 125
Ben-Gay Extra Strength Balm for Arthritis 97
Ben-Gay Gel for Sports 97
Ben-Gay Ointment 97
Beneficial Insurance 63
Beneficial Management Consumer Financial Services 37
Beneteau Yachts 111
Benetton Retail Sweater Stores 123
Bennett's Sauces & Toppings 107
Berentzen 23
Beret Line 51
Berkley Publishing 3
Berliner & Marx Plume De Veau Veal 23
Bermuda Tourism 57
Berotec 15
Best Catalog Showrooms 125
Best Foods New Products 37
Bethlehem Steel & Steel Products 57
Betty Crocker Big Batch Cookie Mix 103
Betty Crocker Creamy Deluxe Frosting 103
Betty Crocker Pancake Mixes 37

The Agency Book **139**

Brand Index

Be–Bo

Betty Crocker Potato Buds **31**
Betty Crocker Specialty Potatoes **31**
Bialosky Bears **119**
Big Boy of America **49**
Big Boy Restaurant **49**
Big League Chew **103**
Big Red Chewing Tobacco **37**
Bill Blass for Hanes Fashion Underwear **87**
Binney & Smith Creative Development Products **103**
Bisquick All-Purpose Baking Mix **103**
Black Velvet Scotch Whiskey **99**
H&R Block Spanish Advertising **123**
Block Drug New Products **109**
Blue Bonnet Butter Blend **47**
Blue Bonnet Margarine **47**
Blue Cross & Blue Shield of Alabama **91**
Blue Seal Cheese Food **123**
Blue Stratos Men's Frangrance **37**
Blue Streak Ignition Products **61**
Blue-Plate Mayonnaise **109**
Boeing Aerospace **35**
Boeing Commercial Airplanes **35**
Boeing Electronics **35**
Boeing Marine Systems **35**
Boeing Military Airplanes **35**
Boeing Recruitment **35**
Boeing Vertol Aircraft Systems & Helicopters **127**
Boise Cascade Building Products **37**
Boise Cascade Forests **37**
Boise Cascade Office Products **37**
Boise Cascade Packaging **37**
Boise Cascade Paper **37**
Bojangles Chicken & Biscuit Fast Food **115**
Bold 'n Spicy Deli Mustard **123**
Bolt Paper Towels **115**
Bon Bons Ice Cream **57**
Bonkers **37**
Bonkers Cat Food **99**
Bonne Maman Preserves **129**
Book-of-the-Month Club **43**
Booth Newspapers National Trade Media Advertising **123**

Bo–Bu

Booth's High & Dry Gin **123**
Borateem **41**
Boraxo **41**
Borden Dairy Products **125**
Borg-Warner Corporate Advertising **57**
BoRics Haircare Centres **123**
Bounty Microwave **37**
Bounty Paper Towels **37**
Boy Scouts **57**
Boy Scouts Explorers **57**
Brador Malt Liquor **65**
Brahma Beer **3**
Bran Buds **123**
Bran Flakes **123**
Bran Muffin Crisp **103**
Brawny Paper Towels & Tissues **115**
Breath Savers Mints **37**
Breyer Toys **39**
Breyers Yogurt **11**
Bridal Originals **3**
Bridgestone Tires & Rubber Products **29**
Britains Toys **39**
Brite For No-Wax Floors **57**
Brite-Tone Crayons **119**
British Airways **113**
British Columbia Ministry of Agriculture **35**
British Columbia Ministry of Industry & Small Business Development **35**
British Columbia Ministry of International Trade & Investment **35**
British Sterling **65**
Brittania **3**
Brown Gold **57**
Brownberry Bread **57**
Brown's Velvet Dairy **53**
Bruno Magli **3**
Brut **21**
Bryant Air Conditioners & Heating Equipment **11**
Bubble Yum Bubble Gum **37**
Buc*Wheats **31**
Bud Light **103**
Bufferin **79**
Bulgari Jewelers **21**
Bulova Watches **43**

Bu–Ca

Bumble Bee Clams **123**
Bumble Bee Oysters **123**
Bumble Bee Salmon **123**
Bumble Bee Tuna **123**
Burger King Fast Food Restaurants **123**
Burmah-Castrol Lubricants **115**
Burmah-Castrol Motor Oil **115**
Burnes of Boston **3**
Burrough's English Vodka **3**
Burroughs-Wellcome Corporate Advertising **111**
Burroughs-Wellcome New Head Lice Product **123**
Busch Beer **103**
Busch Entertainment Corporation **103**
Bushnell Consumer Optical Products **37**
Butcher Bones Dog Snacks **51**
Butter Buds **65**
Butter Flavored Crisco **113**
Butterball Deli Turkey Breast **131**
Butterfinger **21**
Butternut Bread **31**
Buttrey Food Stoes **21**
CBN Cable Network **57**
CBS/Fox Pre-recorded Video Cassettes & Videodiscs **47**
C and H Sugars **57**
CIT Commercial Finance **111**
CIT Corporate Finance **111**
CIT Financial Corporation Corporate Advertising **111**
CIT International Sales Corporation **111**
C&P Telephone Company of Maryland **107**
CVS Drug Stores **65**
Cachet Line **51**
Cafe Del Bueno **55**
Cafes de Veracruz New Liqueur Product **37**
Calais **23**
Calamari King **81**
California Milk Advisory Board Dairy Promotions **57**
California Milk Advisory Board New Products **57**
California Redwood Lumber & Plywood **57**
California State Lottery **103**

Ca–Ca

Calrab Raisins **57**
Calvin Klein Eyewear **7**
Camay **23**
Cambridge **23**
Camel Cigarettes **99**
Camel Cigarettes Special Events **87**
Campbell Beans **103**
Campbell Soup Consumer Projects **57**
Campbell Soup Corporate Trade Programs **57**
Campbell Soup Foodservice Projects **57**
Campbell Soup Military Sales **57**
Campbell Soup New Products **13**
Campbell Soup Specialty Foods **57**
Campbell's Condensed Soup Line **13**
Campbell's Tomato Juice **13**
Campus Sportswear **43**
Camus Cognac **31**
Canada Cooler **125**
Canadian Club **97**
Canadian Imperial Bank U.S. Commercial Banking **19**
Canadian Mist **25**
Canadian Windsor **79**
Capitol Broadcasting DC 101 AM/FM Radio Station **123**
Captain Crunch Cereal **13**
Captain Morgan Spiced Dum **47**
Car Care Council Automotive Maintenance **123**
Cardiac Pacemakers Insulin Pumps **123**
Cardiac Pacemakers Pacemakers **123**
Cardinal Savings & Loan **49**
Care*Free Sugarless Chewing Gum **37**
Cargill Flour Division **31**
Cargill Salt Division **31**
Carhartt Work & Hunting Wear **123**
Carl Buddig Packaged Smoked Meats **11**
Carl's Jr. Restaurants **43**
Carlton Cigarettes **79**
Carnation Cat Food **57**
Carnation Instant Diet Product **57**
Carnation New Products **57**

Brand Index

Ca–Ch

Carnation Specialty Ice Cream 57
Carolee Jewelry 95
Carpet One 73
Carrington 109
Carr's Crackers 81
Carte Blanche Travel & Entertainment Card 11
CasaBlanca Fans 41
Cascade 113
Casino Natural Cheese 123
Catapres 15
Catapres TTS 15
Caterpillar Equipment 59
James Catto & Co. New Products 13
Catto's Gold Label Scotch 13
Ceclor 123
Ceco Concrete Construction 59
Cefobid 123
Celanese Fibers 47
Celeste Frozen Pizza 13
Celestial Seasonings New Products 57
Celestial Seasonings Specialty Teas 57
Celicote Air Pollution Control Equipment 69
Celicote Corrosion-control Coatings 69
Celiprolol 123
Cella Wines 25
Cellular One of Harrisburg 49
Cellular One of Lehigh Valley 49
Cellular One of North East Pennsylvania 49
Century Furniture 87
Cerruti Pantyhose 57
Champ Service Products 61
Champion Corporate Advertising 109
Champion Home Builders Recreational Vehicles 123
Champion Spark Plug Aviation Oil Filters 123
Champion Spark Plug Ceramic Products 123
Champion Spark Plugs 123
Chanel Apparel 47
Chanel Cosmetics 47
Chanel Fragrances 47
Charles of the Ritz 89

Ch–Ch

Charles of the Ritz New Products 109
Charlie 115
Charter Ethical Pharmaceuticals 57
Chase Consumer Advertising 115
Chase Corporate Advertising 115
Chase Electronic Banking Division 109
Chase International Advertising 115
Chase Maryland 109
Chase MasterCard 109
Chase Ohio 109
Chase Personal Financial Services 109
Chase Vista 109
Chase Wholesale Advertising 115
Chateau Ste. Michelle Wine 35
CheckRobot Intelligent Check-Out Systems 89
Check-Up Toothpaste 21
Cheer 23
Cheerios 37
Cheese Nips Crackers 51
CHEE-TOS Cheese Flavored Snacks 103
Cheez Whiz 123
Chef Francisco Kissle 123
Chef Francisco New Food Products 123
Chef Pierre 65
Chemical Bank Corporate Advertising 89
Cherry Coke 25
Chesebrough-Pond's Corporate Program 51
Chessie Railroad System 49
Chesterfield Eyewear 7
Chevrolet Cars & Trucks 29
Chevron Aviation & Maritime Fuels 123
Chevron Bulk Products 123
Chevron Elastomeric Liners/Coating 123
Chevron Gasolines 123
Chevron Motor Oils 123
Chevron Road Pavement 123
Chevron Tires/Batteries/Automotive Accessories 123
Chevron Travel Club Credit Cards 123

Ch–Ci

Chevy Chase Savings & Loan 49
Chewels Gum 123
Chewy Granola Bars 13
Chi-Chi's Restaurants 31
Chicago and North Western Transportation Corporate Advertising 31
Chicken Helper 103
Chief Auto Parts 41
Child World 117
Children's Co-Tylenol 113
Chimere Line 51
Chips Ahoy 37
Chivas Regal 47
Chivas Royal Salute 47
Chloraseptic Lozenges 23
Chloraseptic Spray 23
Chrysler Fifth Avenue 21
Chrysler Laser XT 21
Chrysler LeBaron 21
Chrysler LeBaron GTS 21
Chrysler Limousine 21
Chrysler New Yorker 21
Chunky Candy Bar 123
Cie Fragrance 37
CIGNA Corporate Advertising 47
CIGNA Employee Benefits & Health Care Group 47
CIGNA Healthplan of Connecticut 47
CIGNA Healthplan of Delaware 47
CIGNA Healthplan of Maryland 47
CIGNA Healthplan of Massachusetts 47
CIGNA Healthplan of New Jersey 47
CIGNA Healthplan of Pennsylvania 47
CIGNA Healthplan of Washington 47
CIGNA Individual Financial Group 47
CIGNA Investment Group 47
CIGNA Property & Casualty Group 47
CIGNA Worldwide 47
Cinnamon Toast Crunch 31
Cinobac 123
Circle Line Sightseeing Cruises 123
Citibank Corporate Banking Services 57

Ci–Co

Citibank Global Electronic Banking 97
Citicorp CHOICE card 107
Citicorp Diners Club 47
Citicorp Savings of Illinois Savings & Loan 11
Citicorp Travelers Checks 47
Clairol Creme Formula 57
Clairol Essence Shampoos 57
Clairol Shampoo Formula 57
Classy Curl 25
Claussen Pickles 123
Clean 'n Clear 123
Clinique Laboratories 3
Clorets Breath Mints & Gum 123
Clorox Liquid Bleach 57
Clorox New Products 57
Clorox Pre-Wash 103
Clorox 2 All Fabric Bleach 57
Close-Up Toothpaste 123
Clover Stores 49
Club Med Packaged Tour Operator 11
Co-Tylenol 113
Coast Hotels 35
Cobra Answering Machines 31
Cobra Corded & Cordless Telephones 31
Cobra Radar Detectors 31
Coca-Cola Brand 25
Coca-Cola International 25
Cocktails for Two 23
Cocoa Krispies 23
Cocoa Puffs 37
Codex Networking Equipment 65
Coffee, National Association 97
Cointreau America 43
Colgate-Palmolive New Products 57
Colibri Cigarette Lighters 109
Colibri Pens 109
Colombo Yogurt 65
Colorado Tourism 125
Columbia Crest Wine 35
Columbia Medical Plan Health Maintenance Organization 127
Columbia Motion Pictures 115
Columbia Pictures (St. Louis) 73
Combipres 15
Comet Cleanser 113

Brand Index

Co–Co

Comet Liquid **113**
Commander Business Aircrafts **29**
Commodity Exchange, The **43**
Commonwealth Edison Electric Utility **23**
Complete Furniture Polish **123**
Compound W Wart Remover **51**
Compri Hotels **37**
CompuShop **125**
Computer Depot Computer Retailers **31**
Computer Greetings Giant Banner Greeting Card **123**
Comtrex **79**
Con-Tact Decorative Coverings **103**
Concord **23**
Concorde Hotels **7**
Condition After-Shampoo Treatment **57**
Condition Beauty Pack **57**
Condition Hot Oil Treatment **57**
Condition Shampoo **57**
Condition Styling Mousse **57**
Connecticut Mutual Insurance **65**
Connecticut Savings Financial & Banking Services **77**
Connoisseur Magazine **95**
Conoco/DuPont Corporate Advertising **105**
Consolidated Edison Consumer & Corporate Advertising **37**
Consort Hair Spray **21**
Contel Corporate Advertising **89**
Continental Airlines Passenger & Cargo Service **115**
Continental Insurance Direct Marketing **37**
Continental Manufacturing Sanitary Maintenance Equipment **73**
Control **113**
Control Data Automated Wagering for Washington State Lottery **57**
Control Data Computer Storage Devices & Storage Media **31**
Control Data Computer Systems **31**
Control Data Scientific & Engineering Applications **31**
Control Data Services **31**
Conway Salad Dressings **31**
Cook Electric Components **123**
Cooking & Crafts Book Club **43**

Co–Cu

Cook's Champagne **37**
CooperVision **43**
Coors Beer **57**
Coors Expansion **57**
Coors Light **57**
Coors New Products **57**
Copco Enamel Cookware **123**
Copco Enamel Housewares **123**
Coppertone Suntan Products **43**
Cordran **123**
CoreStates Financial Services Holding Company **127**
Corgi Toys **39**
CORIAN **11**
Corn Flakes **23**
Corn Pops **23**
Coronet Brandy **23**
Cortizone 5 **113**
Country Living Magazine **129**
County Line Cheese **21**
Courtyard by Marriott **115**
Courvoisier Cognac **123**
Cracker Barrel Cheeses **123**
Cracklin' Oat Bran **123**
Craft Master Crafts **37**
Crayola Crayons **103**
Crayola Markers **103**
Cream of Rice **47**
Cream of Wheat **47**
Cream of Wheat Mix'n Eat **47**
Creamsicle **37**
Crest **25**
Cresta Blanca **37**
Cribari **37**
Crisco Oil **113**
Crisco Shortening **113**
Crispix Cereal **123**
Crispy Wheats 'n Raisins **31**
Critikan Medical/Surgical Devices **57**
Crouch & Fitzgerald Leather Goods **39**
Crowley Dairy Products **105**
Crown Gasoline **107**
Crown Royal Canadian Whiskey **47**
Cruzan **23**
Cruzan Rum **23**
Cunard Princess/Countess **113**
Cuppenheimer **27**
Curaco Tourist Board **49**

Cu–De

Curad Bandages **57**
Curity Diapers & Infantwear **65**
Cutex Products **129**
Cutlass **23**
Cutler-Hammer Components & Systems **31**
Cutler-Hammer Electronic Devices **31**
CyberTel BeepCall Paging Services **73**
CyberTel Cellular Telephone Services **73**
d-Con Insecticides **55**
Dairy Deli Derby **81**
Dairy Queen **31**
Dairyland Foods **35**
Daisy II Pregnancy Test **99**
Dakota Health Bread **123**
Damon Men's Sportswear **39**
Dana Automotive Components **57**
Dana Truck Components **57**
Dart & Kraft Corporate Advertising **123**
Darvocet **123**
Darvon **123**
Data General Corporate Advertising **57**
Data General Microcomputers **57**
Data General Minicomputers **57**
Data General Office & Industrial Automation Systems **57**
Datamax Office Systems **73**
Dauphin Deposit Bank & Trust **107**
Davidoff Cigarettes **107**
Day & Night Air Conditioning **11**
De Beers Diamonds **11**
Dean Witter Financial Services **89**
Decker Processed Meats **21**
Deere Agriculture & Industrial Products **11**
Deere Lawn & Leisure Products **11**
Del E. Webb Retirement Homes **123**
Del Monte Beverages New Products **57**
Del Taco Fast Food Restaurants **75**
Delaware Group **107**
Delice de France **81**
Deloitte Haskins & Sells U.S. Firmwide Advertising **19**
DeLong Sportswear **59**

De–Do

Delta 88 **23**
Delta Faucets **109**
Delta Gold **57**
Delta Tobacco **107**
Denny's Restaurants **57**
Dental Research Corporation Direct Marketing **37**
Depend Absorbent Products **31**
DeskTop Investors' Software Services **37**
Desmond & Duff **55**
Dewar's **23**
Dewar's 12 **23**
Dexatrim **113**
Di Fini Sportswear **7**
Dial-A-Chipmunk **81**
Dial-A-Muppet **81**
DIAL ONE Franchised Property Services **37**
Dial Santa **81**
Dial Soap **103**
Dialight Optoelectronics **61**
Diamond Foil **123**
Diaparene **55**
Diar-Aid **113**
Diebold Security Systems **69**
Diet Center Weight Loss Program **123**
Diet Coke **25**
Diet Delight **37**
Diet Pepsi **123**
Diet Rite Colas **37**
Diet 7-Up **23**
Diet Sunkist Plus **57**
Digital Equipment Computer Systems **117**
Dillard Department Stores **125**
Dimensia System **23**
Dimension Shampoo & Conditioners **123**
Dimetapp Allergy Relief **115**
Dole Pineapple Sauce **123**
Dole Pineapple Solid Pack & Juice In Cans **123**
Dole Pure 'n Light 100% Juices **123**
Dolly Madison Cakes & Pies **31**
Dolphin Book Club **43**
Domino's Pizza **59**
Don Diego Cigars **21**
Don Emilio **111**

Brand Index

Do–Du

Donnelley Directory Project P **37**
Donnelley Information Special Projects **37**
Donutz **37**
Doral Cigarettes **87**
Dorcol **103**
DORITOS Tortilla Chips **125**
Doubleday Book Clubs/New Member Acquisition **37**
Dourthe Wine **31**
Dove Dishwashing Detergent **123**
DoveBars **131**
Dow Bathroom Cleaner **43**
Dow Chemical Construction Products **69**
Dow Jones Circulation Direct Mail **71**
Dow Jones Corporate Advertising **71**
Dow Jones Information Services Special Projects **71**
Dow Jones International Marketing Services **71**
Doxsee Clam Products **107**
Dr. McGillicuddy Menthol Mint Schnapps **47**
Dramamine **103**
Drambuie Liqueur **123**
Dreft **37**
Dreft Direct Marketing **37**
Dremel Power Tools **11**
Drexel Burnham Lambert Hotel Group **27**
Dreyfus Financial Services **79**
Dristan **99**
Dristan Tablets & Capsules **51**
Dristan Ultra **51**
Drum Tobacco **57**
Dubonnet **23**
Dubonnet Splash **23**
Dubouchett **23**
Dubuque Meats **59**
Duffy-Mott Juices **115**
Duffy-Mott New Products **115**
Duffy-Mott Sauces **115**
Dulcolax **15**
Duncan Hines Brownies/Muffins **113**
Duncan Hines Cake Mixes **113**
Duncan Hines Cookie Mix **113**
Duncan Hines Frosting **113**

Du–EB

Dunhill Accessories **129**
Dunhill Smokers' Products **129**
Duofold **3**
DuPont Applied Technology **11**
DuPont Consumer Paints & Refinishes **11**
DuPont Corporate Automotive Communications **11**
DuPont Diagnostic & BioResearch Systems Division **15**
DuPont Elastomers **11**
DuPont Engineering Plastic Materials & Fluoropolymers **11**
DuPont Ethylene Polymers **11**
DuPont Film **11**
DuPont Industrial Fibers **11**
DuPont Industrial Finishes **11**
DuPont Instruments Photosystems **11**
DuPont Medical X-Ray **15**
DuPont New Products **11**
DuPont Pharmaceuticals **15**
DuPont Plastic Products **11**
DuPont Spunbonded Fibers **11**
Durango Chewing Tobacco **37**
Dutch Hearth Bread **31**
Dutch Master Cigars **21**
Dutch Mill **81**
Dynamo Heavy Duty Detergent **57**
e.p.t. **123**
E.T. Cereal **37**
Eagle Brand Snacks **73**
Eagle Shirtmakers **95**
Eagle's Eye **107**
Earl's Restaurants **35**
Early Detector **123**
Eastern Air Lines **29**
Easy Cheese Spreads **51**
Easy Menders, The **39**
EasyLink Electronic Mail Service **37**
Eaton Agency for Media Placement **31**
Eaton Electronic Control Devices **31**
Eaton Production Monitor/Controls **31**
Eaton Truck Axles & Brakes **69**
Eaton Truck Components **69**
EBASCO Services **53**

Eb–Em

Eberhard Faber Chameleon Pencils **5**
Eberhard Faber Clipper Pens **5**
Eberhard Faber Design Markers **5**
Eberhard Faber Designaire Marker Spray **5**
Eberhard Faber Funcils **5**
Eberhard Faber NSM Artist Portfolios **5**
Eberhard Faber Rolling Writer Pens **5**
Eberhard Faber Vu-rite Visual Systems **5**
Eckerd Drugs Pharmaceutical Division **123**
Eckrich Bologna **131**
Eckrich Lean Supreme **23**
Eckrich Smoked Sausage **23**
Economics Laboratory New Products **77**
Economics Laboratory New Products **105**
Ecuatoriana Airlines **3**
EDDA Taste Show **81**
Eddie Bauer Outdoor Equipment **57**
Eddie Bauer Outdoor Garments **57**
Eddy's Bread **31**
Edelbrock High Performance Parts, Cam Shafts & Manifolds **37**
Edge Shaving Gel **123**
Egg Beaters **123**
Egg Beaters with Cheez **123**
EgyptAir **3**
1873 **111**
El Producto Cigars **21**
El Sol **55**
Elanco Chickens **123**
Elanco Cows **123**
Elanco Pigs **123**
Elasta Eyewear **7**
Electronic Products Magazine **61**
Eli Cutter Cigarettes **29**
Eli Lilly All Products **123**
Elkem **3**
Emerson Quiet Kool Dehumidifiers **57**
Emerson Quiet Kool Kerosene Heaters **57**
Emerson Quiet Kool Room Air Conditioners **57**

Em–Ex

Emery Air Express Delivery Services **123**
Encaprin **37**
Encaprin Direct Marketing **37**
Encare **113**
Encyclopedia Britannica **65**
Endust **79**
Energizer **51**
Enhance Shampoo & Conditioner **123**
Enjoli **109**
Ensign Banks New York and Florida **95**
Entre Computer Centers **37**
Epic Faucets **109**
Epson Computer Printers **57**
Epson Miniature Televisions **57**
Epson Personal Computers **57**
Equitable Life Assurance EVLICO **115**
Equitable Pension Operations **27**
Era Plus Liquid Detergent **23**
Erno Lazlo Institute **129**
ESCO Heavy Equipment & Parts **35**
Eskimo Freezer Paper **123**
Essen Hardware Stores **73**
Esskay Meats **107**
Estee Lauder **3**
Estrella Wines **31**
Evan Picone **65**
Evans Retailer Furrier **123**
Eveready General Purpose Batteries & Flashlights **51**
Eveready Lighting Products **51**
Eveready Rechargeable Batteries **51**
Eveready Super Heavy Duty Batteries & Flashlights **51**
Eveready Watch, Photo, & Hearing Aid **51**
Excedrin **47**
Excedrin P.M. **47**
Executive Life Insurance **75**
Exide Automotive Batteries **57**
Exide Industrial Batteries **57**
Exide Specialty Batteries **57**
Exploration Cruise Line **103**
Extra Strength Dexatrim **113**
Extra Strength Tylenol **113**
Extrom **3**

Brand Index

Ex–Fi

Exxon Corporate Advertising 97
Exxon Corporation Arts/Public Broadcasting 97
F.B.M. Distillery Bacardi Rum 111
F.B.M. Distillery Gold Reserve 111
FHP/HMOs 35
Fab Detergent 57
Fact Pregnancy Test Kit 99
Falcon Jet Corporation Aircraft 97
Famous Grouse 99
Far Eastern Economic Review 71
Farmers Auto Insurance 57
Farmers Commercial Insurance 57
Farmers Fire Insurance 57
Farmers Home Insurance 57
Farmers Truck Insurance 57
Faspak 123
Favor Furniture Polish 123
FECO Thermal & Process Systems 69
Federal Home Loan Investor Relations 123
Federal Home Loan Secondary Mortgages 123
Felipe II 55
Fender Musical Instruments 35
Ferrari Eyewear 7
Ferre Eyewear 7
Fertil-A-Chron 123
Fiberall 79
Fidelity and Deposit Company 107
Fidelity Banking Services 57
Figaro Cat Food 123
Film Guard Plastic Sheeting 31
Final Net 47
Financial Guaranty Insurance 43
Finesse Conditioner 13
Finesse Hair Spray 13
Finesse Mousse 13
Finesse New Products 13
Finesse Shampoo 13
Finn Crisp 81
Fioricet 103
Firenza 23
Fireside Antiques 53
1st Claims Group-Insurance Claim Services 77
First Federal of Michigan 29
First Interstate Bank of Arizona 57

Fi–Fo

First Interstate Bank of California 57
First Interstate Bank of Denver 57
First Interstate Bank of Nevada 11
First Interstate Bank of Oregon 57
First Interstate of Nevada 57
First National Bank of Chicago 57
First National Bank of Chicago 63
1st Nationwide Savings Financial Services 47
1st Nationwide Savings Regional Servicing 47
First Pennsylvania Bank 49
Fisher Nuts 23
Fisher Office Furniture 43
Fitting Pretty Pantyhose 87
501 Jeans 57
Flambe Fanfare 81
Flame Glow 79
Flavorland Foods 41
Fleischmann's Egg Beaters 47
Fleischmann's Light 47
Fleischmann's Light Margarine 123
Fleischmann's Margarine 47
Fleischmann's Margarine 123
Fleischmann's Sweet Unsalted Margarine 123
Fleischmann's Yeast 47
Flexco Commercial Flooring 123
Flexolite Eyewear 7
Florida Citrus 81
Fluff-Out Facial Tissue 55
Fluorigard Dental Rinse 57
Footjoy 65
Ford Authorized Leasing System 123
Ford Bronco 123
Ford Bronco II 123
Ford Club Wagon 123
Ford Dealers-Northwest 35
Ford Direct Marketing 123
Ford Division 15
Ford Division 123
Ford Econoline Van 123
Ford Escort 123
Ford EXP 123
Ford Fleet Cars 123
Ford LTD 123
Ford LTD Crown Victoria 123

Fo–Fr

Ford Medium & Heavy Trucks 123
Ford Motorsports 123
Ford Mustang 123
Ford North East Division 123
Ford Pickup 123
Ford Ranger 123
Ford Recreational Vehicles 123
Ford Rent-A-Car 123
Ford Tempo 123
Ford Thunderbird 123
Forest City Home Centers 93
Forest Products Association, Southern 35
Forever Krystle 109
Formula 409 Spray Cleaner 57
Fortune Book Club 43
FORTUNE Magazine 103
Fostex 79
Four Seasons Air Conditioning Products 61
4C Bread Crumbs 109
4C Iced Tea 109
Francisco French/Italian Breads 57
Franco-American Products 103
Franzia Wines 35
Fred Joaillier 123
Free State Health Maintenance 127
French Quarter French Bread 103
French's Cuisine Dishes Specialty Potatoes 123
French's Foodservice Potato Products 123
French's Instant Mashed Potatoes 123
French's Military Food Products 123
French's Mustard 123
French's Sauce & Gravy Mixes 123
French's Specialty Potatoes 123
Fresh Chef Salads 103
Fresh Chef Sauces 103
Fresh Chef Soups 103
Freshlike Canned & Frozen Vegetables 31
Frette Fine Linens 39
Frigidaire Household Appliances 103
Frito-Lay Canned Dips 125
Frito-Lay Corporate Advertising 125

Fr–Ge

Frito-Lay New Products 57
Frito-Lay Rumbles 57
Frito-Lay Stuffers 57
Frito-Lay Variety Pack 125
Fritos Corn Chips 57
Frontier Airlines 125
Frosted Flakes 23
Frosted Mini Wheats 23
Fruit Corners Fruit Bars 103
Fruit Loops 23
Fruit Roll-Ups 103
Fruitful Bran 123
Fudgesicle 37
Fuji Audio/Video Tapes 89
Fuji Floppy Disks 89
Fulton Lobster 81
Funyuns Fried Onion Snacks 125
Future Floor Finish 57
Futuro Healthcare Equipment 7
GM Defense Group 11
GMAC Automotive & Major Industrial Financing 29
GTE Communication Services 47
GTE Communications Systems 47
GTE Consumer Communications Products 47
GTE Corporate Advertising 47
GTE Directories Corp. 47
GTE Lighting 47
GTE Mobilnet 47
GTE Precision Materials 47
GTE Sprint Corporate Advertising 35
GTE Sprint Telephone Services 123
GTE Telemessager 47
GTE Telenet Communication 47
GTE Telephone Operating Companies 47
Gala Paper Towels & Tissues 115
Gallery Hotels 59
GameTime Park & Playground Equipment 91
Gant for Women 65
Gatorade 13
Gaviscon Antacid 125
GEICO Auto Insurance 49
GEICO Insurance & Annuity 49
Gemeinhardt Flutes 35

Brand Index

Ge–Gl

General Electric Corporate Marketing Media Communications **71**
General Electric Information Services **129**
General Electric Projects **77**
General Electric Rechargeable Batteries **37**
General Mills New Food Products **37**
General Mills New Products **31**
General Mills New Products **37**
General Motors Corporate Advertising **11**
General Motors Public Affairs Advertising **11**
Genesee Beer **51**
Genesee Cream Ale **51**
Genesee Cream Ale Light **51**
Genesee Light Beer **51**
Genesee 12 Horse Ale **51**
GenRad Management Products & Systems **117**
Genstar/Sakrete Products **107**
Gentle-Treatment **25**
George Dickel **23**
Georgia Interchange Statewide ATM Card **123**
Georgia Power Company **25**
Gerber Baby Foods **123**
German National Tourist Office **3**
Gianfranco Ruffini **3**
Giant Food Stores Supermarkets **127**
Gillette Company New Products **11**
Gillette Paper Mate Division **99**
Gitano Pantyhose **87**
Givenchy Hosiery **109**
Glad Plastic Bags & Wrap **23**
Glade Air Fresheners **123**
Glade Spin-Fresh Bathroom Air Freshener **123**
Glamour Magazine **39**
Glatfelter Paper **39**
Gleem **23**
Glen Grant **47**
Glen Ordie **23**
Glendale Federal Savings & Loan **41**
Glenfarclas Single-malt Scotch Whisky **31**
Glenmorangie Scotch **89**

Gl–Gr

Global Homes **123**
Globe Life Insurance **11**
Gloria Vanderbilt Eyewear **95**
GoBot Toy Products **73**
Godfather's Pizza **91**
Gold Jewelry Co-op Program **47**
Gold Jewelry Information Center **47**
Gold Jewelry Promotion **47**
Gold Kist **43**
gold MasterCard **51**
Gold Medal Flour **37**
Gold Reserve Rum **111**
Golden Grahams **31**
Golden Griddle Syrup **37**
Golden Image Imitation Cheese **123**
Golden Skillet Stores **31**
Goldline Laboratories **27**
Goldrush Ice Cream Bars **103**
Good & Plenty **11**
Good Stuff **21**
Good Taste Seminars **81**
Goodyear Aerospace Products **123**
Goodyear Auto Service **123**
Goodyear Automotive Replacement Belts **123**
Goodyear Automotive Replacement Hoses **123**
Goodyear Chemicals **123**
Goodyear Eagle Performance Tire Line **123**
Goodyear Engineered Products **123**
Goodyear Farm Tires **123**
Goodyear Film Products **123**
Goodyear Industrial Products **123**
Goodyear Retail **123**
Goodyear Roofing Systems **123**
Goodyear Shoe Products **123**
Goodyear Truck Tires **123**
Goodyear Vector All-season Radials **123**
Goodyear Wrangler On/Off Road Radials **123**
Gorton's Frozen Fish **79**
Gourmandise **81**
Grace Home Centers West **41**
Grapefruit Products, State of Florida **37**

Gr–Ha

Great Bear Natural Spring Water **123**
Great Clips Haircutting Shops **31**
Great Western Champagne **47**
Greater New York Savings Bank **111**
Green Giant Canned Vegetables **23**
Green Giant Frozen Entrees **23**
Green Giant Frozen Vegetables **23**
Green Giant New Products **23**
Greer Aircraft Propulsion Engines **123**
Greer Armored Vehicle Turbine Engines & Power Systems **123**
Greer Electronic and Electro-mechanical Components & Systems **123**
Greer Environmental Control Systems **123**
Greer Gas Turbine Powerplants **123**
Greer Heavy Truck Turbine Engines **123**
Greer Industrial Regenerators **123**
Greer Industrial Tools & Supplies **123**
Greer Industrial Turbine Engines **123**
Greer Inflatable Rescue Equipment **123**
Greer Military Power Systems **123**
Greer Pollution Control Devices **123**
Greer Power Systems for Urban Rail Transportation **123**
Greer Rapid Transit Systmes **123**
Greyhound Bus Lines **21**
GuadalaHARRY'S Restaurant Chain **77**
Guardian Federal Savings, Connecticut **39**
Guest Quarters Hotel Chain **97**
Gulf & Western Corporate Advertising **105**
Gulf Air **39**
Guy LaRoche **99**
HMO **113**
HON Office Furniture **59**
Haagen-Dazs Cream Liqueur **97**
Haagen-Dazs Ice Cream **99**
Haggar Apparel **125**
Haggar Menswear **125**
Haggar Outerwear **125**

Ha–He

Haig Scotch **111**
Halo Lighting **31**
Halsa Swedish Botanical Shampoos & Conditioners **123**
Hamburger Helper **103**
Hamilton Bank Commercial & Consumer Banking **127**
Handi-Wrap **43**
Hanes Brand Knitwear **87**
Hanes Hosiery **37**
Hanes Men's & Boys' Underwear **87**
Hanes New Products **37**
Hanes Too **37**
Hanes Understatement **37**
Hansen Beverage Dispensing Products **69**
Hansen Quick-Connect Couplings **69**
Harbor Court Hotels & Restaurants **127**
Hardee's **35**
Harlequin Eyewear **95**
Harlequin Fiction Books **11**
Harris Corp. Corporate Advertising **57**
Harris-Lanier Personal Computing Systems **57**
Harris-Lanier Thought Processing Systems **57**
Harris-Lanier Word Processing Systems **57**
Harris Trust & Savings Banking Services **23**
Harshaw/Filtrol Filtering Media **69**
Hartford Business, Auto, Home & Life Insurance **97**
Hartmarx Corporate Division **27**
Hartmarx Retail Division **27**
Harwick Clothes **91**
Haspel **65**
Havoline Motor Oil **51**
Hayes Microcomputer Products **43**
Head & Chest Cold Medicine **23**
Head Racquetball Racquets **49**
Head Shoes **49**
Head Squash Racquets **49**
Head Tennis Racquets **49**
Health & Tennis Corporation of America Clubs **123**
Health Care General Med Health Plan **37**

Brand Index

He–Ho

Health Care Liberty Care Health Plan 37
Health Care United HMO 125
Health-tex 3
Hearst Corporation Corporate Advertising 79
Heartlines 123
Heaven Ice Cream Bars 57
Heet Liniment 51
Heineken Beer 55
Heinz Chili Sauce 23
Heinz Frozen Potatoes 47
Heinz Gravy 23
Heinz Instant Baby Food 23
Heinz Ketchup 23
Heinz New Products 23
Heinz Pickles 23
Heinz Seafood Cocktail Sauce 23
Heinz Squeeze Bottle Ketchup 23
J. A. Henckels 3
Hennessy Cognacs 89
Herman Footwear 65
Herman Joseph's 57
Herr Foods 93
Hershey's Syrup 47
Hertz Buy-A-Car 115
Hertz Car Leasing 115
Hertz Rent-A-Car 115
Hertz Rent-A-Truck 115
Hess's 49
Hewlett-Packard Business Computing Products 23
Hewlett-Packard CIS Growth Power 37
Hewlett-Packard Computer Systems 37
Hewlett-Packard Personal Computing Products 23
Hewlett-Packard Shaw Systems 37
Hewlett-Packard Test Instrumentation Equipment 37
Hewlett-Packard Unix 37
HiComp Car Stereo 61
High Point Ground/Instant Coffee 113
Hiram Walker Cordials-All Flavors 97
Hiram Walker New Products 97
Hoechst-Roussel Ethical Pharmaceuticals 57
Holiday Inns 63

Ho–IB

Holland Cheese 111
Holsum Bread 31
Home Federal Savings & Loan 103
Homericorp Retail Manufactured Homes 123
Honda Automobiles 103
Honda Dealer Advertising Associations 103
Honey & Nut Corn Flakes 23
Honey Maid Grahams 51
Honey Nut Cheerios 37
Honey Roasted Nuts 23
Honey Smacks 23
Honeywell Electronic Air Cleaners 31
Honeywell Industrial Process Instrumentation 57
Honeywell Product Advertising 11
Honeywell Switches & Industrial Controls 11
Honeywell Thermostats 31
H. P. Hood Dairy Products 57
Horsburgh & Scott Industrial Gears & Speed Reducers 69
House Beautiful Magazine 95
House of Almonds 21
Household Finance 103
Howard Johnsons Hotels 29
Howmedica Surgical Devices 57
Hubba Bubba Bubble Gum 103
Hughes Aerospace Systems 57
Hughes Electronic Components 57
Hughes Laboratories Corporate Advertising 105
Hughes Missiles 57
Hummel Figurines 65
Humulin 123
Hungry Jack Biscuits 23
Hush Puppies Footwear 103
Hyatt Hotels 123
Hyatt International Corporate Advertising 123
Hyatt Mexico Out-of-Market Advertising 123
Hygrade Carbuerator Products 61
Hyundai Motor America All Models 13
IBM AT Software 123
IBM Authorized Typewriter Dealers 47
IBM Copiers 47
IBM Corporate Advertising 89

IB–It

IBM Customer Service Division 113
IBM Entry Systems Division 113
IBM Local Branch Advertising 47
IBM National Accounts Division 113
IBM National Distribution Division 113
IBM National Marketing Division 113
IBM Personal Computer Software 89
IBM Personal Computers 89
IBM Product Centers Personal Computers 47
IBM Product Centers Software 47
IBM Product Centers Supplies & Furniture 47
IBM Product Centers Typewriters 47
IBM System 34 47
IBM System 36 47
IBM System 38 47
IBM Typewriters 47
ISC Brandy 57
ISC Champagne 57
ISC Wine 57
ITT Corporate Advertising 19
ITT Dialcom 49
ITT International Telecom 19
IW Harper 23
Iberia Airlines 11
Idaho First National Banking Services 37
Idaho Spuds Instant Potatoes 123
Iletin 123
Illinois Bell Voice & Data Transmission 11
Ilosone 123
Imperial Leather Bath Soap 57
Imperial Sugar 125
"The Incredible Edible Egg" 31
Inmac Direct Response 37
Institute for Health Maintenance Diet Products 123
Institute for Health Maintenance Obesity Clinics 123
Intercontinental Hotels 49
Investors Life Insurance 35
Isotoner Pantyhose 87
Itel Corporation Marine & Rail Container Leasing 37

Iv–Jo

Iveco Medium Duty Diesel Trucks 57
Ivory Liquid 113
Ivory Soap 113
J & B Rare Scotch 13
JCPenney Casualty Insurance 11
JCPenney Life Insurance 11
JCPenney National Retail Advertising 11
JCPenney New Products 11
J & J O'Darby Various 111
Jack Daniel Corporate Advertising 35
Jack Daniel's 25
Jack Daniel's Whisky 111
Jackie Stewart Programs 123
Jacobs Coffee 89
James River New Products 115
Jameson Irish Whiskey 47
Janneau Armagnac 31
Jarlsberg Cheese 77
Jays Snack Foods 59
JAZ-Paris 3
Je Reviens Parfume 95
Jean Lassale 3
Jean Nate 109
Jeanswear 57
Jeep Cherokee 113
Jeep CJ 5 113
Jeep CJ 7 113
Jeep Comanche 113
Jeep Grand Wagoneer 113
Jeep Scrambler 113
Jeep Truck 113
Jeep Vans & Wagons 113
Jeep Wagoneer 113
Jerkey Treats 23
Jet 25
Jewel Food Stores 21
Jewel T Discount Grocery 119
Jhirmack Hair Care Products 109
Jiffy Kits Carbuerator Products 61
Jim Beam Bourbon 21
Jobe's Fertilizer Spikes 109
John Morrell Meats 31
John Weitz 65
Johnson Moisture Formula Cosmetics 25
Johnson & Johnson Baby Bar Soap 99

Brand Index

Jo–Ke

Johnson & Johnson Hospital Service Programs **57**
Johnson & Son Commercial Products Group **31**
Johnson & Son New Products **123**
Johnson & Son New Products **57**
Johnson & Son Specialty Chemicals Group **31**
Jordache Eyewear **95**
Juki Computer Peripherals **7**
Juki Software **7**
Julius Kayser Wine **47**
K2 Skis **35**
Kaepa Athletic Shoes **75**
Kaiser Foundation National HMO & Hospitals **123**
Kaiser Industrial & Specialty Chemicals **69**
Kame Oriental Foods **81**
KangaROOS, U.S.A. **3**
Karo Syrup **37**
Kava Coffee **21**
Kavli Crispbread **77**
Kawasaki Motorcycles **21**
Keds **65**
Keebler Cookies **23**
Keebler Crackers **23**
Keebler New Products **23**
Keebler Pie Crusts **23**
Keebler Snacks **23**
Keebler Soft Batch Cookies **23**
Keepsake **3**
Keflex **123**
Keflin **123**
Kefzol **123**
Kelly Temporary Help Services **11**
Kelly Temporary Help Services **29**
Kemper Group Property & Casualty Insurance **123**
Ken-L Ration All Canned Products **123**
Ken-L Ration Biskit **123**
Ken-L Ration Burger **123**
Ken-L Ration Kibbles 'n Bits **123**
Ken-L Ration Meal **123**
Ken-L Ration Puppy Kibbles 'n Bits **123**
Ken-L Ration Sausages **123**
Ken-L Ration Smorgasburger **123**
Ken-L Ration Special Broil **123**
Ken-L Ration Treats **123**

Ke–Ko

Kenner Preschool Toys **37**
Kentucky Fried Chicken Philadelphia Franchises **49**
Kenworth Trucks **35**
Keri Lotion **79**
Kessler American Whiskey **47**
Killian's Red **57**
Kimberly-Clark Disposable Surgical Products **57**
Kimberly-Clark Home Health Care Division **31**
Kimberly-Clark New Products **31**
Kimberly-Clark New Products **57**
Kimberly-Clark Virucidal Tissues **57**
Kincaid's Brand Potato Chips **125**
Kinder-Care Child Learning Centers **91**
Kindness Permanent Waves **57**
Kingsford Charcoal **103**
Kit Kat **47**
KitchenAid Cooking Equipment **11**
KitchenAid Dishwashers **11**
KitchenAid Food Processors **11**
KitchenAid Kitchen Appliances **11**
KitchenAid Mixers **11**
Kiwi Household Chemical Products **57**
Kiwi Shoe Care **57**
Kix **37**
Kleenex Softique Tissue **57**
Kleenex Tissues **57**
Klorane Conditioners **57**
Klorane Shampoos **57**
Klorane Soaps **57**
Kneip Corned Beef **23**
Knightsbridge Tobacco **107**
Knockando Single Malt Scotch **13**
Knorr Bouillon **55**
Knott's Food Products **41**
Knox Gelatine **21**
Kodak Copier/Duplicator Equipment **123**
Kodak Customer Equipment Service **123**
Kodak Dealer Advertising **123**
Kodak Disc Cameras **123**
Kodak Disc Film **123**
Kodak Government Systems Division **123**

Ko–Kr

Kodak International Special Assignments **123**
Kodak Military & Premium Products **123**
Kodak New Products **123**
Kodak Photo Fan **123**
Kodak Photographic Paper **123**
Kodak Processing Laboratories **123**
Kodak Professional Motion Picture Film **123**
Kodak Radiographic Film Processors & Chemicals **123**
Kodak Radiographic Film, Screens & Cassettes **123**
Kodak Traditional Film **123**
Kodak Traditional Still Camera **123**
Kohler Faucets **31**
Kohler Leisure Products **31**
Kohler Plumbing Fixtures **31**
Kool Cigarettes **47**
Kraft Barbecue Sauce **57**
Kraft Carmels **57**
Kraft Cheese Classic Frozen Foods **123**
Kraft Dairy Group **123**
Kraft Deluxe Slices **123**
Kraft European Valley Cheeses **103**
Kraft Food Service & Industrial Group **123**
Kraft Grated Cheeses **123**
Kraft Handi Snacks **103**
Kraft Home Economics & Teen Age **57**
Kraft Horseradish Sauce **123**
Kraft Jar Cheese **123**
Kraft Jellies & Preserves **103**
Kraft Marshmallow Creme **57**
Kraft Marshmallows **57**
Kraft Multi-product Promotional Advertising **123**
Kraft New Foodservice Products **31**
Kraft New Products **11**
Kraft New Products **23**
Kraft New Products **57**
Kraft New Products **123**
Kraft Packaged Dinners **57**
Kraft Pourable Dressings **123**
Kraft-Pour-On-The-Cheese Cheese Topping **103**

Kr–La

Kraft Premium Dips **123**
Kraft Quality Dips **123**
Kraft Real Mayonnaise **123**
Kraft Reduced Calorie Dressings **103**
Kraft Reduced Calorie Pourable Dressings **123**
Kraft Retail Food Division **123**
Kraft Select Natural Cheese **123**
Kraft Singles **123**
Kraft Special Projects **31**
Kroger Ag-Products **31**
Kroger Bakery Products **31**
Kroger Dairy Products **31**
Kroger Grocery Products **31**
Kroger Supermarkets **31**
Krystal Fast Food Restaurants **113**
Kubota Farm Tractors & Implements **103**
LTU German Airlines **75**
La Petite Boulangerie Bread Shops **103**
La Pina Flour **37**
La Quinta Motor Inns **125**
Labatt Beer **35**
Labatt Beer **125**
LaChoy Packaged Oriental Foods **123**
Ladies' Home Journal **111**
Lady Speed Stick **55**
Lady's Choice Anti-perspirant **37**
Laird's Blended Apple Jack **123**
Lamaur New Products **31**
Lamaur Perma Soft Shampoo & Conditioner **31**
Lamaur Shampoos & Conditioners **31**
Lamaur Style Hairsprays **31**
Lamborghini West **41**
Lancome **99**
Land O'Lakes Butter **31**
Land O'Lakes Country Morning Blend **31**
Land O'Lakes Food Processing **31**
Land O'Lakes Foodservice **31**
Land O'Lakes 4-Quart Cheese **31**
Land O'Lakes Margarine **31**
Land O'Lakes New Products **31**
Landmaster Herbicide **59**
Lane Action Recliners **21**
Lane Cedar Chests **21**

Brand Index

La–Li

Lanson Champagne 31
Lark Luggage 23
Lassale 3
Last Elegant Bear 119
Lauder for Men 3
Laura Scudder's Snack Foods 75
Lava 23
Lavoris Mouthwash 113
LAY'S Potato Chips 125
Lean Cuisine 65
Lee Jeans 21
L'eggs Active Support 37
L'eggs Control Top Pantyhose 37
L'eggs Direct Marketing 37
L'eggs Knee Highs 37
L'eggs Pantyhose 25
L'eggs Regular Pantyhose 37
L'eggs Sheer Energy Pantyhose 37
Leisure Dynamics/Lakeside Aggravation 119
Leisure Dynamics/Lakeside Perfection 119
Leisure Dynamics/Lakeside Tubtown 119
Lemon Scented Cascade 113
Leroux Cordials 47
Leslie Fay 3
Leslie Fay Petite 3
Lestoil Heavy Duty Cleaner 51
Lever Brothers New Products 123
Levi Strauss Hispanic 57
Levi Strauss Menswear 57
Levi Strauss Pan-Divisional 57
Levi Strauss U.S.A. 57
Levi Strauss Womenswear 57
Levi Strauss Youthwear 57
Levy's Rye Bread 57
Libby Lite Fruit 37
Libby-Owens-Ford Glass 29
Libby-Owens-Ford Plastics 29
Libby-Owens-Ford Power & Fluid Components 29
Libby-Owens-Ford Precision Tools 29
Liberty National Life Insurance 91
Life Savers New Products 37
Life Savers Roll Candy 37
Lifestyles Prophylactics 123
Light N' Fluffy Pasta Products 65

Li–Lo

Light N' Lively Low Fat Cheese 123
Ligne-Roset 3
Like Cola 23
Lillet 23
Lilliput Eyewear 7
Lilt Permanent 23
Lilt Shampoo & Conditioner 23
Lindt Chocolates 129
Lionel Electric Trains 37
Lip Quencher 79
Lipton New Products 57
Lipton Noodles n' Sauce 21
Lipton Rice n' Sauce 21
Liquid Clorox Two 57
Liquid Ivory Soap 113
Liquid-Plumr 103
Listerine 123
Listerine Antiseptic 123
Lite-line Powdered Drink Mixes 47
Literary Guild of America Book Club 57
Little Debbie Snack Cakes 91
Lloyds Bank of California 43
London Fog 3
Long John Silver's Restaurants 57
L'Oreal Cosmetics 99
L'Oreal Hair Care 99
L'Oreal Hair Color 99
L'Oreal Mousse 99
Lorillard New Products 37
Lorus 3
Lou Ana Foods 53
Louis Vuitton Leather Goods 39
Louisiana Dental Association 53
Louisiana Department of Commerce & Industry 53
Louisiana Investor-Owned Electric Companies 53
Louisiana Land & Exploration Co. 53
Louisiana Land Offshore Exploration 53
Louisiana Power & Light Consumer Services 53
Louisiana Power & Light Public Relations 53
Loving Care Foam 57
Loving Care Lotion 57
Lowenbrau Special 123
Lowenbrau Special Dark 123

Lo–Ma

Lowrey's Meat Snacks 23
Lubriderm 123
Lucas Boring Mills & Machining Centers 69
Lucite Paint 103
Lucky Charms 37
Lucky Strike Cigarettes 47
Lucky Strike Cigarettes 79
Luden's Cough Drops & Confections 113
Lufthansa German Airlines 99
Lukens Steel 107
Lumex Healthcare Equipment 7
Lunch Wagon Process Cheese 123
LUVS Direct Marketing 37
LUVS Disposable Diapers 37
Lux Beauty Soap 123
Luzianne Tea 109
MPC Model Kits 37
MSD AGVET Animal Health Products 37
Macmillan Book Club Direct Marketing Testing 37
MacNaughton 23
Magnum Malt Liquor 13
Makit & Bakit Oven 37
Malaysian International Airline System 123
Malibu Rum Liqueur 13
Malta Dukesa 55
Mandol 123
Manville Corporation Building & Forest Products 37
Marathon Custom Materials Handling Systems 123
Marathon Custom Steel Fabrication 123
Marathon Instrumentation for Aviation & Electronics Industries 123
Marathon LeTourneau Heavy Materials Handling Equipment 123
Marathon LeTourneau Offshore Oil Rigs 123
Marathon Morco Sulfonates 123
Marathon Morco White Mineral Oil 123
Marathon Nickel Cadmium Batteries 123
Marcal Napkins 55
Marcal Paper Products 49
Marie Brizard Liquers & Cordials 89

Ma–Ma

Marie's Salad Dressing 31
Mark 1 Auto Service Centers 73
Marklin Toys 39
Marlboro Lights 23
Marlboro Red 23
Marriott Hotels & Resorts 57
Marriott Lifecare Residences 115
Mars Bar 23
Mars New Products 23
Marshmallow Krispies 23
Martell Cognac 25
Martha White Foods 21
Martini & Rossi Vermouth & Wines 99
Martinson 57
Marvella 3
Maryland Blue Cross Blue Shield Insurance 127
Maryland Bureau of Industrial Development 107
Maryland Department of Transportation 107
Maryland Economic Growth Associates 107
Maryland Office of Tourism Development 107
Masonite Interior Doors 31
Masonite New Products 31
Masonite Paneling 31
Masonite Roofing 31
Masonite Siding 31
MasterCard 51
MasterCard Corporate Card 51
MasterCard Travelers Cheque 51
MasterCard II 51
Masters Beer 37
MasterTeller 51
Maurice St. Michel Eyewear 7
Maxell Battery Division 3
Maxell Computer Products Division 3
Maxell Professional/Industrial Division 3
Maxell Recording Tapes 115
Maximum Strength Anacin 51
Maximum Strength Tylenol Sinus Medication 113
Maytag Dishwasher 23
Maytag Disposer 23
Maytag Dryer 23
Maytag Microwave Oven 23

Brand Index

Ma–Mc

Maytag Range 23
Maytag Washer 23
Mazda Automobiles 57
Mazda Trucks 57
Mazola Margarine 37
Mazola No-Stick 37
Mazola Oil 37
McCall's 83
McCaw Communications Paging Services 73
McCracken's Apple Chips 125
McCulloch Chain Saws 123
McCulloch Generators 123
McCulloch Log Splitters 123
McCulloch New Products 123
McCulloch Shredders 123
McCulloch String Trimmers 123
McCulloch Water Pumps 123
McDonalds 65
McDonald's Advertising Associations 103
McDonald's Central Coast Operators Association 41
McDonald's Central Valley Operators Association 41
McDonald's Domestic Restaurants 23
McDonald's Restaurants, Association of Chicagoland 23
McDonnell Douglas Data Processing Services 123
McDonnell Douglas Electronic Systems 123
McDonnell Douglas Launching Rockets for Scientific & Military Purposes 123
McDonnell Douglas Medical Monitoring Systems 123
McDonnell Douglas Military Aircraft 123
McDonnell Douglas Offensive & Defensive Military Missiles 123
McDonnell Douglas Optical Equipment 123
McDonnell Douglas Passenger & Cargo Jets for Commerical Airlines 123
McDonnell Douglas Simulators 123
McDonnell Douglas Space Vehicles & Satellites 123
McDonnell Douglas Third Stage Rockets for Scientific Systems 123
McIlhenny Bloody Mary Mix 53

Mc–Mi

McIlhenny Picante Sauce 53
McSorley's Ale 57
McVities 81
Mead Johnson New Products 31
Meaty Bones 23
Medaglia D'Oro 57
Megaphone Company Information Access Services 37
Meister Bräu 13
Mello-Yello 25
MEMTEC Memory Technology 117
Memtex Audio Cassettes 23
Memtex Batteries 23
Memtex Computer Accessories 23
Memtex Video Cassettes 23
Mennen Afta Shave Lotion 99
Mennen Baby Magic Line 29
Mennen Lady Speed Stick 99
Mennen New Products 29
Mennen Skin Bracer 29
Mennen Speed Stick Deodorant 99
Mercedes-Benz Automobiles 97
Merck Sharp & Dohme Ethical Pharmaceuticals 57
Merit Box Cigarettes 23
Merit Cigarettes 23
Merit Ultra Light Cigarettes 23
Meritene 103
Merle Norman Cosmetics 43
Merrill Lynch—Unit Investment Trust 21
Metamucil 103
Metromedia Telecommunications 43
Metropolitan Osteopathic Hospital 127
Mexican Resort Development 37
Mexican Tourism 37
Mexican Velveeta 23
Mexicana International Airlines 123
Micatin Athlete's Foot Remedy 99
Michelin Maps & Guides 47
Michelin Passenger 47
Michelin Performance 47
Michelin Truck 47
Michelin Two-wheel Tires 47
Michelob Classic Dark 103
Michelob Light 103
Microsoft Computer Software 75

Mi–Mo

Midol 55
Midway Airlines 31
Mighty Milk 81
Miles Laboratories, Bayvet Division 107
Milk-Bone Dog Biscuits Line 51
Milk Duds 11
Millbrook Bread 31
Miller Brewing New Products 13
Miller Brewing New Products 23
Miller High Life 123
Miller Lite Beer 13
Milwaukee's Best 13
Mink Difference Hair Spray 11
Mink International Promotion 123
Minolta Cameras 51
Minolta Copiers 21
Minolta Micrographics 21
Minolta Video Equipment 51
Miracle Whip Salad Dressing 123
Mirro Housewares 31
Mirro Outdoor Living Division 31
Missoni Eyewear 7
Mister Salty Pretzels 51
Mitchum Anti-Perspirant 115
Mobil Lubricants 65
Mobil Oil 47
Mobil Oil College Recruiting & Minority Advertising 47
Mobil Oil Gasoline 47
Mobil Oil Public Affairs 47
Molson Ale 37
Molson Canadian Beer 65
Molson Export Ale 65
Molson Golden Beer 37
Molson Light Beer 65
Momentum Muscular Backache Formula 51
Monet Jewelers New Products 123
Monet Jewelry 27
Monitor Home Electronics 95
Monroe Shock Absorbers 123
Monroe Struts & Cartridges 123
Monster Cereals 37
Montgomery Ward 31
Mor-Flo Water Heaters 69
More Cigarettes Special Events 87
Morey's Seafood Products 31
Morton Agricultural Salt Products 103

Mo–Na

Morton Consumer & Industrial Salt Products 103
Morton Garlic Salt 103
Morton Lite Salt 103
Morton Salt Water Conditioning Products 103
Morton Seasoned Salt 103
Mounds 37
Mountain Bell Telephone 125
Mountain Dew 123
Mountain High Yogurt 21
Moxam 123
Mr. Automatic 57
Mr. Build 43
Mr. Goodbar 47
Mr. Muscle 79
Mr. Turkey Hams, Hot-Dogs & Deli Meats 29
Mrs Baird's Bakeries 125
Mrs. Dash 123
Mrs. Dash Salt Substitute 21
Mrs. Filbert's Margarine 21
Mrs. Karls Bread 31
Mrs. Paul's Au Natural Fish Filets 103
Mrs. Paul's Fish Sticks & Fish Filets 103
Mrs. Paul's Light & Natural Fish Filets 103
Mrs. Paul's Light Seafood Entrees 103
Mrs. Smith's Eggo Waffles 23
Mrs. Smith's Frozen Pies 23
Mumm Champagne 47
Mumm VSOP Cognac 47
Muriel Cigars 21
Murine Ear Drops 79
Murphy's Oil Soap 105
My Way Desk Accessories 131
Myers's Rum 47
NBI Office Automation Systems 31
NCR Corporate Advertising 13
NCR Personal Computers 13
NCR United States Data/Processing Group 13
Nabisco Brands New Products 123
Nairn Floors 107
Nalfon 123
Napier Costume Jewelry 89
Nashville Network, The 103
Nassau Royale 111

Brand Index

Na–Ne

National Car Rental 29
National Demographics & Lifestyles 125
National Geographic Magazine 95
National Guard Bureau 103
Nature Valley Chewy Granola Bars 31
Nature Valley Dandy Bar 31
Nature Valley Granola & Fruit Bars 31
Nature Valley Granola Bars 31
Nature Valley Granola Cereals 31
Nature Valley Granola Clusters 31
Nature Valley Granola Crisp 31
Nature Valley Light & Crunchy 31
Nebcin 123
Nehi Cola 37
neo-Citran 103
Neosporin 111
Nescafe 99
Nestea Products 123
Nestle Milk Chocolate Bar 123
Nestle Milk Chocolate Bar with Almonds 123
Nestle New Chocolate Products 123
Nestle's Quik 99
Netherlander Cheese 105
Networx Computer Supplies & Accessories 61
Neurologics, Inc. Brain Monitor 123
New York Air 83
New York Deli Cheesecake 21
New York Life Insurance Annuities 113
New York Life Insurance Life, Health & Group Insurance 113
New York Life Insurance Pension Plans 113
New York State Lottery Instant Game 111
New York State Lottery Lotto Game 111
New York State Lottery Numbers Game 111
New York State Lottery Win4 Game 111
New York Stock Exchange Corporate Advertising 89
New York Stock Exchange Futures & Options 97

Ne–No

New Yorker Magazine Circulation & Advertising Promotion 89
Newtons Cookies Line 51
Nibs 47
Nicholas Laboratories Hospital Supplies 57
Nikon Eyewear 7
Nikon 35mm Cameras & Accessories 115
9-Lives Canned 23
9-Lives Crunchy Meals 23
9-Lives Tender Meals 23
Ninety-Eight 23
Nissan Cars & Trucks 51
Nivea Creme 105
Nivea Hand & Body Lotion 105
Nivea New Products 105
Nivea Oil 105
Nivea Sun Care 105
Norelco Beauty Care Products 97
Norelco Clean Air Machines 97
Norelco Dictation Systems 61
Norelco Garment Care Products 97
Norelco Health Care Products 97
Norelco Home Products 97
Norelco Kitchen Appliances 97
Norelco Men's & Ladies' Razors 97
Norelco New Products 97
Norelco Travel Care 97
Norfolk Southern National Railroad/Freight Company 123
C.A. Norgren Fluid Power Products 69
Normolax Laxative 113
North Shore Gas Co. 57
Northeast Electronics Telephone Test Systems & Equipment 123
Northeastern International Airways 49
Northern Bathroom Tissue 115
Northern Telecom Cellular/Mobile Phone Systems 123
Northern Telecom Common Carrier Equipment 123
Northern Telecom Data Processing Systems 123
Northern Telecom Data Processing Terminals 123
Northern Telecom Data Test Equipment & Systems 123

No–Oh

Northern Telecom Data Transmission/Switching Systems 123
Northern Telecom Digital Switches 123
Northern Telecom Home Telephones 123
Northern Telecom Memory Systems, Data Tape & Disc Drives 123
Northern Telecom Telecommunications Systems 123
Northern Telecom Vantage Small Business Systems 123
Northern Trust Company Banking Services 123
Northwestern Mutual Life & Disability Insurance 123
Northwestern Mutual Life Insurance Annuities 123
Northwestern Mutual Life Insurance IRA's 123
Norton Co. Chemical Process Materials & Equipment 69
Norton Co. Health Care Medical Products 69
Norwest Banks & Financial Companies 31
Noxzema Instant Shave Cream 51
Nu-Salt 65
Nucoa Margarine 37
NuPrime Windows & Doors 69
Nutri-Grain Cereals 123
Nutri-Grain Waffles 23
Nutter Butter Sandwich Cookies 51
OCLI Computer Glare Guard System 37
O.F.C. Canadian 23
O.H. Materials Environmental Services 69
Oasis Water 129
Ocean Spray Cranberry Juices 21
Ocean Spray Grapefruit & Other Bottled Citrus Drinks 57
Ocean Spray Orange Juice 21
O'Darby 111
Off! Insect Repellent 57
O'Grady's Potato Chips 57
Oh Henry! Candy Bar 123
Ohio Health Choice Health Care Services 69
Ohrbach's 43

Ok–Os

Oki Telecom/Cellular Telephone Division 71
Old Charter 23
Old Smuggler Scotch Whisky 123
Old Spice Deodorant 37
Old Spice Solid Anti-perspirant 37
Old Wisconsin Sausage 11
Oldsmobile Dealers of New England 65
Oliver de France 3
Omark Sporting Goods 35
On-Cor 59
On-Cor Lite 59
On Tap 123
100% Bran 47
Oneida Crystal 39
Oneida Stainless & Silverware 39
Orange Products, State of Florida 37
Ore-Ida Frozen Potatoes 47
Oregon Beef Council 35
Oregon Credit Union League 35
Oregon Dairy Products Commission 35
Oregon Farms Frozen Cakes & Dessert Products 123
Oregon Farms Frozen Soup 123
Oregon Sheep Commission 35
Oreo Cookies n' Cream Ice Cream 37
Oreo Sandwich Cookies 51
Original Appalachian Artworks Collectible Toy Animals 123
Orion Motion Pictures 57
Orkin Lawn Care 123
Orkin Termite & Pest Control 123
Os-Cal Calcium Supplement 125
Oscar de la Renta Perfumes 89
Oscar Mayer Bacon 123
Oscar Mayer Chef's Pantry Items 123
Oscar Mayer Cold Cuts 123
Oscar Mayer Ham 123
Oscar Mayer New Products 123
Oscar Mayer Pork Sausage 123
Oscar Mayer Saran Tube Items 123
Oscar Mayer Smokie Links 123
Oscar Mayer Stuffin' Burgers 123
Oscar Mayer Wieners/Franks 123
Osco Drug 21

Brand Index

Ou–Pa

Our Gang/Our Girl **3**
Ovaltine **103**
Oxipor Psoriasis Lotion **51**
Oxydol **37**
Ozarka Bottled Water **123**
PMC Specialty Chemicals **69**
Pac-Man Cereal **37**
PACE Electronic Systems Repair Products **127**
PACE Membership Warehouses **125**
Pace Picante **21**
Pacific Bell Business-to-Business MTS Services **37**
Pacific Fruit Express Shippers **123**
Pacific Northwest Bell Telecommunications **37**
Pacific Southwest Airlines **43**
Pacific Telesis Business Advertising **57**
Pacific Telesis Corporate Advertising **57**
Pacific Telesis Financial Advertising **57**
Pacific Telesis Other Divisions/Major Products **57**
Pacific Telesis Positioning & Products **57**
Pacific Telesis Residence **57**
Pacific Telesis Yellow Pages **57**
Pacific Western Airlines **35**
Pacquin Hand Cream **97**
Pacquin with Aloe Skin Cream **97**
Paddington Corporation New Products **13**
Pagagni Wines **31**
Paine Webber Corporate, Product & Financial Services **113**
Pan-American Life Insurance **53**
Panadol **55**
Paramount Pictures Midwest **73**
Parkay Light Spread **103**
Parkay Margarine **103**
Parker Brothers Games **65**
Parker Brothers Games & Electronic Cartridges **37**
Parliament Cigarettes **13**
Parlodel **103**
Partager French Wine **47**
Partners Group Health Insurance **89**
Pastabilities Restaurants **105**

Pa–Pe

Patek Philippe Watches **109**
Paul Masson **47**
Paul Masson Vineyards **47**
Payless Shoesource **57**
Payne Air Conditioning **11**
Peanut Butter Boppers **103**
Pearl Drops Smoker's Tooth Polish **103**
Pearl Drops Tooth Polish **103**
Pearle Dental Services **57**
Pearle Prescription Eyewear **57**
Pediatric Tylenol **113**
Peerless Faucets **109**
Penn Dairy Products **57**
Pennsylvania Gas & Water Company **49**
Pennsylvania State Lottery **57**
Penta Hotels-New York **105**
Pentax Binoculars **31**
Pentax Cameras **31**
Pentax Lenses **31**
Pentax New Products **31**
Pentax Surveying Instruments **31**
Pentax Telescopes **31**
People's Bank of Connecticut **39**
Peoples Gas Light & Coke Company **57**
Pep Boys **49**
Pepsi-Cola **123**
Pepsi-Cola Bottling Group **125**
Pepsi-Cola New Products **123**
Pepsi Light **125**
Perdue Chicken Franks **115**
Perdue Chicken Parts **115**
Perdue Fresh Chickens **115**
Perdue Fresh Prepared Chicken Dishes **115**
Perdue Shenandoah Turkeys **115**
Perkin-Elmer Corporate Development **3**
Perkin-Elmer Data Systems **3**
Perkin-Elmer Instrument Group **3**
Perque Carpet & Drapery **53**
Perrier Mineral Water **129**
Perry Ellis Perfumes **89**
Persantine **15**
Personal Touch **123**
Pert Rinse & Conditioner **23**
Pert Shampoo **23**
Pet Grocery Division **31**

Pe–Pl

Peter Pan Seafoods **35**
Petro-Lewis Oil & Gas Products, Investments **37**
Pevely Dairy **73**
Pfizer Inc. New Products **97**
Phelps Dodge Product & Corporate Advertising **113**
Philadelphia Brand Cream Cheeses **123**
Philadelphia Brand Dressings **103**
Philadelphia National Bank Banking Services **127**
Philip Morris New Products **13**
Philip Morris New Products **23**
Phillips' Milk of Magnesia **55**
Phillips Petroleum Products **125**
Philon Compilers **3**
Phone-Mate Telephone Answering Machines **123**
Pierre Cardin **95**
Pillsbury Best Cookies **23**
Pillsbury Best Sweet Rolls **23**
Pillsbury Cinnamon Rolls with Icing **23**
Pillsbury Crescent Rolls **23**
Pillsbury New Products **23**
Pillsbury Soft Breadsticks **23**
Pioneer Consumer Electronics **37**
Pioneer-Standard Components, Systems & Instrumentation **69**
Pipin' Hot Loaf **23**
Pitney Bowes Financial Services **77**
Pittsburgh Automotive Primers, Finishes & Coatings **29**
Pizza Hut **93**
Plaid Pantry Markets **35**
Plaisir Cheese **21**
Planters Cannister Snacks **21**
Planters Nuts **21**
PLATO Instructional Systems **31**
Play Doh **37**
Players Lights 25's **23**
Playtex Gloves **109**
Pledge Furniture Polish **123**
Plumpers Hot Dogs **59**
Plymouth Caravelle **21**
Plymouth Duster **21**
Plymouth Gran Fury **21**
Plymouth Horizon **21**
Plymouth Reliant **21**
Plymouth Sundance **21**

Pl–Pr

Plymouth Turismo Duster **21**
Plymouth Voyager **21**
Pol Sol Vitamins **21**
Poland Spring Water **129**
Polar B'ar **11**
Pond's Cream & Cocoa Butter Lotion **51**
Pond's Face Products **51**
Pontiac Dealer Association, Nassau-Suffolk **39**
Pontiac Dealer Association, New York, New Jersey, Connecticut **39**
Pontiac Dealer Association, Northern New York Region **39**
Pontiac Dealer Association, Southern Connecticut **39**
Pop-Tarts **23**
Popeyes Famous Fried Chicken & Biscuits **53**
Popsicle **37**
Popsicle Industries Novelties **37**
Popular Mechanics **109**
Porcelanosa **53**
Posture Calcium Supplement **113**
Pour Lui **89**
PowerHouse **37**
Powers Irish Whiskey **23**
Precise **25**
Preferred Meal Systems **31**
Preformed Line Electric Power & Telecommunication Products **69**
Prelu-2 **15**
Preludin **15**
Premium Saltines **51**
Prentice-Hall **5**
Preparation H Cleansing Pads **51**
Preparation H Ointment & Suppositories **51**
Prescriptives **3**
T. Rowe Price Discount Brokerage **97**
T. Rowe Price Mutual Funds **97**
T. Rowe Price Real Estate Funds **97**
Primo Del Ray Cigars **21**
Prince Matchabelli Line **51**
Prince Tennis Equipment **129**
Princess Cruises **125**
Pro Comm Windows & Doors **69**
Proctor & Gamble Drug Trade **113**
Proctor & Gamble Grocery Trade **113**

Brand Index

Pr–Rc

Proctor & Gamble Industrial Chemical 113
Proctor & Gamble Institutional/Industrial Division 113
Proctor & Gamble Military Trade 113
Proctor & Gamble New Products 23
Product 19 23
Promise Spread 99
Prompt 103
Protector Automotive Security Products 61
Provident Institution for Savings 65
Puerto Rico Industrial Development Administration 111
Puerto Rico Tourism 97
Puget Sound National Bank 35
Pulte-Virginia 49
Pure & Natural Soap 103
Pusser's Rum 13
Q-Vel 15
QMS Laser Computer Printers 91
Quaker Granola Dipps 123
Quaker Granola Whipps 123
Quaker Oats Children's Pre-Sweetened Cereals 13
Quaker Oats Corn Bran 13
Quaker Oats Foodservice Division 31
Quaker Oats Foodservice Public Relations 31
Quaker Oats New Products 13
Quaker Oats New Products 123
Quaker Oats Oak Bran 13
Quality Care 3
Quality Paperback Book Club 43
Quasar Audio Products 103
Quasar Microwave Ovens 103
Quasar Televisions 103
Quasar Video Cassette Recorders 103
Queen Elizabeth II 113
Quiche Cookie 81
Quiet World Sleeping Aid 51
Quinn's Cooler 37
RC Cola 37
RC 100 Cola 37
RCA Color TVs 23
RCA Cylix 39
RCA Global Communications 39

Rc–Re

RCA Mail 39
RCA Telex 39
RCA VCRs 23
RCA Video Cameras 23
ROLM Voice & Data Communications 75
RPM Fashions 3
Radio Page America 39
Radisson Hotels 49
Radisson Hotels 57
Ragu' Foods 129
Raid Insecticides 57
Raisin Bran 23
Raisin Squares 23
Ralston-Purina Breakfast Products 115
Ralston-Purina Patient Feeding 31
Ralston-Purina Pet Foods 115
Ramada Inns Hotel Group 103
Reader's Digest International Editions 71
Reader's Digest Sweepstakes Support Advertising 123
ReaLemon Lemon Juice 47
Realities by Omega Eyewear 7
Red Band Flour 37
Red Devil Paints & Chemicals 129
Red Pack Tomato Product 37
Redbook 109
Redi-Pans 123
Redi-Serve 59
Redi-Vision Video Leasing 65
Reed and Barton Silversmiths 65
Reese's Pieces 47
Renaissance International Hotels 103
Renault Alliance 113
Renault Encore 113
Renuzit 79
Replex Medication 105
Republic Airlines 37
Republic Airlines Frequent Traveler Programs 37
Republic Health Substance Abuse Treatment Centers 125
Resource 103
Respbid 15
Reuben Meat Products 31
Revlon New Products 115
Reynolds Food Service Market Products 123

Re–SW

Reynolds New Products 123
Reynolds Plastic Wrap 123
Reynolds Wrap 123
Rheaban 97
Rice Council Market Development 11
Rice Krispies 23
Rice Krispies Bars 23
Richardson-Vicks New Products 57
Rigaud Candles 95
Rinso 123
Riopan 113
Ritz Crackers 51
Robitussin Cough Remedies 115
Rockwell International 29
Roerig Ethical Pharmaceuticals 57
Rolex Watches 123
Rolls-Royce Motors 43
Ron Castillo 111
Ron Chereskin 3
Rooster 3
William H. Rorer Ethical & OTC Pharmaceuticals 57
Rosarita Canned & Pre-packaged Mexican Foods 123
Rose-Petal Place 37
Rotek Large Ball & Roller Bearings 69
Round-The-Clock Hosiery 109
Roundup Herbicide 59
Roxane Ethical Pharmaceuticals 57
Roy Rogers 49
Royal Ages Scotch 13
Royal Paisley Scotch 47
Rubbermaid Housewares Products 103
Ruffles Perfume 89
Ruffies Plastic Bags 31
Ruffles Potato Chips 103
Rums of Puerto Rico 113
Russ Berrie Impulse Gifts 111
Russian Prince 111
Ryan Homes 93
Ryder Truck Rental & Leasing 123
S.O. Ezy 47
S.O.S. Oven Cleaning Pads 47
S.O.S. Soap Pads 47
SPS Car Stereo 61
SPS High Technology Products 57
S&W Canned Fruits & Vegetables 37

Sa–Se

Sacramento Brand Tomato Juice 37
SAFECO Insurance 35
Safeway Stores 49
Sagafjord 113
Saint Laurie Men's & Women's Tailored Clothing 95
Salada Tea Bags 23
Salem Cigarettes 51
Sally Hansen 79
Samsonite Luggage 23
Samsung Electronics 39
San Giorgio Pasta 65
Sandoz Corporate Advertising 103
Sandy Mac 81
Sani-Flush Line 51
Santa Monica Bank Banking Services 11
Sarah Lee Frozen Cakes, Pies & Pastries 57
Sarah Lee Frozen Croissants 57
Saran Wrap 43
Saratoga 23
Sarron Ridge Wine 35
Sason Ac'cent 123
Satellite Orbit Magazine 39
Sauza Tequila 79
Sav-On Drug Centers 21
Savarin 57
Scenic America Paper Towels 55
Scheaffer-Eaton Writing Instruments & Stationery Supplies 29
Schering Ethical Pharmaceuticals 57
Schick Razors & Blades 123
Schmidt's Classic Beer 57
Schmidt's Lite Beer 57
Schmidt's Premium Beer 57
Schmidt's Regular Beer 57
F. Schumacher Fabrics & Wallcoverings 89
Schwinn Bicycles 31
Scientific Magazine Advertising Promotion 89
O. M. Scott Consumer Lawn Products 47
Scott Paper Company Value Line Advertising 123
ScotTissue 123
ScotTowels 123
ScotTowels Jr. 123
Sea Breeze 47

Brand Index

Se–Si

Seafood Broiler Restaurants 119
Seagram's Mixers 43
Sealtest Cottage Cheese 11
Sealtest Ice Cream 11
Sealtest Milk 11
Sears Discover Card 123
Sears Financial Network 57
Sears Home Fashions 103
Sears Infant, Children's & Teens Clothing 103
Sears Men's & Women's Apparel 103
Sears Merchandise Group 103
Sears Payment Systems Services 123
Sears Retail Sales 123
Sears Savings & Loans 123
Secret 23
Seiko Watches 3
Seikosha Printer 3
Selsun Blue 79
Serengeti Eyewear 57
Serentil 15
ServiStar 93
"The 700 Club" Project Bible 113
"The 700 Club" Specials 113
7-Up 23
Seven-Up Company New Products 23
1776 Tobacco 107
Shakey's 107
Sharp Electronics Consumer & Industrial Divisions 115
Sheer Elegance Pantyhose 37
Sheetz Convenience Stores 93
Sheraton Corporate Advertising 49
Sheraton Hotels 49
Sheraton Hotels & Inns 65
Sheraton Music City/Nashville 49
Shop N' Sav 119
Short Brothers Commuter Aircraft Manufacturing 57
Shout Laundry Soil & Stain Remover 57
Showtime 123
ShowToons 87
Shredded Wheat and Bran 47
Shredded Wheat & Spoon Size Shredded Wheat 47
Signetics Integrated Circuits 37

Si–So

Silo Retail Discount Appliance Chain 57
SilverStone Non-Stick Cookware 11
Simac Small Appliances 99
Simborg Medical Software 35
Richard Simmons Anatomy Asylums 123
Simpson Paper 35
Sinclair Electronic Products 117
Sine-Aid 113
Singer Knitting Machines 39
Singer Sewing Machines 39
Sinutab 123
Sippin'pak Fruit Juices 47
Sitmar Cruises 57
Skaggs Alpha Beta Combo Stores 21
Skaggs Drug Centers 21
Skin Bracer 55
Skinner Pasta 65
Skintastic Body Gel 123
Skippy Peanut Butter 37
Skor 47
Sleepinal 113
Slice 123
Slice 'n Bake Cookies 23
Slim-Fast 113
Smirnoff Vodka 99
Smith-Corona Portable Typewriters 109
SmithKline Beckman Pharmaceuticals 127
S'mores Crunch 31
Smurfs Vitamins 21
Sof-Pac Bathroom Tissue 55
Soft Scrub Cleanser 57
Soft Sense Hand & Body Lotion 123
Solo Detergent 37
Sony Compact Disc 99
Sony Professional Audio & Information Products 99
Sony Professional Audio/Video Equipment 89
Sony Trinitron TV 99
Sony Video Communications 99
Sony Walkman 99
Sophia Loren Eyewear 95
South Central Bell 91
Southern California Gas Company 57

So–St

Southern Living Magazine 103
Southern New England Telephone Cellular Mobile Division 105
Southern New England Telephone Yellow Pages/Directory Services Division 105
SouthTrust Banking Services 91
Special Effects Frost'n Tip 47
Special Effects Light Effects 47
Special Effects Quiet Touch 47
Special Effects Summer Blonde 47
Special K 23
Specialty Brands, Inc. New Products 31
Speed Stick 55
Speidel Watchbands 65
Sperry Computers 57
Sperry New Products 37
Spice Islands 31
Sporting Eyewear 7
Spread 'n Bake Brownies 23
Spring City 3
Sprite 25
Squeeze Parkay 103
Squibb/Connaught Immunologic Agents 57
Ssips 81
St. Paul Financial Services 31
St. Paul Insurance 31
Stanback Headache Powders 87
Stanback Max 87
Standard Ignition Products 61
Standish Farms Bread 31
Stanley Blacker 3
Stanley Garage Door Openers 65
Stanley Hardware 65
Stanley Tools 65
Star Markets 21
Star-Kist New products 23
Star-Kist Tuna 23
Star-Kist Tuna Light 23
Starline Design Eyewear 7
State Farm Fire & Casualty 103
State Farm Life & Accident Assurance 103
State Farm Life Insurance 103
State Farm Mutual Automobile Insurance 103
State of California Tourism 75
State of Florida Department of Citrus School Marketing 37

St–Su

State of Israel U. S. Tourism 19
Statue of Liberty Advertising 123
Stauffer Agricultural Chemicals 37
Stayfree Silhouettes 113
Steak-umm 47
Steelcase Furniture 29
Steidl's Wine Cooler 13
Steiff Toys 39
Steinway Pianos 89
Step Saver Floor Polish 123
Stetson Eyewear 95
Sticklets Gum 123
Stock Cordials 23
Stock Vermouth 23
Strawberry Shortcake Cereal 37
Strawbridge & Clothier 49
Streets & Co. 39
STREN Monofilament Fishing Line 11
Stroh Light 25
Stroh's 25
Suave Toiletries 13
Subaru Dealers of New England 65
Subaru Regional Distributors 83
Sudafed 111
Sugar Association 57
Sugar-Free Like Cola 23
Sun Carpet & Floor Centers 73
Sun Company Corporate Advertising 11
Sun Giant Foods 21
Sun Line 3
SunChips Brand Corn Chips 125
Sunkist Bottled Products 57
Sunkist Corporate Advertising 57
Sunkist Corporate Trademark Advertising 57
Sunkist Foodservice 57
Sunkist Fresh Citrus Fruits 57
Sunkist Frozen & Canned Products 57
Sunkist Fruit Rolls 57
Sunkist Natural 57
Sunkist Orange Juice 57
Sunkist Orange Soda 57
Sunrise Instant Coffee 123
Sunset Books 37
Sunset Magazine 37
Sunshine Biscuits 43
Super Pop Popcorn 21

Brand Index

Su–Te

Supercuts Retail Haircutters 57
Superior Casing Crews 53
Superiore 103
Superjuice 81
Superpretzel 81
Superstix Crayons 119
SupeRx Drugs 31
Surge Farm Sanitation Chemicals 31
Surge Milk Handling Systems 31
Suzanne Gibson Dolls 39
Suzuki Automobiles 75
Sweet N' Low 65
Sweetheart Bread 31
Swiss Knight 81
Swiss Miss Hot Cocoa Mix 21
Swiss Miss Pudding 21
Swiss Miss Pudding Pops 21
Swift Premium Hard Salami 131
Switzer Candies & Confections 11
Switzer Corporate Advertising 11
Switzer Licorice 11
Syntech Terminals for Lottery Games 111
TAP Air Portugal 3
TRW Performance Group 123
TV Guide Magazine 11
Tab 25
Tabasco Sauce 53
Tackle 57
Taco Bell Restaurants 125
Take Five Candy Bar 47
Take-Off Make-Up Remove Cloths 113
Tameran Micropgrahics & Reproduction Equipment 69
Tampax Tampons 51
Tank II Bowl Cleaner 51
Tappan Kitchen Appliances 57
Taster's Choice 65
Taster's Choice Decaffeinated Coffee 123
Tatung Electronic Products 37
Teachers Scotch 111
Team Flakes 47
TearGard 15
Teem 123
TEFLON Cookware 11
Tele-Sav Long Distance Service 73
Telos Computer Software 123

Te–To

Tender Leaf Tea 37
Tes-Tape 123
Tetley Ice Tea Mixes 57
Tetley New Products 57
Tetley Soluble Teas 57
Tetley Tea Bags 57
Texaco Anti-Freeze 51
Texaco Corporate Programs 51
Texaco Gasolines 51
Texas Monthly Magazine 125
Thalitone 15
Thermal-Gard Windows & Doors 69
Thermogrip Glue Guns 65
Thomas Cook 63
Thompson Medical New Products 111
Thomson Computer Monitors 37
Thomson Diagnostic, Imaging & Radiotherapy Equipment 89
3 Minute Brand Oat Meal 21
3 Musketeers 23
3M Commercial Chemicals Division 31
3M Commercial Graphics Division 31
3M Corporate Division 31
3M Household Products Division 31
3M Photo Color Systems Division 31
3M Thinsulate 3
3M Transportation 31
Tia Maria Liqueur 123
Tickle 47
Tidal Wave 103
Tide 113
Tide Liquid 113
Tide Unscented 113
Tiffen 3
Tilex 57
Time Saver Stores 53
Timotei Shampoo 123
Tissot 27
Titleist 65
Tofutti 29
Toll House Morsels 123
Tombstone Pizza 31
Tom's Potato Chips & Other Snack Foods 123
Tomy Toys 75

To–Tr

Tone Soap 57
Top Job 113
Topol Toothpolish 113
Toranado 23
Torchmark Financial Services 91
Torecan 15
Toro Garden Tillers 31
Toro Lawn & Garden Appliances 31
Toro Lawn Mowers 31
Toro New Products 31
Toro Snow Throwers 31
Tort and Insurance Practice Section 49
Toshiba Electronic Components 11
Toshiba Personal Computers 11
Toshiba Plain Paper Copiers 11
Toshiba Printers 11
Toshiba Word Processors 11
TOSTITOS Tortilla Chips 125
Total 37
Touch of Butter Margerine 57
Tough Act 43
Tour Eiffel 81
Tower Air 19
Toyota Automobiles & Trucks 37
Toyota Dealer Advertising 37
Toyota Dealers Advertising Association-Northwest 41
Toyota Dealers Advertising Association-Southern California 41
Toyota Dealers Association-Mid-Atlantic 41
Toyota Distributors-Mid-Atlantic 41
Trane Commercial Air Conditioning 31
Trane Heating & Ventilating Systems 31
Traveler Magazine 95
Travelers Corporation Financial Services 51
Traveline 3
Tree Ripe Cocktail Mix 81
Tri-Star Productions (St. Louis) 73
Triaminic 103
Triangle Manufacturing 107
Trifari 3
Trinidad & Tobago Tourist Board 99
Triumph Cigarettes 37
Triune Bottled Water 21

Tr–Ul

Trix 37
Tronolane 79
Tropicana Orange Juice 23
True Cigarettes 37
Trus Joist Structural Building Products 35
Trusthouse Forte North America 3
Tuffies Plastic Bags 31
Tuffy 47
Tuna Helper 103
Turtles Boxed Candy 123
Tuttorosso Tomato Product 37
Twentieth Century Fox Film Corporation (Midwest) 73
20 Mule Team 41
20/20 Wine Coolers 35
Twice As Fresh Air Freshener 57
Twinlab Health & Nutritional Products 61
Twinsport Nutritional Supplements 61
Twix 23
Twizzlers 47
2000 Flushes 109
Tyco Toys 21
Tylenol 113
Tyndale Religious Books 113
UFO Eyewear 7
U.S. Army Recruiting Command 11
U.S. Army Reserve Office Training Corp. 11
U.S. Army Reserve 11
U.S. Marine Corp. Recruiting 123
U.S. National Bank of Oregon 35
U.S. News & World Report Trade & Consumer Magazine Advertising 37
U.S. Steel Product & Corporate Advertising 113
U.S. Tobacco New Products 57
U.S. Travel & Tourism from Overseas 11
USA Cable Network 43
USAir Passenger & Cargo Airline 123
USF&G Insurance 107
USSA Federal Savings Bank 63
Ultra Brite Toothpaste 57
Ultra Sheen Conditioner & Hair Dress 25
Ultra Sheen Cosmetics 25

Brand Index

Ul–Ve

Ultra Sheen Hair Food 25
Ultra Sheen Professional 25
Ultra Sheen Relaxers 25
Ultra Star Curls & Waves for Men 25
Undie-L'eggs 37
Uniden 27
Union Carbide Silicones and Urethane Division 103
Union 76 Accessories 23
Union 76 Batteries 23
Union 76 Gasolines 23
Union 76 Lubricants 23
Union 76 Tires 23
Unisa America Accessories 111
Unisa America Shoes 111
United Airlines Asia 23
United Airlines Passenger Service 23
United Airlines Vacations 23
United Banks of Colorado 125
United HealthCare HMOs 31
United States Department of Treasury 99
United States Fidelity & Guaranty Company Insurance 127
United States Golf Associates Membership Program 37
United Telecom Long Distance & Other Telecom Services 57
Universal Pictures 47
Universal Pictures (St. Louis) 73
Upmann Cigars 21
Upper 10 37
V-Cillin K 123
V-8 Juice 13
VLI Health Care Products 75
Valentino Perfume 89
Valvoline 21
Van Heusen 27
Vanish 79
Vantage Cigarettes Special Events 87
Vaseline Dermatology Formula Lotion & Cream 51
Vaseline Intensive Care Lotion & Cream 51
Vaseline Petroleum Jelly 51
Vat 69 Scotch 79
Veg-All Foodservice 31
Velveeta Extra Thick Slices 23

Ve–We

Velveeta Loaf 23
Velveeta Slices 23
Venetian Cream Liqueur 123
Viadent Toothpaste & Oral Rinse 95
Viceroy Cigarettes 47
Virginia Industrial Chemicals 127
Virginia Slims Cigarettes 23
Virginia Slims Lights Cigarettes 23
Virginia Slims 120's Cigarettes 23
ViroMed Tablets & Liquid 51
Vise-Grip Locking Tools 21
Vistafjord 113
Vistakon Contact Lenses 57
Vitasoy Natural Food Drink 37
Vive La Dijon! 123
Vivitar Cameras/Accessories 75
Vixen Yachts 117
Vizcaya 23
Volkswagen Cabriolet 47
Volkswagen Golf 47
Volkswagen GTI 47
Volkswagen Jetta 47
Volkswagen Jetta GLI 47
Volkswagen Quantum 47
Volkswagen Scirocco 47
Volkswagen Vanagon 47
Voltron Toy Products 73
Volvo Automobiles 115
Walker Exhaust Systems 123
Wall Street Journal, The—Advertising Promotion 71
Wall Street Journal/Asian, The 71
Wall Street Journal/Europe, The 71
Wall Street Journal/International, The 71
Wall Street Journal Weekly/Asian, The 71
Walt Disney Pictures (St. Louis) 73
Warner-Lambert New Products 123
Washington State Economic Development 35
Washington State Tourism 35
Waterford Crystal 107
Waverly Crackers 51
WAWA 49
Weather Channel, The 123
Weatherby Rifles 21
Webb Decorative Windows, Louvers, Grilles & Cupolas 69

We–Wi

Weber Bar-B-Ques 21
Webers Bread 31
Wedgwood Imported China Tableware 123
Wedgwood Imported Chrystal 123
Wedgwood Jewelry & Giftware 123
Weighco-Weight Watchers Franchisee 93
Weight Watchers Franchised Weight Control Program 47
Weight Watchers Frozen Food 47
Weisfield's Jewelry 35
Welch Foodservice Products 31
Welch Public Relations 31
Wendy's Restaurant Chain 37
West Company Disposal Medication Devices 57
West Company Pharmaceutical & Beverages Closures 57
West Tobacco 107
Western Supermarkets 91
Western Union Electronic Cash Transfer 115
Western Union Mailgram 115
Westin Hotels Development 35
Westinghouse Defense & Electronic Systems Center 127
Westvaco Chemicals 97
Westvaco Corporate Advertising 97
Westvaco Fine Printing Papers 97
Westvaco Packaging 97
Weyerhaeuser Information Systems 35
Weyerhaeuser Paperboard Packaging 35
Weyerhaeuser Personal Care Products 35
Weyerhaeuser Wood Products 35
Whatchamacallit 47
Wheat Hearts Hot Cereal 37
Wheaties 103
Wheatsworth Crackers 51
White Cloud 23
White Rain Hair Spray 11
Whitney's Yogurt 23
Whole Wheat Bisquick 103
Wick Fowler's 2-Alarm Chili 51
Wild Turkey Premium Spirits 27
Williams & Humbert Dry Sack 111
Wilmington Trust 107
Wilson Foods Pork Processing & Meat Packing 31

Wi–Yu

Wilton Bakery & Cooking Pans 123
Wilton Cake & Food Decorating Products 123
Wilton Candy-making Kits 123
Winchell's Donut Houses 57
Winchester Ammunition & Defense Products 73
Wind Song Line 51
Wines Papillon 111
Winsight Software 19
Winston Cigarettes 99
Winston Cigarettes Special Events 87
Wish-Bone Salad Dressing 57
WIX Filters 87
Woman's World Magazine 3
Women's Way 49
Womphopper's Restaurants 57
Wondra Flour 37
Woolite Gentle Cycle Powder 51
Worcestershire Sauce 123
World Wide Travel Services 73
Worth Parfumes 95
Wrangler Domestic Products 37
Wyler Powdered Drink Mixes 47
X-14 Mildew Cleaner 109
Xerox Copiers 103
Xerox Duplicators 103
Xerox Electronic Printers 103
Xerox Facsimile Machines 103
Xerox Interrelated Office Systems 103
Xerox Memorywriter Typewriters 103
Xerox Networks 103
Xerox Voice Message Exchanges 103
Xerox Work Stations 103
Xomed Microelectronic Devices 57
Yamaha Audio Components/Systems 11
Yamaha Combo Products 11
Yamaha Keyboard Products 11
Yamaha Specialty Products 11
Yamaha Sporting Goods 11
Yokohama Tires 35
Yoplait New Products 37
Yoplait Yogurt 37
York Peppermint Pattie 37
W. F. Young Foot Powder 123
Yugo Cars 109

Brand Index

ZB–Zi

Z-Bec Vitamins **115**
Zact Toothpaste **79**
Zenith Cable TV Products **57**
Zenith Corporate Advertising **57**
Zenith Data Systems **57**
Zenith Desktop Computers **57**
Zenith TV Sets **57**
Zenith Video Cassette Recorders **57**
Zenith Video Components & Parts **57**
Ziff-Davis Information Retrieval Systems **69**
Ziploc Bags **43**

Client Index

AA–Al

AAA Automobile Club of Missouri **73**
AAA Midwest Conference Group **73**
AAI Corporation **127**
ABT Associates, Inc. **21**
ACEMESA **123**
A.E. Engine Parts, Inc. **69**
A.E. Group **69**
A&G Development **49**
AMC International Operations **113**
AMF Ben Hogan Company **125**
AMF Tire Equipment, Gaither's Tire Tool **17**
AMP Inc. **57**
AT&T Communications **21**
AT&T Communications **99**
A&W Food Services of Canada Ltd. **35**
AWACS **127**
AWI, Inc. **53**
Abbott Laboratories-Diagnostic Division **123**
Abbotts Dairy Products **81**
Accurate Box Company, Inc. **81**
Acme Markets **21**
Adam, Meldrum & Anderson **67**
adidas, U.S.A. **27**
Adirondack Direct **7**
Advanced Care Products **121**
Advanced Micro Devices **75**
Advertising Checking Bureau **3**
Advertising Council-Committee for Prevention of Child Abuse **29**
Advertising Council-Crime Prevention **37**
Advertising Council-International Youth Exchange **107**
Advest, Inc. **45**
Agri-Diagnostics Associates **37**
Agway Country Foods **67**
Air Afrique **39**
Air Canada **97**
Air Products & Chemicals, Inc. **57**
Airborne Express **43**
Airbus Industries of North America, Inc. **49**
Alabama Gas Corporation **91**
Alameda County Fair **35**
Alaska Tourism **57**
Alberta Alcoholism & Drug Abuse Commission **35**

Al–Am

Alberto-Culver Company **21**
Alberto-Culver Company **123**
Albertsons **57**
Alconox, Inc. **7**
ALDI Foods, Incorporated **59**
Alex/Pinata Foods **17**
Algonquin Gas Transmission Co. **45**
All American Sports **37**
Allegheny International **17**
Allen & Company Incorporated **45**
Allied Corporation **21**
Allied Corporation **111**
Allied Imaging Co. **45**
Allied-Signal Inc. **47**
Allis-Chalmers Corporation **31**
Allstate Insurance **123**
Allstate Insurance Companies **23**
Almay, Inc. **113**
Alpenrose Dairy **35**
Alpha Beta Markets **21**
Alpha Chemical & Plastics Corp. **7**
Alpha Microsystems **75**
AlpWater USA, Inc. **37**
Aluminum Company of America **65**
Alvin Ailey **83**
Amana Refrigeration **57**
AMBAC Municipal Bond Insurance **5**
Amchem Products, Inc. **57**
Amdahl Corporation **37**
American Aging Association **123**
American Airlines, Inc. **21**
American Association of Retired Persons **49**
American Automobile Association **37**
American Bar Association **49**
American Brands **65**
American Brands **79**
American Broadcasting Companies, Inc. **97**
American Broadcasting Company **11**
American Can Co.-Container Division **57**
American Cancer Society **9**
American Cast Iron Pipe Company **91**
American Cyanamid Company-Animal Health Division **107**

Am–An

American Egg Board **31**
American Express Company **95**
American Express Company **99**
American Federation of Information Processing Societies **49**
American Floral Marketing Council **49**
American Greetings Corp. **47**
American Hardware Supply Company/ServiStar **93**
American Hawaii Cruises **75**
American Home Products Corp. **99**
American Home Products Corp.-Boyle-Midway **51**
American Home Products Corp.-Whitehall Laboratories **51**
American Honda Motor Company, Inc. **103**
American International Group **21**
American Isuzu Motors **43**
American Lamb Council **11**
American Motors Corporation-Jeep Corporation **113**
American Postal Workers Union **123**
American Red Cross-PenJer Chapter **107**
American Safety Razor **79**
American Satellite Company **127**
American Security Bank **49**
American Stores Company **21**
American Telephone & Telegraph Co. **11**
American Telephone Services, Inc. **73**
American Thread **77**
American Tourister **29**
American Video Teleconferencing **3**
Ameritech **123**
Ames Laboratories **123**
AMPAD **5**
Amsterdam Corporation **7**
AMTRAK **49**
AMTRAK **103**
Amurol Products Co. **103**
Analog & Digital Systems, Inc. **89**
Andersen Corporation **31**
Anderson Co., The **123**
Andrea, Inc. **21**
Anheuser-Busch Co., Inc. **103**
Animed Inc. **37**
Anne Klein II **89**

Ap–Av

Apollinaris **81**
Apple Computer, Inc. **33**
Aramis **3**
Arby's, Inc. **93**
Arco Chemical Co. **57**
Argenti **27**
Arizona Lottery **57**
Armour-Dial Co. **57**
Armour-Dial, Inc. **103**
Armour Food Company **21**
Armstrong Rubber Company **21**
Armstrong World Industries **49**
Arnold Bakers **57**
Arnold Foods Company, Inc. **57**
Arnold Foods Company, Inc.-Brownberry Division **57**
Arrow Company, The **3**
Arrow Electronics, Inc.-Commercial Systems Group **73**
Arrowhead Puritas Waters, Inc. **123**
Ashley's Outlet Stores **31**
Ashton-Tate **33**
Asian Art Museum **37**
Ask Computer Systems, Inc. **33**
Assa, Inc. **69**
Associated Press Broadcast Services **103**
Associates Commercial Corporation **59**
Association of American Railroads **21**
Association of Chicagoland, McDonald's Restaurants **23**
Astoria Federal Savings & Loan Association **61**
Astra Pharmaceuticals **21**
Audi of America, Inc. **47**
Audiosears Corporation **7**
Audiovox **61**
Australia & New Zealand Banking Group **83**
Australian Tourist Commission **11**
Australian Trade Commission **11**
Automated Packaging Systems, Inc. **69**
Automobile Club of Southern California **11**
Avalon Industries **119**
Avis **27**
Avis Rent A Car Systems, Inc. **21**
Avis Rent A Car Systems, Inc. **61**

Client Index

Av–Ba

Avon Products, Inc. **11**
Avondale Mills **91**
Avondale Shipyards **53**
Ayerst Laboratories **113**
Ayerst Laboratories **121**
BASF Systems Corp. **65**
BASF Wyandotte Corporation **121**
BDP Company-Day & Night Air Conditioning **11**
BDP Company-Payne Air Conditioning **11**
Babson Bros. Co. **31**
Bacardi & Company-Nassau **111**
Bacardi Corporation **111**
Bacardi Imports, Inc. **111**
Bacardi International, Ltd.-Bermuda **111**
Bachman Quality Snacks **107**
Bahamas Express **7**
Bahamas Ministry of Tourism, The **11**
Bahamasair **7**
Baird & Co. Incorporated, Robert W. **45**
Baird & Warner **63**
Baker Instruments Corporation **121**
Baldwin Piano **35**
Bali Co. **37**
Baltimore Federal Financial **107**
Baltimore Gas & Electric Company **107**
Baltimore Sun, The **49**
Baltimore Symphony Orchestra **49**
Banca Serfin **5**
Bandini Fertilizer **41**
Bangor Punta Operations, Inc.-FECO Division **69**
Bank & Olufsen **21**
Bank Leumi **21**
Bank of America **5**
Bank of Boston **65**
Bank of New England **21**
Bank of New York, The **9**
Bank of Pennsylvania **107**
Bank of Virginia **49**
Bankers Trust Company **45**
Banquet Frozen Foods **57**
Barclays Bank of California **37**
Barcus-Berry Electronics, Inc. **45**
Bardahl Manufacturing Corp. **35**

Ba–Be

Barnes-Hind Inc. **121**
Barton Brands, Ltd. **31**
Baskin-Robbins **35**
Baskin-Robbins **123**
Bateman Eichler, Hill Richards, Incorporated **45**
Bauer, Inc., Eddie **57**
Bayless Markets **103**
Beam Distilling Co., James B. **21**
Bear Brand Ranch **17**
Bear, Stearns & Co. **45**
Beatrice Companies, Inc. **23**
Beatrice Companies, Inc. **123**
Beatrice Foods Co. **99**
Beatrice Foods Co. **109**
Beatrice Foods Co.-Dairy Division **21**
Beatrice Foods Co.-Martha White Foods Division **21**
Beatrice Foods Co.-Sanna Division **21**
Beatrice/Hunt-Wesson Foods **119**
Beatrice Meats, Inc.-Deli Division **131**
Beatrice U.S. Food **25**
Beck/Arnley **93**
Beck's Beer **43**
Bedford Toyota-Volvo **69**
Beech-Nut Nutrition Corporation **43**
Beech-Nut Nutrition Corporation **121**
Beiersdorf **105**
Bell & Howell Co. **37**
Bell Atlantic Corporation **57**
Bell Atlantic Mobile Systems **57**
Bell Atlantic Yellow Pages **57**
Bell Helicopter/Textron **21**
Bell Laboratories **57**
Bell of Pennsylvania **57**
BellSouth Advanced Systems **91**
BellSouth Advertising & Publishing **91**
BellSouth Mobility, Inc. **123**
Belo Broadcasting Corporation **21**
Benefacts, Inc. **127**
Beneficial Insurance Group, Inc. **63**
Beneficial Management Corp. **37**
Beneteau Yachts **111**
Benetton **123**
Berkley Publishing **3**

Be–Bo

Berlex Laboratories Inc. **121**
Bermuda Department of Tourism **57**
Best Products Co., Inc. **125**
Bethlehem Steel Corp. **57**
Biehl & Co. **53**
Big Boy Restaurants **49**
Bil-Mar Foods **29**
Binney & Smith, Inc. **103**
Bio Products, Inc. **15**
Biosonics, Inc. **15**
Birkenstock Footprint Sandals, Inc. **45**
Bisso & Son, Inc., E.N. **53**
Blair & Co., Inc., D.H. **5**
Blair & Company, William **45**
Block Drug Co. **109**
Block, Inc., H&R **123**
Blount International, Ltd. **91**
Blue Bell, Inc. **37**
Blue Bell, Inc.-Wrangler Division **87**
Blue Cross/Blue Shield **49**
Blue Cross/Blue Shield **123**
Blue Cross/Blue Shield of Alabama **91**
Blue Cross/Blue Shield of Texas **21**
Blumenthal & Company, Jack W. **49**
Blunt Ellis & Loewi Incorporated **45**
Blyth Eastman Paine Webber **5**
Boca Investors Inc. **89**
Boca Investors Realty, Inc. **89**
Boca Raton Museum of Art **89**
Boehringer Ingelheim, Ltd. **113**
Boehringer Ingelheim Pharmaceuticals, Inc. **15**
Boehringer Mannheim Diagnostics **15**
Boeing **35**
Boeing Vertol Company **127**
Boettcher & Company, Inc. **45**
Boise Cascade Corporation **37**
Bojangles of America, Inc. **115**
Bongrain International American Corporation **81**
Bonneville Power **35**
Book-Of-The-Month Club **43**
Booth Newspapers, Inc. **123**
Borax-U.S. **41**
Borden, Inc. **21**

Bo–Bu

Borden, Inc. **47**
Borden, Inc. **125**
Borg-Warner Corp. **57**
BoRics Haircare Centers **123**
Boston Magazine **49**
Bounty Hybrid Wheat **21**
Boy Scouts of America **57**
Bradford & Co. Incorporated, J.C. **45**
Brahma Beer **3**
Brandeis Department Stores **21**
Brick Institute of America **49**
Bridal Originals **3**
Bridgestone Tire Company of America **29**
Bristol-Myers Company **79**
Bristol-Myers Company-Clairol Products Division **57**
Bristol-Myers Company-Products Division **9**
Bristol-Myers Company-Products Division **47**
British Airways **113**
British Columbia Ministry of Agriculture **35**
British Columbia Ministry of Industry & Small Business Development **35**
British Columbia Ministry of International Trade & Investment **35**
British Petroleum **39**
British Sterling **65**
Brittania **3**
Brown, Inc., Alex. **107**
Brown & Sons, Alex. **5**
Brown & Sons, Alex. **45**
Brown & Williamson Tobacco Corp. **29**
Brown & Williamson Tobacco Corp. **47**
Brown Brothers Harriman & Co. **45**
Brown-Forman Distillers **25**
Brown's Velvet Dairy, Inc. **53**
Bryan Foods, Inc. **9**
Bryant Air Conditioning Co. **11**
Buddig and Company, Carl **11**
Buffalo General Hospital **67**
Bulgari Jewelers **21**
Bull & Bear Group **45**
Bullock, Ltd., Calvin **45**

Client Index

Bu–Ca

Bulova Watch Company **43**
Bumble Bee Seafoods **123**
Burger King Corp. **123**
Burmah-Castrol, Inc. **115**
Burnes of Boston **3**
Burroughs-Wellcome **111**
Burroughs-Wellcome **123**
Burroughs Wellcome-Canada Corporate **111**
Bushnell **37**
Business Week **21**
Businessland **33**
Butcher & Company **5**
Buttrey Food Stores **21**
CBN Cable Network **57**
CBS Broadcast Group **47**
CBS/Fox Video **47**
CBS Publications **39**
CIT Commercial Finance **111**
CIT Corporate Finance **111**
CIT Financial Corporation **111**
CIT International Sales Corporation **111**
C&P Telephone Company of Maryland **107**
CPC International, Inc. **55**
CPC International, Inc.-Best Foods Division **37**
C&S National Bank of South Carolina **21**
Cadbury-U.S.A. **37**
Caddex Corporation **35**
Cafes de Veracruz **37**
California & Hawaiian Sugar Co. **57**
California Angels **17**
California Cooler, Inc. **33**
California Milk Advisory Board **57**
California Redwood Association **57**
California Sports, Inc. **41**
California State Fair **17**
California State Lottery **103**
Calrab **57**
Calvert Company **49**
Campbell Soup Company **13**
Campbell Soup Company **57**
Campbell Soup Company **103**
Campbell Soup Company-Triangle Manufacturing **107**
Campus Sportswear **43**
Canadian Imperial Bank Group-U.S. **19**

Ca–Ch

Capital Cities Broadcasting Corp. **57**
Capital Cities Broadcasting-WJR Radio **29**
Car Care Council **123**
Cardiac Pacemaker, Inc. **123**
Cardinal Savings & Loan **49**
Career Labs, Inc. **49**
Carey, W.P. **5**
Cargill, Inc. **31**
Carhartt, Inc. **123**
Carlin Communications **81**
Carl's Jr. Restaurants **43**
Carlson Properties **21**
Carnation Co. **57**
Carolee, Inc. **95**
Carpet One **73**
Carrera Casting Corporation **7**
Cartan Tours, Inc. **63**
Carte Blanche **11**
Carter Investments, Inc. **91**
Carter-Wallace, Inc. **103**
CasaBlanca Fan Company **41**
Cash Station, Inc. **63**
Casio, Inc. **45**
Castle & Cooke **65**
Castle & Cooke Foods **123**
Cataract Center **49**
Caterpillar Tractor Company **59**
Catto & Co., James **13**
Cavalcade Tours **7**
Ceco Corporation **59**
Cedar Point Amusement Park **93**
Celanese Fibers **47**
Celestial Seasonings **57**
Cellular One **49**
Cellular One **103**
Central Marine Service, Inc. **53**
Central Savings **17**
Century Furniture Co. **87**
Century 21/Stanmeyer **45**
Champion Home Builders Co. **123**
Champion International Corp. **109**
Champion Spark Plug Company **123**
Chanel, Inc. **47**
Charles of the Ritz **109**
Charles of the Ritz Group Ltd. **89**
Charter Pharmaceuticals **57**
Chase Manhattan Bank **45**

Ch–Co

Chase Manhattan Bank **109**
Chase Manhattan Bank **115**
Chateau Ste. Michelle **35**
Chef Francisco Inc. **123**
Chemical Bank **43**
Chemical Bank **89**
Chesebrough-Ponds, Inc. **129**
Chesebrough-Pond's Inc.-Corporate Program **51**
Chesebrough-Pond's Inc.-Health & Beauty Products Division **51**
Chesebrough-Pond's Inc.-Prince Matchabelli Division **51**
Chessie Railroad System **49**
Chevron U.S.A. Inc. **123**
Chevy Chase Savings & Loan **49**
Chicago and North Western Transportation Co. **31**
Chicago Board of Trade **45**
Chicago Corporation, The **45**
Chicago SUN-TIMES **31**
Chicago Symphony Orchestra **31**
Chief Auto Parts **41**
Child World **117**
Christian Broadcasting Network **113**
Christian Dior **33**
Christian Schmidt Brewing Co. **57**
Chrysler Corp. **21**
Church of the Nazarene **111**
CIBA Consumer Pharmaceuticals **9**
Ciba-Geigy **65**
CIGNA Corporation **47**
Circle Line Sightseeing Yachts, The **123**
CIRRUS System, Inc. **63**
Citibank, N.A. **57**
Citibank, N.A. **97**
Citicorp **5**
Citicorp-Card Acceptance Division **107**
Citicorp Savings of Illinois **11**
Citicorp Services Inc. **47**
Citizen Watch **83**
Clairol Incorporated **47**
Clinique Laboratories **3**
Clorox Co., The **57**
Clorox Co., The **103**
Clover Stores **49**
Club Med Inc. **11**
Coast Hotels Ltd. **35**

Co–Co

Coca-Cola Bottlers **91**
Coca-Cola Company, International **25**
Coca-Cola U.S.A. **25**
Coca-Cola U.S.A. **99**
Cointreau America **43**
Coldwell Banker **45**
Colgate-Palmolive Company **57**
Colgate-Palmolive Company **65**
Colgate-Palmolive International **121**
Colibri **109**
Collaborative Research **21**
Collagen Corporation **33**
Colombo, Inc. **65**
Colonial Penn Insurance Co. **123**
Colorado Tourism Board **125**
Columbia Chase **5**
Columbia Medical Plan, Inc. **127**
Columbia Pictures **115**
Columbia Pictures-St. Louis **73**
Columbia Presbyterian Hospital **123**
Combustion Engineering **65**
Commercial Credit **49**
Commercial Trust Company **21**
Commodity Exchange, The **43**
Commonwealth Edison Company **23**
Commonwealth of Pennsylvania-Department of Revenue **57**
CommTek Publishing **39**
Compco **21**
Compri Hotel Corporation **37**
CompuShop Incorporated **125**
Computer Depot **31**
Computer Greetings Corp. **123**
Computer Identics Corporation **45**
ConAgra **21**
Concorde Hotels International **7**
Connecticut Mutual Insurance Company **65**
Connecticut Natural Gas **45**
Connecticut Savings Bank **77**
Conoco/DuPont **105**
Conrad Rice Mill **53**
Conseil Interprofessionnel du Vin de Bordeaux **3**
Consolidated Cigar Corp. **21**
Consolidated Edison Co. of New York, Inc. **37**

Client Index

Co–Da

Consolidated Foods **65**
Consul Restaurant Corporation **31**
Contel **89**
Continental Airlines **115**
Continental Can Company **63**
Continental Illinois National Bank **45**
Continental Insurance Companies **37**
Continental Manufacturing **73**
Continental Telephone **21**
Control Data Corp. **31**
Control Data Corp.-Automated Wagering Division **57**
Control Data Education Delivery Services **21**
Convenient Food Marts **67**
Conway Import Company, Inc. **31**
CooperVision **43**
Coors Co., Adolph **57**
Coppertone Suntan Products **43**
CoreStates Financial Corp. **127**
Corning Glass Works-Technical Products Division **57**
Cos Medica **121**
Cosmair, Inc.-L'Oreal Division **99**
Countrywide Credit Industries **5**
Critikan, Inc. **57**
Crouch & Fitzgerald **39**
Crowley Foods **105**
Crown Gasoline **107**
Cruise Lines International Association **47**
Cumberland Packing Corp. **65**
Cunard Line Ltd./Norwegian American Cruises **113**
Curaco Tourist Board **49**
Currie, Coopers & Lybrand **35**
Cushman & Wakefield **21**
Custom Computer Specialists **61**
Custom Optics **7**
Cyber Digital, Inc. **61**
CyberTel BeepCall **73**
CyberTel Cellular Telephone Company **73**
d-Con Company, The **55**
Daewoo Corp. **123**
Dairyland Foods **35**
Dallas Morning News, The **125**
Dalton and Assoc., J.F. **45**
Dalton Bookseller, B. **21**

Da–Di

Damon **39**
Dan River **21**
Dana Corp. **57**
Dana Corp.-WIX Division **87**
Dart & Kraft, Inc. **123**
Dart & Kraft, Inc.-Dairy Food Group **123**
Data General **57**
Datamax Office Systems, Inc. **73**
Datamedia **45**
Dataspeed **35**
Dauphin Deposit Bank & Trust **107**
De Beers Consolidated Mines, Ltd. **11**
de Castro, Inc., Robert F. **53**
Dean Witter Reynolds Inc. **89**
Dean Witter Reynolds Inc. **123**
Dearborn Park **63**
Decision Resources, Inc. **123**
Deere & Company-Domestic **11**
Deere & Company-International **11**
Del Laboratories **79**
Del Monte Franchised Beverages **57**
Del Taco **75**
Delaware Group **107**
Deloitte Haskins & Sells **19**
DeLong Sportswear **59**
Delta Dental Plan **45**
Delta Faucet Co. **109**
DeLuxe Laboratories **123**
Denny's, Inc. **57**
Dental Research Corporation **37**
Derata Corporation **15**
Designers Orthopedics **7**
DeskTop Broker, Inc. **37**
Di Fini Originals **7**
DIAL ONE International, Inc. **37**
Diamond Benefits Plan Insurance **17**
Dicomed **21**
Diebold, Incorporated **69**
Diet Center, Inc. **123**
Digital Equipment Corporation **117**
Digitech, Inc. **73**
Dillard Department Stores **125**
Dillon, Read & Co. Inc. **45**
Dime Savings Bank of New York, The **45**

Di–du

Disney On Ice of Northern California **41**
Dista Products Co. **123**
Dominion Resources, Inc. **21**
Domino's Pizza, Midwest **59**
Donaldson, Lufkin & Jenrette **45**
Donnelley Directory **37**
Donnelley Information Publishing **37**
Dorsey Laboratories, Inc. **103**
Doubleday & Co. **123**
Doubleday Book Clubs **37**
DoveBar International **131**
Dow Chemical **43**
Dow Chemical U.S.A. **69**
Dow Jones & Company, Inc. **5**
Dow Jones & Company, Inc. **71**
Dow Jones News Service **21**
Doxsee Food Corporation **107**
Drackett Co. **79**
Drake Hotel **21**
Dremel **11**
Drexel Burnham Lambert, Inc. **5**
Drexel Burnham Lambert, Inc. **27**
Drexel Burnham Lambert, Inc. **33**
Dreyfus Corp. **79**
Duffy-Mott Company, Inc. **115**
Duke Ziebert Restaurant **49**
Dunhill Of London, Inc., Alfred **129**
Dunkin' Donuts of America, Inc. **9**
Duofold **3**
du Pont de Nemours & Co., E.I. **15**
du Pont de Nemours & Co., E.I. **107**
du Pont de Nemours & Co., E.I.-Chemicals, Dyes & Pigments Department **11**
du Pont de Nemours & Co., E.I.-Employee Relations Department **11**
du Pont de Nemours & Co., E.I.-Fabric & Finishes Department **11**
du Pont de Nemours & Co., E.I.-Petrochemical Department **11**
du Pont de Nemours & Co., E.I.-Photo Products Department **11**
du Pont de Nemours & Co., E.I.-Polymer Products Department **11**
du Pont de Nemours & Co., E.I.-Textile Fibers Department **11**

du–Em

du Pont Pharmaceuticals **121**
Dutch Mill Baking Company **81**
Dynascan, Inc. **31**
E-Systems, Inc. **21**
ESPN **123**
Eagle Brand Snacks **73**
Eagle Crest **35**
Eagle's Eye, Inc. **107**
Earl's Restaurants **35**
Eastco **45**
Eastern Air Lines, Inc. **29**
Eastern Brewing Corporation **55**
Eastern Dairy Deli Association **81**
Eastman Kodak Company **67**
Eastman Kodak Company **99**
Eastman Kodak Company **123**
Eaton Corporation-Automation Products Division **31**
Eaton Corporation-Axle & Brake Division **69**
Eaton Corporation-Cutler-Hammer Division **31**
Eaton Corporation-Truck Components Marketing **69**
EBASCO Services, Inc. **53**
Eberhard Faber, Inc. **5**
Eckerd Drug Company-Pharmacy Division **123**
Economics Laboratory **77**
Economics Laboratory **105**
Ecuatoriana Airlines **3**
Edelbrock Corp. **37**
Edleman, Inc., Daniel J. **53**
EgyptAir **3**
Eiki Film Projectors **17**
El San Juan Hotel & Casino **3**
Elanco **123**
Elderplan Inc. **71**
Electrical Association **49**
Electrolux Corp.-Tappan Appliance Division **57**
Electronic Data Systems **21**
Eli Lilly & Company **123**
Elkem **3**
Embassy Pictures, Inc. **103**
Emerson Quiet Cool Corp. **57**
Emery Worldwide **123**
Emhart Corp. **65**
Empress Travel **7**
Emra Corp.-Supercuts **57**

Client Index

En–Fi

Encyclopedia Britannica, Inc. **65**
Ensign Bank FSB **95**
ENTEX, Inc. **21**
Entre Computer Centers, Inc. **37**
Epson America, Inc. **57**
Equibank **93**
Equitable, The **27**
Equitable Life Assurance Society of the United States, The **115**
Equitec **123**
Ernst & Whinney **91**
ESCO Corporation **35**
Esprit Systems, Inc. **61**
Essen Hardware Stores **73**
Esskay Meats **107**
Estee Corporation **15**
Estee Lauder **3**
Evans, Inc. **123**
Exchange National Bank **131**
Executive Fitness Center **5**
Executive Life Insurance **75**
Exide Corp. **57**
Extrom **3**
Exxon Corporation **97**
F.B.M. Distillery Company, Ltd.-Canada **111**
FDL Marketing, Inc. **59**
FHP/Arizona **35**
FHP/Boise **35**
FHP/California **35**
FHP/New Mexico **35**
FHP/Utah **35**
Faberge **21**
Fairchild Industrial Products Co. **87**
Fairchild Publications-"M" Magazine **5**
Falcon Jet Corporation **97**
Farm Credit Banks of Omaha **21**
Farm Credit System **21**
Farmers Insurance Group **57**
Federal Express Corporation **9**
Federal Farm Credit Banks **5**
Federal Home Loan Mortgage Corp. **123**
Federal Land Bank **21**
Fender Musical Instruments **35**
Fertil-A-Chron **123**
Fidelity and Deposit Company **107**
Fidelity Bank, N.A. **57**
Filbert, J.H. **21**

Fi–Fr

Financial Guaranty Insurance Corp. **43**
Fireside Antiques **53**
First Boston Corporation, The **45**
First Chicago Building Corporation **63**
1st Claims Group **77**
First Data Resources **21**
First Federal of Michigan **29**
First Interstate Bancorp. **45**
First Interstate Bancorp. **57**
First Interstate Bank Ltd. **57**
First Interstate Bank of Arizona **57**
First Interstate Bank of California **57**
First Interstate Bank of Denver **57**
First Interstate Bank of Nevada **11**
First Interstate Bank of Oregon **57**
First Interstate of Nevada **57**
First National Bank of Chicago, The **57**
First National Bank of Chicago, The **63**
First National Bank of Omaha **21**
1st Nationwide Financial Corporation **47**
1st Nationwide Savings **47**
First Pennsylvania Bank **49**
FirsTel Information Sytems **21**
Fisher Office Furniture **43**
Flavorland Foods, Inc. **41**
Fleet Fuel Management, Inc. **53**
Flexco Company **123**
Foodways National, Inc. **47**
Forbes, Inc. **45**
Ford Dealer Advertising Association **123**
Ford Export Corp. **123**
Ford Motor Company **25**
Ford Motor Company-Ford Division **123**
Ford Regional Marketing **123**
Forest City **93**
Fortune Magazine **103**
Foundation for Savings Institutions, The **13**
4C Foods Corp. **109**
Foxboro Company, The **65**
Frankel Enterprises, E.J. **49**
Franklin Group of Funds, The **45**
Franklin Institute **49**

Fr–Ge

Fred Joaillier, Inc. **123**
Free State Health Plan, Inc. **127**
Freeport-McMoran **53**
FreightMaster **21**
French American Banking Corp. **45**
French Company, The R.T. **123**
Fresh Air Fund **37**
Frette Fine Linens **39**
Frigidaire Co. **103**
Frito-Lay, Inc. **57**
Frito-Lay, Inc. **103**
Frito-Lay, Inc. **125**
Frontier Airlines **125**
Frye Company, The **9**
Fuji Photo Film U.S.A., Inc.-Magnetic Products Division **89**
Fulton Lobster Company **81**
Fundimensions **37**
Futuro Company, The **7**
GTE Corporation **47**
GTE Sprint Communications Corp. **123**
GTE Sprint Corporation **35**
Gagliardi Brothers, Inc. **47**
Gaines Foods, Inc. **33**
GameTime, Inc. **91**
Garneau Company, Joseph **25**
Garrett Corporation, The **123**
GEICO Insurance **49**
Gemeinhardt Flutes **35**
General Automation Computers **17**
General Business Services, Inc. **127**
General Datacom **45**
General Electric Company **37**
General Electric Company **71**
General Electric Company **77**
General Electric Company **129**
General Electric Company-Aircraft Engine Group **45**
General Electric Credit Corp. **45**
General Foods Corporation **121**
General Mills, Inc. **21**
General Mills, Inc. **31**
General Mills, Inc. **79**
General Mills, Inc. **103**
General Mills, Inc.-Big G Division **37**
General Mills, Inc.-New Business Division **37**

Ge–Go

General Mills, Inc.-Sperry Division **37**
General Motors Corporation **11**
General Motors Corporation **23**
General Motors Corporation-AC-DELCO Division **29**
General Motors Corporation-Chevrolet Motor Division **29**
General Motors Corporation-GMAC **29**
General Signal Corporation-Ceilcote Company **69**
Genesee Brewing Company, Inc. **51**
GenRad, Inc. **117**
Genstar/Sakrete Products **107**
Georgetown University School of Nursing **45**
Georgia Interchange Network **123**
Georgia Power Company **25**
Gerber Products Co. **123**
German Convention Bureau **3**
German National Tourist Office **3**
Gianfranco Ruffini **3**
Giant Food Stores, Inc. **127**
Gibor Textile Enterprises **57**
Gillette Company, The **99**
Gillette Company, The-Personal Care Division **11**
Gillette Oral-B Laboratories **33**
Gingiss Formalwear International **131**
Gioia Macaroni Co., Inc. **67**
Glamour Magazine **39**
Glatfelter Company, P.H. **39**
Glenbrook Laboratories **55**
Glendale Federal Savings & Loan Association **41**
Glenmore Distilleries **55**
Global Homes, Inc. **123**
Globe Life and Accident Insurance Company **11**
Godfather's Pizza **35**
Goebel, W. **65**
Gold Kist **43**
Goldline Laboratories **27**
Goldman, Sachs & Co. **45**
Good Food Magazine **21**
Goodyear Tire & Rubber Co., The **123**
Gould, Inc. **21**

Client Index

Go–Ha

Government Employees Insurance Co. **45**
Grace, W.R.-Organic Chemicals Division **21**
Grace Home Centers West **41**
Gravely International, Inc. **87**
Great Bear Spring Co. **123**
Great Clips, Inc. **31**
Greater New York Blook Program, The **47**
Greater New York Savings Bank, The **111**
Green Giant Company **23**
Greyhound Lines, Inc. **21**
Griphoist **45**
Grumman Data Systems **61**
Guest Quarters **97**
Guild Wineries & Distillers **37**
Gulf Air **39**
Gulf & Western **105**
Gulfstream Aerospace **29**
Gund, Inc. **119**
Gus Paulos Chevrolet **35**
HON Company, The **59**
Haagen-Dazs **99**
Haggar Apparel Company **125**
Halliburton Services **21**
Halo Lighting, Cooper Industries **31**
Hambletonian Society **49**
Hambrecht & Quist Incorporated **5**
Hambrecht & Quist Incorporated **45**
Hamilton Bank **127**
Hanes Corporation **37**
Hanes Hosiery **87**
Hanes Knitwear **87**
Hannan Company **69**
Harbor Court **127**
Harbor Linen **7**
Harcourt Brace Jovanovitch **65**
Hardwick Clothes, Inc. **91**
Harlequin Enterprises Ltd. **11**
Harness Tracks of America **49**
Harris Corp. **57**
Harris-Lanier Business Products **57**
Harris Technical Systems **21**
Harris Trust and Savings Bank **23**
Harshaw/Filtrol Partnership **69**
Hartford Insurance Group, The **97**

Ha–Ho

Hartmarx **27**
Harvard Business Review **45**
Hayes Microcomputer Products **43**
Head Racquet Sports **49**
Health & Tennis Corp. of America **123**
Health Care COMPARE **45**
Health Care Plan **67**
Health Care United **125**
Health Care USA **37**
Health-tex **3**
HealthAmerica Corporation **43**
Hearst Business Communications, Inc. **61**
Hearst Corporation, The **79**
Hearst Corporation, The **95**
Hearst Corporation, The **109**
Hearst Corporation, The **129**
Hechinger Company **49**
Heilig-Myers Company **49**
Heinz Company, H.J. **23**
Helene Curtis **37**
Helene Curtis Industries, Inc. **13**
Heller Financial, Inc. **31**
Henckels, J.A. **3**
Henke Machine, Inc. **21**
Henkel Corporation **21**
Hercules **65**
Herr Foods, Inc. **93**
Hershey Chocolate Company **47**
Hershey Entertainment & Resort Company **127**
Hershey Foods Corporation **47**
Hershey Foods Corporation **65**
Hertz Corporation **115**
Hess's **49**
Heublein, Inc. **99**
Hewlett-Packard Company **23**
Hewlett-Packard Company **37**
Hewlett Packard-Microwave & Communications Instrument Group **37**
Highlander Eyewear **95**
Hiram Walker Incorporated **97**
Hoechst-Roussel Pharm., Inc. **57**
Holiday Inns **21**
Holiday Inns **63**
Holland Cheese Exporters Association **111**
Hollister, Inc. **131**
Holy Cross College **53**

Ho–IT

Home Federal Savings & Loan **103**
Home Team Sports **49**
Homericorp **123**
Honda Cars of Cleveland **69**
Honda Dealer Advertising Associations **103**
Honeywell, Inc. **31**
Honeywell, Inc.-Process Control Division **57**
Honeywell, Inc.-MICRO SWITCH Division **11**
Honeywell Aerospace and Defense **21**
Honeywell Commercial Aviation Operations **21**
Hood Inc., H.P. **57**
Horsburgh & Scott Co. **69**
Hotel Plaza Athenee, New York **3**
House of Lawrence **81**
Household Finance Corp. **103**
Household Research Institute **35**
Howard Johnsons Hotels **29**
Howard Research & Development **49**
Howard Security Services **49**
Howard, Weil, Labouisse, Friedrichs Inc. **53**
Hubbard's Cupboard **81**
Huber Brewing Company, Joseph **131**
Hue Vision Corporation **7**
Hughes Aircraft Company **57**
Hughes Laboratories **105**
Hutton & Company Inc., E.F. **45**
Hyatt Hotels Corp. **123**
Hyatt International Corp. **123**
Hyster Company **21**
Hyundai Motor America **13**
IBM Corporation **47**
IBM Corporation **89**
IBM Corporation **113**
IBM Entry Systems Data **89**
IBM Entry Systems Division **89**
IBM World Trade Americas/Far East Corp.-Latin America Division **89**
ICI Americas **107**
ISC Wines of California **57**
ITT Consumer Financial Corp. **21**
ITT Corporation-Corporate **19**
ITT Corporation-International Telecom **19**

IT–Ja

ITT Dialcom, Inc. **49**
Iberia Airlines **11**
Idaho First National Bank **37**
Illinois Bell Telephone Company **11**
Illinois State Lottery **21**
Imperial Sugar Company **125**
Impulse, Ltd. **73**
Indian Summer, Incorporated **59**
Infomag **35**
Infomatics **49**
Information Handling Services **125**
Ingersoll Rand **21**
Inhilco, Inc. **95**
Inland Steel Company **21**
Inmac **37**
Insilco Corporation **129**
Institute for Health Maintenance **123**
Intech Systems Corporation **15**
Intel Corporation **33**
InterAmerican Foods **55**
Intercontinental Hotels **49**
InterFirst Corporation **125**
Intermedics **21**
International Dairy Queen, Inc. **31**
International Executive Service Co. **123**
International Gold Corporation, Ltd. **47**
International Information Network **83**
International Multifoods **31**
International Securities Corp. **69**
International Spike, Inc. **109**
InterNorth, Inc. **21**
Interstate Brands **31**
Interstate General Corporation **49**
Inverness Properties **91**
Investment Company Institute **47**
Investors Insurance Corp. **35**
Iona College **77**
Ipsen Industries **45**
Iselin & Company, William **111**
Isram Tour Operators **7**
Itel Corporation **37**
Iveco Trucks of North America, Inc. **57**
J & J Snack Foods Corporation **81**
J I Case **21**
Jack Daniel Distillery **25**

Client Index

Ja–Ka

Jack Daniel Distillery **35**
Jacobs Coffee Company, The **89**
James River Corporation **115**
Jartran, Inc. **21**
Javits Convention Center of New York, The Jacob K. **3**
Jays Foods, Incorporated **59**
JAZ-Paris **3**
Jean Lassale **3**
Jefferson Performing Arts Society **53**
Jefferson-Pilot Corp. **87**
Jefferson Standard Life Insurance Co. **87**
Jerdon, Inc. **95**
Jergens Company, The Andrew **9**
Jet America Airlines **17**
Jewel Food Stores **21**
Johanna Farms, Inc. **81**
John Wayne/Ontario Airports **17**
Johnson & Higgins **27**
Johnson & Johnson **99**
Johnson & Johnson **113**
Johnson & Johnson-Health Care Division **121**
Johnson & Johnson Hospital Services **57**
Johnson & Son, Inc., S.C. **31**
Johnson & Son, Inc., S.C. **57**
Johnson & Son, Inc., S.C. **79**
Johnson & Son, Inc., S.C. **123**
Johnson & Son, Inc., S.C. **129**
Johnson Products Company, Inc. **25**
Johnson Publishing Company **25**
Johnson, Lane, Space, Smith & Co., Inc. **45**
Jones Intercable, Inc. **125**
Juki Office Machine Corporation **7**
K2 Ski Corporation **35**
K & B, Inc. **53**
KABC-TV **41**
KCET-TV **43**
KGO-TV **41**
KSL Radio **35**
KUTV **35**
Kaepa, Inc. **75**
Kaiser Chemicals **69**
Kaiser Foundation Health Plan **123**
KangaROOS, U.S.A. **3**
Karastan Rug Mills **9**

Ka–Kr

Karl/Lorimar Home Video **21**
Karsh & Hagan, Inc. **57**
Kawasaki Motors Corp. **21**
Keebler Company **23**
Keefe, Bruyette & Woods, Inc. **45**
Keepsake **3**
Kellogg Company **23**
Kellogg Company **123**
Kellogg Rust, Inc. **91**
Kelly Services, Inc. **29**
Kelly Services-Direct Response **11**
Kemper Group **123**
Kenner Parker, Inc. **65**
Kenner Products **37**
Kennywood Park **93**
Kentucky Fried Chicken-Philadelphia Franchises **49**
Kenworth **35**
Kidder, Peabody & Co., Incorporated **45**
Kimberly-Clark Corp. **31**
Kimberly-Clark Corp.-Consumer Division **57**
Kimberly-Clark Corp.-Health Care Division **57**
Kinder-Care, Inc. **91**
King & Co., Inc., D.F. **5**
King & Co., Inc., D.F. **45**
Kings Dominion **49**
KitchenAid **11**
Kiwi Polish Co. **57**
Kleinwort Benson Group **45**
Knoll International **83**
Knott's Berry Farm Amusement Park **41**
Knott's Food Products **41**
Kobrand Corporation **3**
Kohler Co. **31**
Kraft, Inc. **23**
Kraft, Inc. **31**
Kraft, Inc. **57**
Kraft, Inc. **103**
Kraft, Inc.-Dairy Products Group **11**
Kraft, Inc.-Food Service/Industrial **123**
Kraft, Inc.-U.S. Retail Food Group **123**
Kroger Company, The **31**
Kroger Company, The **55**
Kroger Manufacturing Group **31**

Kr–Li

Kronenbourg U.S.A. **83**
Krystal Company, The **113**
Kubota Tractor Corp. **103**
Kyanize Paints, Inc. **45**
LTU German Airlines **75**
La Belle Creole Hotel **3**
La Costa Resort **21**
La Petite Boulangerie **103**
La Quinta Motor Inns **125**
Labatt Breweries of B.C. Ltd. **35**
Labatt Importers, Inc. **125**
Ladenburg, Thalmann & Co. Inc. **45**
Ladies' Home Journal **111**
Lamaur, Inc. **31**
Lamb-Weston **35**
Lamborghini West **41**
Land O'Lakes, Inc. **31**
Lane Company **21**
Lane Publishing Company **37**
Larsen Company, The **31**
Lassale **3**
Lauder for Men **3**
Laura Scudder's **75**
Lazard Freres & Co. **45**
Leaf, Inc.-Switzer-Clark Division **11**
Leathercraft Process **7**
Lee Company **21**
Legg Mason, Inc. **49**
Leggat McCall & Werner, Inc. **117**
L'eggs Products **25**
L'eggs Products **87**
L'eggs-Direct Marketing Division **37**
Leisure Dynamics, Inc. **119**
Lennox Industries, Inc. **21**
L'erin Cosmetics **21**
Leslie Fay **3**
Leslie Fay Petite **3**
Lever Brothers Company, The **99**
Lever Brothers Company, The **123**
Lever Brothers-Household Products Division **121**
Lever Brothers-Personal Products Division **121**
Levi Strauss & Co. **57**
Lexidata **21**
Libbey-Owens-Ford **29**
Libby, McNeil & Libby, Inc. **33**

Li–MC

Liberty National Life Insurance **91**
Library of America, The **89**
Liebert, Short, Fitzpatrick and Hirshland **49**
Life Savers, Inc. **37**
Lighthouse, The-New York Association for the Blind **15**
Ligne-Roset **3**
Lipton, Inc., Thomas J. **21**
Lipton, Inc., Thomas J. **57**
Liquor Barn **35**
Literary Guild of America, The **57**
Litton Industries-Lucas Machine Division **69**
Lloyds Bank of California **43**
LogicSoft **61**
London Fog **3**
Long & Foster Realtors **49**
Long Beach Transit **17**
Long John Silver's **57**
Lorillard **37**
Lorimar **21**
Lorus **3**
Lorus Canada **3**
Los Angeles County Fair **35**
Los Angeles Visitors & Convention Bureau **41**
Lou Ana Foods, Inc. **53**
Louis Vuitton **39**
Louisiana Dental Association **53**
Louisiana Department of Commerce & Industry **53**
Louisiana Investor-Owned Electric Companies **53**
Louisiana Land & Exploration Co. **53**
Louisiana Land Offshore Exploration **53**
Louisiana Power & Light Company **53**
Lozier Corporation **21**
Luden's Inc. **113**
Lufthansa German Airlines **99**
Lukens Steel **107**
Lumex, Inc. **7**
Luzianne Blue-Plate Foods **109**
Lyon Conklin **49**
MAI/Basic Four Systems **21**
MCA/Universal **47**
MCA/Universal Recreational Services **57**

Client Index

MC–Ma

MCI Communications Corporation 9
M&T Bank 67
Macmillan Book Club 37
Maguire/Thomas Partners 123
Malaysian Airlines System 123
Malmark, Inc. 49
Malrite Communications 21
Management Equities Corporation 53
Management Group, The 59
Management Science America 83
Manor HealthCare Corp. 103
Manufacturers Hanover Trust Co. 37
Manufacturers Hanover Trust Co. 123
Manville Corporation 37
Marathon Carey-McFall Co. 123
Marathon Manufacturing Co. 123
Marcal Paper Mills, Incorporated 55
Marcal Paper Products 49
March of Dimes, The-National Chapter 49
Marielle Foods, Inc. 81
Marine World/Africa U.S.A. 41
Marineland 123
Marion Laboratories, Inc. 125
Mark 1 Auto Service Centers 73
Marriott Corporation 49
Marriott Corporation 115
Marriott Hotels, Inc. 57
Mars, Inc. 23
Martec International 45
Martin Inc., Jeffrey 113
Martin Inc., Jeffrey 121
Martin Marietta Corporation 127
Martin Marietta-Michoud 53
Martlet Importing Co. Inc. 37
Martlet Importing Co. Inc. 65
Marvella 3
Mary Kay Cosmetics, Inc. 21
Maryland Blue Cross Blue Shield 127
Maryland Bureau of Industrial Development 107
Maryland Department of Transportation 107
Maryland Economic Growth Associates 107

Ma–Mc

Maryland Office of Tourism Development 107
Maryland Port Administration 127
Masonite Corporation 31
Massachusetts Mutual Life Insurance 21
MasterCard International Inc. 51
Masters Brewing Company, The 37
Mavar Shrimp & Oyster Co. 53
Maxell Corporation 115
Maxell Corporation-Battery Division 3
Maxell Corporation-Computer Products Division 3
Maxell Corporation-Professional/Industrial Division 3
Maxicare Health Plan 33
Maytag Company, The 23
Mazda Motors of America 57
McCall's 83
McCaw Communications 73
McCormick Properties, Inc. 127
McCulloch Corporation 123
McDonald & Company Securities, Inc. 45
McDonald's Advertising Associations 103
McDonald's Central Coast Operators Association 41
McDonald's Central Valley Operators Association 41
McDonald's Corporation 65
McDonald's Corporation 67
McDonald's Corporation 23
McDonald's Corporation 25
McDonald's Operators Association-Bakersfield 41
McDonald's Operators Association-Medford 41
McDonald's Operators Association-Portland 41
McDonald's Operators Association-Sacramento Central Valley 41
McDonald's Operators Association-Southern California 41
McDonald's Operators Association-San Francisco/Monterey Bay 41
McDonald's Regional Area Restaurants 21
McDonald's Restaurants-Mac Central Co-op 87
McDonnell Douglas Corp. 123

Mc–Mi

McIlhenny Company 53
McKee Baking Company 91
McLean Trucking Co. 87
McMillen Communications 49
McNeil Corp., The Robert A. 123
McNeil Pharmaceutical 121
Mead Corporation 27
Mead Johnson & Company 31
Mead Johnson & Company-Pediatric Vitamins 21
Megaphone Company, The 37
Meguiar's Polish 17
Melville Corporation 65
MEMTEC Incorporated 117
Memtex Products 23
Mennen Company, The 29
Mennen Company, The 55
Mennen Company, The 99
Merce Cunningham 3
Mercedes-Benz of North America, Inc. 97
Mercer Plastics Co., Inc. 7
Merchants Insurance Group 67
Merchants Trading 45
Merck & Company-MSD AGVET Division 37
Merck Sharp & Dohme 57
Merck Sharp & Dohme International 121
Merle Norman Cosmetics 43
Merrell Dow Pharmaceuticals, Inc. 21
Merrill Lynch-Unit Investment Trusts 21
Metromedia Telecommunications 43
Metropolitan Hospital 127
Mexican Foods of America 77
Mexican National Tourist Council 37
Mexican Resort Development-Fonatur 37
Mexicana Airlines 123
Michelin Tire Corp. 47
Microsoft Corporation 75
MidCon Corp. 123
Midway Airlines 31
Miles Laboratories, Inc. 33
Miles Laboratories, Inc.-Bayvet Division 107
Miles Laboratories, Inc.-Grocery Products Division 47

Mi–Mu

Miller Brewing Company 13
Miller Brewing Company 23
Miller Brewing Company 33
Miller Brewing Company 123
Mink International 123
Minneapolis Star and Tribune, The 21
Minnesota Gas Company 21
Minnesota Twins Baseball Club 31
Minnetonka, Inc. 21
Minolta Corporation-Business Equipment Division 21
Minolta Corporation-Photographic Division 51
Minolta USA 47
Mirro Corporation 31
Misdom-Frank Corporation 7
Mitsubishi Electric Sales America, Inc. 33
Mobil Oil Corporation 47
Mobil Oil Corporation 65
Modular Computer Systems, Inc. 45
Monet Jewelers, Inc. 123
Monet Jewelry 27
Monitor Systems, Inc. 95
Monsanto 59
Montgomery Ventures, Ltd. 53
Montgomery Ward 31
Moore & Schley 5
Mor-Flo Industries, Inc. 69
Morgan Guaranty Trust Company of New York 5
Morgan Stanley & Co. Incorporated 45
Morrell & Company, John 31
Morrison-Knudsen Co., Inc. 37
Morrow & Co. 45
Morton Salt 103
Moseley, Hallgarten, Estabrook & Weeden Inc. 45
Motorola, Inc. 65
Mountain Bell Telephone 125
Mr. Build 43
Mrs Baird's Bakeries, Inc. 125
Mrs. Paul's Kitchens, Inc. 103
Mrs. Smith's Frozen Foods Company Co. 23
Multibank Financial Corp. 45
Multiwire 61
Municipal Assistance Corp. 45

Client Index

Mu–Na

Municipal Bond Insurance Association **123**
Murdoch & Coll, Inc. **63**
Murphy-Phoenix Company, The **105**
Musica Sacra **7**
Mutual of Omaha **21**
NBI, Inc. **31**
NCR Corporation **13**
NFL Alumni Association-St. Louis **73**
NY State Electric & Gas **67**
Nabisco Brands, Inc. **123**
Nabisco Brands, Inc.-Biscuit Division **37**
Nabisco Brands, Inc.-Biscuit Division **51**
Nabisco Brands, Inc.-Grocery Division **51**
Nabisco Brands, Inc.-Grocery Products Division **47**
Nabisco Brands, Inc.-Planters/Life Savers Division **21**
Nairn Floors **107**
Nalco Chemical Co.-Oil Field Services Division **21**
Napa Naturals **35**
Napier Company, The **89**
Napp Chemicals **21**
Nashville Network, The **103**
National Adoption Center **49**
National Alliance of Business **31**
National Association Home Builders **123**
National Car Rental System **29**
National Coffee Association **97**
National Council on Alcoholism **11**
National Demographics and Lifestyles **125**
National Distillers **79**
National Education Association **123**
National Federation of Coffee Growers of Columbia **47**
National Geographic Society **95**
National Guard Bureau, The **103**
National Gypsum **21**
National Medical Enterprises **43**
National Oats Company **21**
National Presto Industries, Inc. **21**
National Railroad Passenger Corp. **49**
National Securities & Research **39**

Ne–No

Nestle Company, Inc., The **65**
Nestle Company, Inc., The **81**
Nestle Company, Inc., The **99**
Nestle Company, Inc., The **123**
Netair International Corp. **33**
Neurologics, Inc. **123**
New England Shrimp **21**
New Jersey Bell **21**
New Jersey Division of Commerce & Economic Development **21**
New Jersey Division of Travel & Tourism **21**
New Jersey Education Association **49**
New Jersey National Bank **5**
New Jersey Transit **21**
New Orleans Dental Association **53**
New Orleans Dental Conference **53**
New Orleans Jazz & Heritage Festival **53**
New Orleans Public Service Inc. **53**
New York Air **83**
New York City Opera **111**
New York Hospital-Cornell Medical Center **21**
New York Life Insurance Company **113**
New York Mets **43**
New York State Lottery **111**
New York Stock Exchange, Inc. **89**
New York Stock Exchange, Inc. **97**
New York Telephone Company **21**
New York Times, The **21**
New Yorker Magazine, The **89**
New Zealand Trading Company **35**
Newport News Shipbuilding **21**
Nicholas Laboratories **57**
Nickerson American Plant Breeders **31**
Nike, Inc. **33**
Nikon Inc. **115**
Nikon Precision Incorporated **33**
Nissan Motor Corporation In U.S.A. **51**
Nomura Securities International, Inc. **45**
Norfolk Southern Corp. **123**
Norgren Co., C.A. **69**
Norseland Foods Inc. **77**
North American Philips Co. **61**

No–Or

North American Philips Corporation **97**
Northeastern International Airways **49**
Northeastern University **45**
Northern Business Information **71**
Northern Illinois Gas Company **21**
Northern Natural Gas Co. **21**
Northern Petrochemical Co. **21**
Northern Telecom, Inc. **123**
Northern Trust Company, The **45**
Northern Trust Company, The **123**
Northwest Ford Dealers **35**
Northwestern Bell Telephone Company **21**
Northwestern Mutual Life Insurance **123**
Norton Company **69**
Norwest Corporation **31**
Novo Laboratories, Inc. **21**
Noxell Corporation **51**
Nurses House **15**
Nuveen & Co. Incorporated, John **45**
NYNEX Information Resources **33**
NYNEX Mobile Communications **67**
OCLI Optical Coating Laboratory, Inc. **37**
O.H. Materials Co. **69**
Oakwood Homes Corp. **87**
Ocean Spray Cranberries, Inc. **21**
Ocean Spray Cranberries, Inc. **57**
Ohio Health Choice Plan **69**
Ohrbach's **43**
Okemo Mountain, Inc. **123**
Oki Electric Company Ltd. **71**
Old Stone Corporation **49**
Oldsmobile Dealers of America **65**
Olin Chemical Corporation **121**
Oliver de France **3**
Olympus Corp. **21**
Omaha World-Herald **21**
Omark **35**
Omega Group **7**
On-Cor Frozen Foods **59**
One Magnificent Mile **103**
Oneida Silversmiths **39**
Oppenheimer & Co., Inc. **45**
Ore-Ida Foods, Inc. **47**
Oregon Beef Council **35**

Or–Pe

Oregon Credit Union League **35**
Oregon Dairy Products Commission **35**
Oregon Sheep Commission **35**
Oregonian **35**
Organon Pharmaceuticals **21**
Original Appalachian Artworks, Inc. **123**
Orion Pictures Corp. **57**
Orkin Exterminating Co. **123**
Ortho Pharmaceutical **121**
Oscar Mayer & Co. **123**
Osco Drug **21**
Our Gang/Our Girl **3**
Ozarka Bottled Water **123**
PACCAR International **35**
PMC Specialties Group, Inc. **69**
PACE, Incorporated **127**
Pace Foods, Inc. **21**
PACE Membership Warehouse **125**
Pace University **99**
Pacific Bell **37**
Pacific Fruit Express **123**
Pacific Northwest Bell **37**
Pacific Southwest Airlines **43**
Pacific Telesis Group **57**
Pacific Western Airlines **35**
Paddington Corporation, The **13**
PaineWebber Incorporated **45**
PaineWebber Incorporated **113**
Palm Beach Corporation **95**
Palm Beach, Inc. **65**
Pamida, Inc. **21**
Pan-American Life Insurance Co. **53**
Panafax Corporation **61**
Paramount Pictures-Midwest **73**
Parfums Stern Inc. **89**
Park Avenue Tobacco, Inc. **107**
Park Towne Place **49**
Parke-Davis **121**
Parker Brothers-Canada **37**
Parker Brothers-U.S.A. **37**
ParkWest Ski Resort **35**
Parlux, Inc. **95**
Partners National Health Plans **89**
Pastabilities Restaurants **105**
Peanut Shack of America, Inc. **87**
Pearle Health Service **57**
Peat, Marwick, Mitchell **21**

Client Index

Pe–Ph

Penn Dairies **57**
Penney Company, Inc., JC-Financial Services **11**
Pennsylvania Gas & Water Company **49**
Pennsylvania Horticultural Society **57**
Pennsylvania Trial Lawyers Association **49**
Penta Hotels **105**
Pentagon Federal Credit Union **49**
Pentax Corporation **31**
People's Bank of Connecticut **39**
Peoples Energy Corp. **57**
Pep Boys **49**
Pepsi-Cola Bottling Group **125**
Pepsi-Cola Company **123**
Pepsi-Cola Company **125**
Pepsi-Cola U.S.A.-Food Service Division **125**
PepsiCo Foods International **125**
Perdue Farms, Inc. **115**
Perkin-Elmer-Corporate Development **3**
Perkin-Elmer-Data Systems **3**
Perkin-Elmer-Instrument Group **3**
Perque Carpet & Drapery **53**
Perrier Group, The **129**
Pet, Inc. **31**
Pet Underwood **123**
Peter Pan Seafoods, Inc. **35**
Petersen Manufacturing Co., Inc. **21**
Petro-Lewis Corporation **37**
Pevely Dairy **73**
Pfizer Inc. **97**
Pfizer Inc. **123**
Pfizer Inc.-Leeming/Pacquin Division **9**
Pfizer Inc.-Roerig Division **57**
Pfizer Pharmaceuticals **45**
Pharmaceutical Manufacturers Association **127**
Phelps Dodge Industries, Inc. **113**
Phelps, Dunbar, Marks, Claverie & Sims **53**
Philadelphia Electric Company **49**
Philadelphia Gas Works **49**
Philadelphia Industrial Development Corp. **49**
Philadelphia Magazine **49**
Philadelphia National Bank **127**

Ph–Pr

Philharmonia Virtuosi **3**
Philip Morris Company **23**
Philip Morris U.S.A. **13**
Philips Business Systems, Inc. **61**
Phillips Chemical Company **125**
Phillips Petroleum Company **125**
Phillips-Van Heusen Corporation **27**
Philon Compilers **3**
Phone-Mate, Inc. **123**
Pier 39 **35**
Pillsbury Company, The **23**
Pilot Life Insurance Co. **87**
Pioneer Electronics Inc.-U.S.A. **37**
Pioneer-Standard Electronics, Inc. **69**
Piper, Jaffray & Hopwood **45**
Pitney Bowes Credit Corporation **77**
Pittsburgh Plate Glass-Automotive Finishes Group **29**
Pittsburgh Plate Glass-Coating and Resins Division **29**
Pizza Hut **33**
Pizza Hut **93**
Plaid Pantry Markets **35**
Plaisir de France **21**
Plus Development Corp. **33**
Poly-Tech **31**
Pontiac Dealers of NY/NJ/CT, The **39**
Popeyes Famous Fried Chicken & Biscuits **47**
Popeyes Famous Fried Chicken & Biscuits **53**
Popsicle Industries **37**
Porcelanosa, SA **53**
Porsche Cars North America **33**
Porsche-Audi Motor Cars, Inc. **69**
Port Authority of N.Y. & N.J. **95**
Preferred Financial Corporation **45**
Preferred Meal Systems **31**
Preformed Line Products Company **69**
Prentice-Hall, Inc. **5**
Prescott, Ball & Turben, Inc. **45**
Prescriptives **3**
Price Associates, Inc., T. Rowe **97**
Procter & Gamble Company, The **103**
Procter & Gamble Company, The **113**

Pr–Re

Procter & Gamble Company, The-Direct Marketing **37**
Procter & Gamble Company of Canada, Inc. **37**
Professional Apparel Association **49**
Provident Institution for Savings **65**
Prudential-Bache Securities **5**
Prudential-Bache Securities **21**
Prudential-Bache Securities **45**
Public Service Company of Colorado **125**
Puerto Rico Industrial Development Administration **111**
Puerto Rico Tourism Company **97**
Puget Sound National Bank **35**
Pulte Home Corporation **49**
Q-107 FM **103**
QMS, Inc. **91**
Quaker Oats Company, The **13**
Quaker Oats Company, The **31**
Quaker Oats Company, The **123**
Quality Care **3**
Quasar Co. **103**
RCA Consumer Electronics **23**
RCA Corp. **103**
RCA Global Communications **39**
ROLM **75**
RPM Fashions **3**
Radisson Hotel Corp. **57**
Raddison Mark Plaza Hotel **49**
Raddison Plaza-Austin **49**
Ralphs Grocery Company **41**
Ralston Purina Company **31**
Ralston Purina Company **43**
Ralston Purina Company **115**
Ramada Inns, Inc. **103**
Rauscher Pierce Refsnes, Inc. **45**
Raytheon Corporation **65**
Reader's Digest Association, Inc. **71**
Reader's Digest Association, Inc. **123**
Realty World **21**
Redi-Vision Leasing Systems **65**
Reed and Barton Silversmiths **65**
Reemtsma GmbH **107**
Reeves International **39**
Renfield Importers Ltd. **99**
Republic Airlines, Inc. **37**
Republic Health Corporation **125**

Re–Ro

Republic Money Orders, Inc. **21**
RepublicBank Corporation **21**
Restaurant Associates **27**
Retirement Community Developers **49**
Revlon Healthcare Group **123**
Revlon, Inc. **115**
Reynolds Metals Co. **123**
Reynolds Tobacco Company, R.J. **51**
Reynolds Tobacco Company, R.J. **87**
Reynolds Tobacco Company, R.J. **99**
Rhodes Company, James H. **7**
Rice Council **11**
Rich Co., F.D. **57**
Rich Products Corporation **67**
Richardson-Vicks, Inc. **57**
Riggs, Counselman, Michaels & Downes, Inc. **127**
Ringling Brothers Circus of Northern California **41**
Ritz-Carlton Chicago, The **63**
Riverton Corporation, The **49**
Roadway Package System **93**
Robertson, Colman & Stephens **45**
Robins, A.H. **115**
Robinson-Humphrey Company, Inc., The **45**
Roche Laboratories **121**
Rockwell International **29**
Rocky Mountain Energy **21**
Rolex Watch U.S.A., Inc. **123**
Rolls-Royce Motors **43**
Ron Chereskin **3**
Rooney, Pace Inc. **45**
Rooster **3**
Rorer, Inc., William H. **57**
Rosecroft Raceway **49**
Ross Laboratories **79**
Rotek Incorporated **69**
Rothschild Inc. **45**
Rothschild, Unterberg, Towbin, L.F. **5**
Rothschild, Unterberg, Towbin, L.F. **45**
Round Hill Development Co., Ltd. **57**
Rouse Company, The **49**
Rowntree DeMet's, Inc. **123**
Roxane Laboratories, Inc. **57**

Client Index

Ro–Sc

Roy Rogers **49**
Royal Canadian Mint **123**
Royal Crown Beverage Company of Southern California **37**
Royal Crown Cola Company **37**
Rubbermaid Inc. **103**
Rums of Puerto Rico **113**
Russ Berrie and Company **111**
Russell Corporation **21**
Rust International Corporation **91**
Ryan Homes **93**
Ryder Truck Rental, Inc. **123**
STSC, Inc. **49**
S&W Fine Foods, Inc. **37**
Saab-Scania of America, Inc. **9**
SAFECO **35**
Safety Harbor Spa & Fitness Center **63**
Safeway Stores **49**
Saint Laurie Ltd. **95**
Salada **23**
Salomon Brothers Inc. **45**
Samsung Electronics America **39**
San Diego Union/Tribune **103**
San Francisco Zoological Society **37**
Sanders Associates **21**
Sandoz Nutrition Corp. **103**
Sandoz U.S.A. **103**
Sandy Mac Food Company **81**
Santa Monica Bank **11**
Sanyo Business Systems **27**
Sanyo Electric, Inc.-Home Appliance Division **9**
Sara Lee Corp.-Kitchens of Sara Lee **57**
Sav-On Drug Centers **21**
Schaper Manufacturing Company **21**
Schenley Industries, Inc. **23**
Schering Corp. **57**
Schieffelin & Co. **89**
Scholastic, Inc. **123**
Schott-America **65**
Schumacher & Co., F. **89**
Schwinn Bicycle Company **31**
Scientific American Magazine **89**
Scott & Sons, O.M. **47**
Scott Paper Company **65**
Scott Paper Company **123**

Sc–Sh

Scott Paper Limited **35**
Scripps-Howard **21**
Scudder, Stevens & Clark **49**
Seafood Broiler Restaurants **119**
Seagram & Sons, Inc., Joseph E. **47**
Seagram's Mixers **43**
Sealy of the Carolinas, Inc. **87**
Sealy, Inc. **21**
Searle & Co., G.D. **103**
Sears Financial Credit **123**
Sears, Roebuck & Co. **57**
Sears, Roebuck & Co. **93**
Sears, Roebuck & Co. **103**
Sears, Roebuck & Co. **123**
Sears, Roebuck & Co.-LA Group **123**
Sears, Roebuck & Co.-Mid-California Group **123**
Sears, Roebuck & Co.-Southwest Group **123**
Sears Savings Bank **123**
Season-all Industries **69**
Seattle Times **35**
Security Pacific National Bank **45**
Seidler Amdec Securities Inc. **45**
Seidman & Seidman BDO **95**
Seiko Time Canada, Ltd. **3**
Seiko Time Corp. **3**
Seikosha Printer **3**
Sensormatic-CheckRobot, New Products Division **89**
Seven-Up Company **23**
SEVENTEEN Magazine **21**
Shaffer, Clarke & Co., Inc. **81**
Shakey's **107**
Sharp Electronics **115**
Sharp Health Systems **103**
Sheaffer-Eaton **29**
Shearson Lehman/American Express **5**
Shearson Lehman Brothers **99**
Sheetz Convenience Stores **93**
Sheppard & Enoch Pratt Hospital **107**
Sheraton Hotels **49**
Sheraton Hotels and Inns **65**
Sherburne Corporation **89**
Shokai Far East, Ltd. **7**
Shop N' Sav, Inc. **119**
Short Brothers U.S.A., Inc. **57**

Sh–Sq

Showtime/The Movie Channel, Inc. **123**
Shulton, Inc. **37**
Signet **21**
Signetics Corporation **37**
Silo Inc. **57**
Silver Smith Casino & Resort **35**
Simac Appliances Corp. **99**
Simborg Systems **35**
Simmons Anatomy Asylums, Richard **123**
Simpson Paper **35**
Sinclair Research Limited **117**
Singer Company, The **39**
Sitmar Cruises **57**
Six Flags Great Adventure Amusement Park **43**
Six Flags Magic Mountain Amusement Park **43**
Six Flags Over Georgia **123**
Six Flags Power Plant **107**
Skaggs Alpha Beta Combo Stores **21**
Skaggs Drug Centers **21**
Smith International **21**
Smith-Corona **109**
SmithKline Beckman Corporation **127**
Sony Broadcast Products Company **89**
Sony Corporation of America **99**
Source Telecomputing Corp. **103**
South Central Bell **91**
Southern California Gas Co. **57**
Southern Forest Products Association **35**
Southern Gas Association **21**
Southern Living Magazine **103**
Southern New England Telephone **105**
Southland Canada, Inc. **35**
SouthTrust Corporation **91**
Southwest Washington Hospitals **35**
Southwestern Bell Mobile Phone Systems, Inc. **21**
Special Olympics **37**
Specialty Brands, Inc. **31**
Sperry Corp. **57**
Spring City **3**
SPS Technologies **57**
Squibb/Connaught, Inc. **57**

Sq–Su

Squibb International **121**
St. Charles **49**
St. Paul Companies, Inc., The **31**
St. Paul Federal Savings & Loan Association, Chicago **45**
St. Peters Hospital **73**
Stanback Company **87**
Standard & Poor's Corporation **45**
Standard Insurance **35**
Standard Microsystems Corp. **61**
Standard Motor Products **61**
Standard Pacific-Illinois Corp. **63**
Stanley Blacker **3**
Stanley Works, The **65**
Star Markets **21**
Star-Kist Foods, Incorporated **23**
Starline Optical Corporation **7**
State Farm Insurance Co. **103**
State of California-Tourism/Economic Development **75**
State of Florida-Department of Citrus **37**
State of Israel-Tourist Office **19**
State of Vermont-Travel Division **21**
Stateline Hotel & Casino **35**
Stateline Properties **35**
Stauffer Chemical Company **37**
Steelcase **29**
Stein & Comapny **63**
Steinway & Sons **89**
Stella Artois Imported Beer **17**
Stern Watch Agency, Inc., Henri **109**
Stifel, Nicolaus & Company Incorporated **45**
Store Audits, Inc. **7**
Stouffer Corporation **65**
Strawbridge & Clothier **49**
Streets & Co. **39**
Stride-Rite Corporation **65**
Stroh Brewery Company, The **25**
Stuart Pharmaceuticals **121**
Subaru Dealers of New England **65**
Subaru of America **83**
Subaru Regional Distributors **83**
Suburban Bank **103**
Sugar Association, The **57**
Sun Banks of Florida **9**
Sun Carpet & Floor Centers **73**
Sun Company, The **11**

Client Index

Su–Th

Sun Line **3**
Sunkist Growers, Inc. **57**
Sunn Electronics **35**
Sunshine Biscuits **43**
Superior Casing Crews **53**
Superior Pet Products **21**
Surdyk's Liquor Store **21**
Surgicot, Inc. **21**
Surgikos, Inc. **21**
Suzuki of America Automotive Corporation **75**
Swatch **99**
Syntro Corporation **15**
Sytech International, Inc. **111**
TAP Air Portugal **3**
TRW-Replacement Parts Division **123**
Taco Bell Corporation **125**
Tambrands, Inc. **51**
Tameran, Inc. **69**
Tatung Company of America, Inc. **37**
Tax Management Inc. **127**
Taylor & Co., W.A. **123**
Tel-Plus Communications **83**
Tele-Sav Long Distance Company **73**
Telos Corp. **123**
Temple University **57**
Tenex Corporation **131**
Tenneco Automotive **123**
Tenneco Inc. **21**
Tenneco Realty Development Corp. **21**
Tenneco West **21**
Tennessee Gas Transmission Co. **21**
Teradata **35**
Tetley Inc. **57**
Texaco Inc. **51**
Texas Instruments **21**
Texas Monthly **125**
Textron **65**
Theradyne Corporation **7**
Thomas Cook, Inc. **63**
Thompson Medical **111**
Thompson Medical Company **113**
Thomson CGR-Medical Corporation **89**
Thomson Consumer Products, Inc. **37**

Th–Tr

Thomson McKinnon Securities Inc. **45**
3M **31**
3M-Data Recording Products Division **33**
3M Thinsulate **3**
Tiffen **3**
Time Saver Stores, Inc. **53**
Tissot, S.A. **27**
Titus Food, Inc. **35**
Tofu Time, Inc. **29**
Tombstone Pizza Corporation **31**
Tom's Foods **123**
Tomy Corporation **75**
Tomy Corporation-Aurora Hobby Division **119**
Tony's Pizza Service **21**
Topps Chewing Gum, Inc. **33**
Torchmark Corporation **91**
Toro Company, The **31**
Toshiba America, Inc.-Co-Op Programs **11**
Toshiba America, Inc.-Components Division **11**
Toshiba America, Inc.-Copier Division **11**
Toshiba America, Inc.-Corporate **11**
Toshiba America, Inc.-Information Systems Division **11**
Tower Air **19**
Toyota Canada, Inc. **37**
Toyota Dealer Associations **37**
Toyota Dealers Advertising Association, Northern California **41**
Toyota Dealers Advertising Association, Northwest **41**
Toyota Dealers Advertising Association, Southern California **41**
Toyota Dealers Association, Mid-Atlantic **41**
Toyota Distributors, Inc., Mid-Atlantic **41**
Toyota Motor Sales U.S.A., Inc. **37**
Trafalgar Tours, Inc. **65**
Trane Company, The **31**
TransAmerica Corp. **43**
Travelers Corporation, The **51**
Travelers Insurance Co. **123**
Traveline **3**
Tree Ripe Products, Inc. **81**
Trendline **45**

Tr–Un

Tri-Star Productions-St. Louis **73**
Tri-Valley Growers **37**
Trifari **3**
Trinidad & Tobago Tourist Board **99**
Triune **21**
Trump Casino Hotel **33**
Trus Joist Corporation **35**
Trusthouse Forte North America **3**
Tucker Anthony & R.L. Day Inc. **45**
Tulane Medical Center **53**
Turkish Tourism & Information Office **45**
Tuthill Corporation-Hansen Coupling Division **69**
TV Guide Magazine **11**
Twentieth Century Fox Film Corporation **123**
Twentieth Century Fox Film Corporation-Midwest **73**
Twinlab **61**
Tyco Industries **21**
Tyndale House Publishers **113**
U.C. Berkeley Foundation **33**
UGI Corporation **49**
UMA Shoe Company, Bruno Magli **3**
U.S. Army Recruiting **11**
U.S. Department of Treasury **99**
U.S. Health Care Systems, Inc. **113**
U.S. National Bank of Oregon **35**
U.S. News & World Report **37**
U.S. Office **49**
U.S. Suburban Press, Inc. **21**
U.S. Tobacco Co. **57**
U.S. Travel and Tourism Administration **11**
USA Cable Network **43**
USAir **123**
USF&G Insurance **107**
USSA Federal Savings Bank **63**
Uniden Corporation of America **27**
Uniform Software Co. **123**
Union Bank **45**
Union Carbide Corporation **23**
Union Carbide Corporation **51**
Union Carbide Corporation **103**
Union Pacific Railroad **21**
Union Savings Bank **61**

Un–Vo

Union Texas Petroleum **21**
Union Underwear Co., Inc. **113**
Unisa America, Inc. **111**
United Airlines **23**
United Banks of Colorado **125**
United Division of Howmedica, Inc. **57**
United HealthCare Corporation **31**
United States Fidelity & Guaranty Company, Inc. **127**
United States Forest Service **57**
United States Golf Association **37**
United States Marine Corps **123**
United States Steel Corporation **113**
United Telecom Communications **57**
United Way of Central Maryland **107**
Universal Manufacturing **21**
Universal Pictures-St. Louis **73**
Universal Shellac & Supply Company **7**
Universal Television **123**
University of Alabama Hospitals **91**
Unocal Corporation **23**
Utility Emergency Services Fund **49**
VF Corporation **21**
VGI Corporation **49**
VLI Corporation **75**
Valley Forge Country **49**
Valley Forge Medical Center & Hospital **49**
Valvoline Oil Company **21**
Van Munching & Company **55**
Vancouver Mandarin Hotel **35**
Vari-X Corporation **45**
Vernitron, Inc. **45**
Vipont Laboratories, Inc. **95**
Virginia Chemicals **127**
Vision Industry Council of America **7**
Visolux Inc. **63**
Vista International Hotel **5**
Vistakon, Inc. **57**
Vitasoy U.S.A. Inc. **37**
Vivitar **75**
Vixen Yachts **117**
Volkswagen United States, Inc. **47**
Volume Shoe Corp. **57**

The Agency Book **169**

Client Index

Vo-We

Volvo of America Corp. **115**
Vulcan Materials Company **91**
WAGA-TV5 **21**
WBZ-TV **43**
WCBS-TV **43**
WJBK-TV **131**
WJLA-TV **103**
WLIF-FM **107**
WMAQ Radio **21**
WNBC-TV **89**
WPEN/WMGK Radio **49**
WTTO-TV **91**
WXRX-FM **43**
W.S.R. Futures **45**
Wachovia Bank & Trust Co. **87**
Wall Street Camera Exchange **7**
Wall-to-Wall Sound **49**
Walt Disney Pictures-St. Louis **73**
Warner-Lambert Company **123**
Warner-Lambert International **121**
Warwick, The **49**
Washington Apple Commission **35**
Washington Gas Light **49**
Washington Post, The **103**
Washington State Economic Development **35**
Washington State Tourism **35**
Waterford Crystal **107**
WAWA, Inc. **49**
Weather Channel, The **123**
Weatherby, Inc. **21**
Webb Manufacturing, Inc. **69**
Webb, Del E. **123**
Weber-Stephen Products Co. **21**
Wedbush, Noble, Cooke, Inc. **45**
Wedgwood Inc. **123**
Weighco, Inc. **93**
Weight Watchers International **47**
Weisfield's **35**
Welch Foods, Inc. **31**
Weller-Davis, Inc. **49**
Wendy's International, Inc. **37**
Wertheim & Co., Inc. **45**
West Company, The **57**
West Jersey Health Systems **49**
West Suburban Hospital **59**
Westbury Hotel, New York **3**
Western Supermarkets **91**
Western Union **37**

We-Yo

Western Union **115**
Westin Benson, The **35**
Westin Hotels Development **35**
Westin Mexico **35**
Westinghouse Broadcasting **65**
Westinghouse Electric Corporation **127**
Westvaco **97**
Westwood Pharmaceutical **79**
Weyerhaeuser **35**
Wheat, First Securities, Inc. **45**
Wheeler & Wheeler **49**
Whitehall Laboratories **121**
Whitney Museum of American Art **33**
Whitney's **23**
Wholefoods, Inc. **81**
Wild Turkey Premium Spirits **27**
Wilkes-Barre Times Leader, The **3**
William Grant & Sons, Inc. **33**
Willowbrook Mall **3**
Wilmington Trust **107**
Wilson Foods Corporation **31**
Wilton Enterprises, Inc. **123**
Winchell's Donut House **57**
Winchester Group **73**
Wine Group, The **35**
Winsight **19**
Witter Reynolds Inc., Dean **45**
Wizards Ice Cream & Confectionery Shoppe **63**
Wolverine Boots & Shoes **21**
Wolverine World Wide, Inc. **103**
Woman's World Magazine **3**
Women's Way **49**
World Airways **35**
World Wide Travel **73**
Worlds of Wonder, Inc. **33**
Wright & Co., Inc., E.T. **45**
Wrigley Jr. Co., Wm. **103**
Xerox Corp. **103**
Xomed, Inc. **57**
YMCA **37**
Yamaha Electronics Corporation USA **11**
Yamaha International Corporation **11**
Yamaha Motor Corp., USA **33**
Yokohama Tire Corp. **35**
Yonex Tennis/Golf **17**

Yo-Zy

Yoplait USA, Inc. **37**
Young & Company, Arthur **17**
Young & Company, Arthur **53**
Young, Inc., W.F. **123**
Yugo America **109**
Zale Corporation-Fine Jewelers Guild Division **21**
Zenith Electronics Corp. **57**
Ziff-Davis Corporation-Information Marketing International **69**
Zyloware Corporation **95**

Location Index

Agency
State
Address

AC&R Advertising, Inc.

New York

AC&R Advertising, Inc.
16 East 32nd Street
New York, New York 10016
212-685-2500

AC&R Public Relations[2]
136 Madison Avenue
New York, New York 10016
212-685-8000

Respond Productions[2]
16 East 32nd Street
New York, New York 10016
212-685-2500

AC&R Direct[2]
16 East 32nd Street
New York, New York 10016
212-685-2500

AC&R Rossi[2]
136 Madison Avenue
New York, New York 10016
212-532-1411

Albert Frank-Guenther Law Incorporated

California

Albert-Frank Guenther Law
Incorporated[2]
244 California Street
San Francisco, California 94111
415-989-7020

New York

Albert Frank-Guenther Law
Incorporated
71 Broadway
New York, New York 10006
212-248-5200

Pennsylvania

Albert Frank-Guenther Law
Incorporated[2]
2000 Market Street
Philadelphia, Pennsylvania 19103
215-564-2345

The Alden Group

New York

The Alden Group
535 Fifth Avenue
New York, New York 10017
212-867-6400

J.S. Alden Public Relations Inc.[2]
535 Fifth Avenue
New York, New York 10017
212-867-6400

Ally & Gargano, Inc.

New York

Ally & Gargano, Inc.
805 Third Avenue
New York, New York 10022
212-688-5300

N W Ayer Inc.

California

N W Ayer Inc.[1]
707 Wilshire Boulevard
Los Angeles, California 90017
213-621-1400

Illinois

N W Ayer Inc.[1]
One Illinois Center
111 East Wacker Drive
Chicago, Illinois 60601
312-645-8800

Michigan

N W Ayer Inc.[1]
2000 Fisher Building
Detroit, Michigan 48202
313-874-8500

New York

N W Ayer Inc.
1345 Avenue of the Americas
New York, New York 10105
212-708-5000

Ayer Design[2]
1345 Avenue of the Americas
New York, New York 10105
212-708-5188

Ayer Direct[2]
1345 Avenue of the Americas
New York, New York 10105
212-708-6350

Ayer Public Relations[2]
1345 Avenue of the Americas
New York, New York 10105
212-708-5461

Ayer International[2]
1345 Avenue of the Americas
New York, New York 10105
212-708-5670

Backer & Spielvogel, Inc.

California

Backer & Spielvogel[1]
7711 Center Avenue
Huntington Beach, California 92647
714-895-9926

Illinois

Backer & Spielvogel Chicago, Inc.[1]
479 Merchandise Mart Plaza
Chicago, Illinois 60654
312-222-2511

New York

Backer & Spielvogel, Inc.
11 West 42nd Street
New York, New York 10036
212-556-5200

Barnum Communications, Inc.

New York

Barnum Communications, Inc.
500 Fifth Avenue
New York, New York 10110
212-221-7363

Basso & Associates, Inc.

California

Basso & Associates, Inc.
P. O. Box 8030
3198 Airport Loop Drive
Newport Beach, California 92660
714-641-0111

Biederman & Co.

New York

Biederman & Co.
100 Fifth Avenue
New York, New York 10011
212-929-7200

Betacom, Inc.[2]
100 Fifth Avenue
New York, New York 10011
212-929-7200

Bozell, Jacobs, Kenyon & Eckhardt

Arizona

Bozell, Jacobs, Kenyon & Eckhardt[1]
100 West Clarendon
Suite 2206
Phoenix, Arizona 85013
602-264-9100

Location Index

Agency
State
Address

California

Bozell, Jacobs, Kenyon & Eckhardt[1]
1100 Glendon Avenue
Los Angeles, California 90024
213-208-0220

Bozell, Jacobs, Kenyon & Eckhardt[1]
10850 Wilshire Boulevard
Los Angeles, California 90024
213-879-1800

Bozell, Jacobs, Kenyon & Eckhardt
Yellow Pages[2]
10850 Wilshire Boulevard
Los Angeles, California 90024
213-879-1800

Bozell, Jacobs, Kenyon & Eckhardt
Public Relations[2]
10850 Wilshire Boulevard
Los Angeles, California 90024
213-879-1800

Georgia

Bozell, Jacobs, Kenyon & Eckhardt[1]
One Securities Center
3490 Piedmont Road
Atlanta, Georgia 30305
404-266-2221

Bozell, Jacobs, Kenyon & Eckhardt
Yellow Pages[2]
One Securities Center
3490 Piedmont Road
Atlanta, Georgia 30305
404-226-2221

Bozell, Jacobs, Kenyon & Eckhardt
Public Relations[2]
One Securities Center
3490 Piedmont Road
Atlanta, Georgia 30305
404-226-2221

Group 2 Atlanta[2]
3500 Piedmont Road
Atlanta, Georgia 30305
404-262-3239

Illinois

Bozell, Jacobs, Kenyon & Eckhardt[1]
625 North Michigan Avenue
Chicago, Illinois 60611
312-988-2000

Bozell, Jacobs, Kenyon & Eckhardt
Direct[2]
625 North Michigan Avenue
Chicago, Illinois 60611
312-988-2000

Bozell, Jacobs, Kenyon & Eckhardt
Yellow Pages[2]
625 North Michigan Avenue
Chicago, Illinois 60611
312-988-2000

Bozell, Jacobs, Kenyon & Eckhardt
Public Relations[2]
625 North Michigan Avenue
Chicago, Illinois 60611
312-988-2000

Graphic TypeTech[2]
57 West Grand Avenue
Chicago, Illinois 60601
312-744-0003

Massachusetts

Bozell, Jacobs, Kenyon & Eckhardt[1]
One Boston Place
Boston, Massachusetts 02108
617-367-7300

Bozell, Jacobs, Kenyon & Eckhardt
Direct[2]
One Boston Place
Boston, Massachusetts 02108
617-367-7300

Michigan

Bozell, Jacobs, Kenyon & Eckhardt[1]
30600 Telegraph Road
Birmingham, Michigan 48010
313-645-6170

Minnesota

Bozell, Jacobs, Kenyon & Eckhardt[1]
100 North 6th Street
Minneapolis, Minnesota 55403
612-371-7500

Bozell, Jacobs, Kenyon & Eckhardt
Direct[2]
100 North 6th Street
Minneapolis, Minnesota 55403
612-371-7500

Bozell, Jacobs, Kenyon & Eckhardt
Yellow Pages[2]
100 North 6th Street
Minneapolis, Minnesota 55403
612-371-7500

Bozell, Jacobs, Kenyon & Eckhardt
Public Relations[2]
100 North 6th Street
Minneapolis, Minnesota 55403
612-371-5500

Custom Production Service, Inc.[2]
100 North 6th Street
Minneapolis, Minnesota 55403
612-371-5555

Nebraska

Bozell, Jacobs, Kenyon & Eckhardt[1]
10250 Regency Circle
Omaha, Nebraska 68114
402-397-8660

Bozell, Jacobs, Kenyon & Eckhardt[2]
Visual Communications Center
730 North 109th Court
Omaha, Nebraska 68114
402-397-8660

Bozell, Jacobs, Kenyon & Eckhardt
Yellow Pages[2]
10250 Regency Circle
Omaha, Nebraska 68114
402-397-8660

Bozell, Jacobs, Kenyon & Eckhardt
Co-op Services[2]
10250 Regency Circle
Omaha, Nebraska 68114
402-397-8660

Bozell, Jacobs, Kenyon & Eckhardt
Public Relations[2]
10250 Regency Circle
Omaha, Nebraska 68114
402-397-8660

Bozell, Jacobs, Kenyon & Eckhardt
Agricultural[2]
10250 Regency Circle
Omaha, Nebraska 68114
402-397-8660

Dudycha Group[2]
407 South 27th Avenue
Omaha, Nebraska 68131
402-346-3100

New Jersey

Bozell, Jacobs, Kenyon & Eckhardt[1]
2700 Route 22
Union, New Jersey 07083
201-688-2700

Bozell, Jacobs, Kenyon & Eckhardt
Public Relations[2]
2700 Route 22
Union, New Jersey 07083
201-688-2700

Custom Production Service, Inc.[2]
2700 Route 22
Union, New Jersey 07083
201-688-2700

New York

Bozell, Jacobs, Kenyon & Eckhardt, Inc.
One Dag Hammarskjold Plaza
New York, New York 10017
212-705-6000

---

1 Branch
2 Subsidiary
3 Affiliate
4 Division

Location Index

Agency
State
Address

Bozell, Jacobs, Kenyon & Eckhardt
Direct[2]
40 West 23rd Street
New York, New York 10010
212-206-5000

Bozell, Jacobs, Kenyon & Eckhardt
Healthcare[2]
6 East 43rd Street
New York, New York 10017
212-867-1670

Bozell, Jacobs, Kenyon & Eckhardt
Yellow Pages[2]
6 East 43rd Street
New York, New York 10017
212-916-8500

Bozell, Jacobs, Kenyon & Eckhardt
Co-op Services[2]
6 East 43rd Street
New York, New York 10017
212-916-8500

Bozell, Jacobs, Kenyon & Eckhardt
Public Relations[2]
6 East 43rd Street
New York, New York 10017
212-916-8500

Custom Production Service, Inc.[2]
40 West 23rd Street
New York, New York 10010
212-206-5000

Texas

Bozell, Jacobs, Kenyon & Eckhardt[1]
201 E. Carpenter Freeway
P. O. Box 691200
Dallas/Ft. Worth Airport, Texas
75261-9200
214-556-1100

Bozell, Jacobs, Kenyon & Eckhardt
Direct[2]
201 East Carpenter Freeway
P. O. Box 619200
Dallas/Ft. Worth Airport, Texas
75261-9200
214-556-3427

Bozell, Jacobs, Kenyon & Eckhardt
Yellow Pages[2]
201 East Carpenter Freeway
P. O. Box 619200
Dallas/Ft. Worth Airport, Texas
75261-9200
214-556-1100

Bozell, Jacobs, Kenyon & Eckhardt
Co-op Services[2]
201 East Carpenter Freeway
P. O. Box 619200
Dallas/Ft. Worth Airport, Texas
75261-9200
214-556-1100

Bozell, Jacobs, Kenyon & Eckhardt
Public Relations[2]
201 East Carpenter Freeway
P. O. Box 619200
Dallas/Ft. Worth Airport, Texas
75261-9200
214-556-1000

Custom Production Service, Inc.[2]
201 East Carpenter Freeway
P. O. Box 619200
Dallas/Ft. Worth Airport, Texas
75261-9200
214-830-2432

CPS Camera[2]
201 East Carpenter Freeway
P. O. Box 619200
Dallas/Ft. Worth Airport, Texas
75261-9200
214-830-2490

Group 2[2]
201 East Carpenter Freeway
P. O. Box 619200
Dallas/Ft. Worth Airport, Texas
75261-9200
214-830-2432

Bozell, Jacobs, Kenyon & Eckhardt
Recruitment Advertising[2]
201 East Carpenter Freeway
P. O. Box 619200
Dallas/Ft. Worth Airport, Texas
75261-9200
214-830-2428

Bozell, Jacobs, Kenyon & Eckhardt
Industrial/Technical[2]
201 East Carpenter Freeway
P. O. Box 619200
Dallas/Ft. Worth Airport, Texas
75261-9200
214-830-2432

Graphic Typography[2]
1451 Empire Central, Suite 110
Dallas, Texas 75247
214-630-5661

Bozell, Jacobs, Kenyon & Eckhardt[1]
RepublicBank Center, Suite 3300
700 Louisiana Street
Houston, Texas 77002
713-228-9551

Bozell, Jacbos, Kenyon & Eckhardt
Public Relations[2]
RepublicBank Center, Suite 3300
700 Louisiana Street
Houston, Texas 77002
713-228-9551

Utah

Bozell, Jacobs, Kenyon & Eckhardt[1]
First Interstate Plaza
170 South Main Street, Suite 1230
Salt Lake City, Utah 84101
801-531-6106

Washington DC

Bozell, Jacobs, Kenyon & Eckhardt[1]
1199 North Fairfax Street
Alexandria, Virginia 22314
703-549-0600

Leo Burnett Company, Inc.

Illinois

Leo Burnett Company, Inc.
Prudential Plaza
Chicago, Illinois 60601
312-565-5959

Burrell Advertising Inc.

Georgia

Burrell Advertising Inc./Atlanta[2]
100 Colony Square-Suite 200
Atlanta, Georgia 30361
404-875-1683

Illinois

Burrell Advertising Inc.
625 N. Michigan Avenue
Chicago, Illinois 60611
312-266-4600

Calvillo, Shevack & Partners, Inc.

New York

Calvillo, Shevack & Partners, Inc.
1350 Avenue of the Americas
New York, New York 10019
212-245-7300

Campbell-Ewald Company

California

Campbell-Ewald Company
10920 Wilshire Boulevard
Suite 1100
Los Angeles, California 90024
213-824-1922

Florida

Campbell-Ewald Latina[4]
Koger Executive Center
8525 NW 53rd Terrace
Suite 101
Miami, Florida 33166
305-592-7135

Illinois

Campbell-Ewald Company[1]
120 S. Riverside Plaza
Chicago, Illinois 60606
312-454-1752

Location Index

Agency
State
Address

Massachusetts

Campbell-Ewald Company
88 Broad Street
Boston, Massachusetts 02110
617-423-0121

Michigan

Campbell-Ewald Company
30400 Van Dyke
Warren, Michigan 48093
313-574-3400

CeCo Communications, Inc.[4]
30400 Van Dyke
Warren, Michigan 48093
313-575-9400

New York

Campbell-Ewald of New York, Inc.
1345 Avenue of the Americas
New York, New York 10105
212-489-6200

Pennsylvania

Campbell-Ewald Company[1]
Porter Building
Suite 1101
601 Grant Street
Pittsburgh, Pennsylvania 15219
412-765-1200

Campbell-Mithun Advertising

Illinois

Campbell-Mithun Advertising
737 North Michigan Avenue
Chicago, Illinois 60611
312-565-3800

Minnesota

Campbell-Mithun Advertising
222 South Ninth Street
Minneapolis, Minnesota 55402
612-347-1000

Cash Plus[2]
222 South Ninth Street
Minneapolis, Minnesota 55402
612-347-6901

Promotion Works[2]
222 South Ninth Street
Minneapolis, Minnesota 55402
612-347-1495

Chiat/Day inc. Advertising

California

Chiat/Day inc. Advertising
517 South Olive Street
Los Angeles, California 90013
213-622-7454

Chiat/Day inc. Advertising
77 Maiden Lane
San Francisco, California 94109
415-445-3000

New York

Chiat/Day inc. Advertising
79 Fifth Avenue
New York, New York 10003
212-807-4000

Cole & Weber, Inc.

California

Cole & Weber[1]
2029 Century Park East
Suite 920
Los Angeles, California 90067
213-879-7979

Cole & Weber[1]
10 Lombard Street
San Francisco, California 94111
415-393-2455

Oregon

Morton/Cole & Weber[1]
55 S.W. Yamhill Street
Portland, Oregon 97204
503-226-2821

Utah

TPC/Cole & Weber[1]
375 W. 2nd South
Salt Lake City, Utah 84101
801-364-2740

Washington

Cole & Weber
Riverview Plaza
16040 Christensen Road S.
Seattle, Washington 98188
206-433-6200

Dancer Fitzgerald Sample, Inc.

California

Dancer Fitzgerald Sample
San Francisco[1]
1010 Battery Street
San Francisco, California 94111
415-982-8400

Dancer Fitzgerald Sample
Southern California[1]
3878 Carson Street
Torrance, California 90503
213-540-2554

New York

Dancer Fitzgerald Sample, Inc.
405 Lexington Avenue
New York, New York 10174
212-661-0800

David Deutsch Associates

New York

David Deutsch Associates
655 Third Avenue
New York, New York 10017
212-867-0044

Davis, Johnson, Mogul & Colombatto, Inc.

California

Davis, Johnson, Mogul & Colombatto, Inc.
3435 Wilshire Boulevard
Los Angeles, California 90010
213-251-4500

Ad Latina[4]
3435 Wilshire Boulevard
Suite 720
Los Angeles, California 90010
213-251-4400

Gelman & Gray
Communications, Inc.[2]
Public Relations
3435 Wilshire Boulevard
Suite 908
Los Angeles, California 90010
213-251-4600

Davis, Johnson, Mogul & Colombatto, Inc.[1]
731 Market Street
San Francisco, California 94103
415-546-1100

Maryland

Davis, Johnson, Mogul & Colombatto, Inc.[1]
1615 York Road
Suite 305
Lutherville, Maryland 21093
301-823-7500

Oregon

Davis, Johnson, Mogul & Colombatto, Inc.[1]
101 SW Main Street
Suite 1200
Portland, Oregon 97204
503-241-7781

1 Branch
2 Subsidiary
3 Affiliate
4 Division

Location Index

Agency
State
Address

Della Femina, Travisano & Partners Inc.

California

Della Femina, Travisano & Partners of California, Inc.[1]
5900 Wilshire Boulevard
Los Angeles, California 90036
213-937-8540

Georgia

Della Femina, Travisano & Partners/Atlanta[1]
Waterford Centre
555 Triangle Parkway
Suite 200
Norcross, Georgia 30092
404-263-0500

New York

Della Femina, Travisano & Partners Inc.
625 Madison Avenue
New York, New York 10022
212-421-7180

Della Femina, Travisano, Sherman & Olken, Inc.[4]
625 Madison Avenue
New York, New York 10022
212-421-7180

Doremus & Company

California

Doremus/Los Angeles[1]
10960 Wilshire Boulevard
Suite 1422
Los Angeles, California 90024
213-478-3071

Doremus/San Francisco[1]
825 Battery Street
San Francisco, California 94111
415-981-4020

Illinois

Doremus/Chicago[1]
500 North Michigan Avenue
Suite 400
Chicago, Illinois 60611
312-321-1377

Massachusetts

Doremus/Boston[1]
535 Boylston Street
Boston, Massachusetts 02116
617-266-2600

New York

Doremus & Company
120 Broadway
New York, New York 10271
212-964-0700

Doremus/Marketshare[1]
41 Madison Avenue
New York, New York 10010
212-725-8400

Washington DC

Doremus/Washington[1]
1090 Vermont Avenue, N.W.
Washington, D.C. 20005
202-842-3666

Doyle Dane Bernbach Group Inc.

California

DDB/Los Angeles[1]
5900 Wilshire Boulevard
Los Angeles, California 90036
213-937-5100

Kresser, Craig/D.I.K.[2]
2029 Century Park East
Los Angeles, California 90067
213-553-8254

Rapp & Collins, Inc.[2]
5900 Wilshire Boulevard
Los Angeles, California 90036
213-936-9600

York Alpern/DDB[2]
5757 Wilshire Boulevard
Los Angeles, California 90036
213-931-9000

DDB/San Francisco[1]
530 Bush Street
San Francisco, California 94108
415-398-2669

Colorado

DDB/Denver[1]
#2 Tamarac Square
Suite 416
7535 E. Hampden Avenue
Denver, Colorado 80231
303-337-3500

Georgia

Cargill, Wilson & Acree Inc.[2]
Suite 1150 Tower Place
3340 Peachtree Road, N.E.
Atlanta, Georgia 30026
404-261-8700

Fletcher/Mayo/Associates, Inc.[2]
Five Piedmont Center
Suite 710
Atlanta, Georgia 30305
404-261-0831

Hawaii

Milici Valenti Smith Park Advertising, Inc.[2]
12th Floor
700 Bishop Street
Honolulu, Hawaii 98613
808-536-0881

Illinois

Fletcher/Mayo/Associates, Inc.[2]
211 E. Ontario
15th floor
Chicago, Illinois 60611
312-266-1717

Michigan

DDB/Detroit[1]
Top of Troy Building
755 W. Big Beaver Road
Suite 900
Troy, Michigan 48084
313-362-2339

Missouri

Fletcher/Mayo/Associates, Inc.[2]
427 West 12th Street
Kansas City, Missouri 64105
816-421-1000

Fletcher/Mayo/Associates, Inc.[2]
R.R. #3 John Glenn Road
P. O. Box B, Station E
St. Joseph, Missouri 64505
816-233-8261

New York

DDB/New York[1]
437 Madison Avenue
New York, New York 10022
212-415-2000

Bernard Hodes Advertising[2]
555 Madison Avenue
New York, New York 10022
212-758-2600

Kallir, Philips, Ross, Inc.[2]
605 Third Avenue
New York, New York 10158
212-878-3700

Rapp & Collins Inc.[2]
475 Park Avenue South
New York, New York 10016
212-725-8100

Location Index

Agency
State
Address

Texas

Direct Response Group, Inc.[2]
8701 Carpenter Freeway
Dallas, Texas 75247
214-631-5111

The Earle Palmer Brown Companies

Maryland

The Earle Palmer Brown Companies[2]
100 Saint Paul Plaza Building
Suite 500
Baltimore, Maryland 21202
301-576-8420

The Earle Palmer Brown Companies[2]
6935 Arlington Road
Bethesda, Maryland 20814
301-986-0510

Pennsylvania

The Earle Palmer Brown Companies[2]
1845 Walnut Street
Philadelphia, Pennsylvania 19103
215-299-3800

Virginia

The Earle Palmer Brown Companies[2]
7814 Carousel Lane
Suite 300
Richmond, Virginia 23229
804-747-7666

William Esty Company, Inc.

New York

William Esty Company, Inc.
100 East 42nd Street
New York, New York 10017
212-692-6200

Fitzgerald Advertising Inc.

Louisiana

Fitzgerald Advertising Inc.
1055 St. Charles Avenue
New Orleans, Louisiana 70130
504-529-3161

Font & Vaamonde Associates, Inc.

New York

Font & Vaamonde Associates, Inc.
183 Madison Avenue
Suite 1402
New York, New York 10016
212-679-9170

Foote, Cone & Belding Communications, Inc.

California

Smith-Hemmings-Gosden, Inc.[2]
3360 Flair Drive
El Monte, California 91731
818-571-6600

Foote, Cone & Belding
11601 Wilshire Boulevard
Los Angeles, California 90025-1772
213-312-7000

FCB/Telecom[2]
520 South Lafayette Park Place
Suite 201
Los Angeles, California 90057
213-389-1551

FCB/Entertainment[2]
11601 Wilshire Boulevard
Los Angeles, California 90025-1772
213-312-7000

Foote, Cone & Belding
1255 Battery Street
San Francisco, California 94111
415-398-5200

Vicom Associates, Inc.[2]
901 Battery Street
San Francisco, California 94111
415-391-8700

Deutsch, Shea & Evans[2]
605 Market Street
Suite 706
San Francisco, California 94105
415-543-7222

Connecticut

North Castle Partners
20 Bridge Street
Greenwich, Connecticut 06830
203-622-1122

Wahlstrom & Co.[2]
Holly Pond Plaza
1281 Main Street
Stamford, Connecticut 06902
203-348-7347

Illinois

Foote, Cone & Belding
401 N. Michigan Avenue
Chicago, Illinois 60611
312-467-9200

IMPACT/Chicago[2]
401 N. Michigan Avenue
Chicago, Illinois 60611
312-467-9200

FCB Direct Marketing[2]
401 N. Michigan Avenue
Chicago, Illinois 60611
312-467-9200

Golin/Harris Communications[2]
500 N. Michigan Avenue
Chicago, Illinois 60611
312-836-7100

New York

Foote, Cone & Belding
101 Park Avenue
New York, New York 10178
212-907-1000

Carl Byoir & Associates[2]
380 Madison Avenue
New York, New York 10017
212-986-6100

IMPACT/New York[2]
101 Park Avenue
New York, New York 10178
212-907-1000

Albert-Frank Guenther Law[2]
61 Broadway
New York, New York 10006
212-248-5200

FCB Direct East[2]
101 Park Avenue
New York, New York 10078
212-907-1007

Pennsylvania

Lewis, Gilman & Kynett
1700 Market Street
Philadelphia, Pennsylvania 19103
215-543-3775

HealthCom[2]
1700 Market Street
Philadelphia, Pennsylvania 19103
215-568-3775

Grant/Jacoby, Inc.

Illinois

Grant/Jacoby, Inc.
500 N. Michigan Avenue
Chicago, Illinois 60611
312-664-2055

Greenstone & Rabasca Advertising, Inc.

New York

Greenstone & Rabasca Advertising, Inc.
1 Huntington Quadrangle
Melville, New York 11746
516-249-2121

1 Branch
2 Subsidiary
3 Affiliate
4 Division

Location Index

Agency
State
Address

Haddon Advertising, Inc.

Illinois

Haddon Advertising, Inc.
919 N. Michigan Avenue
Chicago, Illinois 60611
312-943-6266

Haddon, Lynch and
Baughman, Inc.[2]
919 N. Michigan Avenue
Chicago, Illinois 60611
312-649-0371

HBM/CREAMER, Inc.

Connecticut

HBM/CREAMER, Inc.[2]
100 Constitution Plaza
Hartford, Connecticut 16103
203-278-1500

Illinois

HBM/CREAMER, Inc.[2]
410 North Michigan Avenue
Chicago, Illinois 60611
312-222-4900

Massachusetts

HBM/CREAMER, Inc.[2]
One Beacon Street
Boston, Massachusetts 02108
617-723-7770

New York

HBM/CREAMER, Inc.[2]
1633 Broadway
New York, New York 10019
212-887-8000

Pennsylvania

HBM/CREAMER, Inc.[2]
600 Grant Street
Pittsburgh, Pennsylvania 15219
412-456-4500

Rhode Island

HBM/CREAMER, Inc.[2]
800 Turks Head Building
Providence, Rhode Island 02903
401-456-1500

Washington DC

HBM/CREAMER, Inc.[2]
1612 K Street, N.W.
Suite 706
Washington, D.C. 20006
202-775-9320

Healy-Schutte & Company

New York

Healy-Schutte & Company
1207 Delaware Avenue
Buffalo, New York 14209
716-884-2120

Healy-Schutte & Company[2]
Harro East
400 Andrews Street
Rochester, New York 14604
716-325-6830

The Jayme Organization, Inc.

Ohio

The Jayme Organization, Inc.
23200 Chagrin Boulevard
One Commerce Park Square
Cleveland, Ohio 44122
216-831-0110

Publicom Public Relations[3]
23200 Chagrin Boulevard
One Commerce Park Square
Cleveland, Ohio 44122
216-831-0400

Strategic Research Center[3]
23200 Chagrin Boulevard
One Commerce Park Square
Cleveland, Ohio 44122
216-831-2410

The BoardRoom Design &
Promotion[3]
23200 Chagrin Boulevard
One Commerce Park Square
Cleveland, Ohio 44122
216-831-0204

MacDantz Direct[3]
23200 Chagrin Boulevard
One Commerce Park Square
Cleveland, Ohio 44122
216-831-0110

The Johnston & Johnston Group

California

Johnston Thoen & Lindh[2]
5455 Wilshire Boulevard
Los Angeles, California 90036
213-933-7577

New York

Jim Johnston Advertising, Inc.
551 Fifth Avenue
New York, New York 10176
212-490-2121

North Carolina

The Carolina Partnership[2]
P. O. Box 2839
Chapel Hill, North Carolina 27514
919-967-8282

Kerlick, Switzer & Johnson Advertising

Missouri

Kerlick, Switzer & Johnson
Advertising
727 N. First Street
St. Louis, Missouri 63102
314-241-4656

KS & J Direct[2]
727 N. First Street
St. Louis, Missouri 63102
314-241-4656

KS & J Public Relations[2]
727 N. First Street
St. Louis, Missouri 63102
314-241-4656

KS & J Entertainment[2]
727 N. First Street
St. Louis, Missouri 63102
314-241-4656

keye/donna/pearlstein

California

keye/donna/pearlstein
11080 Olympic Boulevard
Los Angeles, California 90064
213-477-0061

Knudsen Moore Schropfer, Inc.

Connecticut

Knudsen Moore Schropfer, Inc.
666 Glenbrook Road
Stamford, Connecticut 06906
203-967-7200

Laurence, Charles, Free & Lawson, Inc.

New York

Laurence, Charles, Free &
Lawson, Inc.
261 Madison Avenue
New York, New York 10016
212-661-0200

The Lempert Company, Inc.

New Jersey

The Lempert Company, Inc.
202 Belleville Avenue
Belleville, New Jersey 07109
201-759-2927

Location Index

Agency
State
Address

Levine, Huntley, Schmidt & Beaver, Inc.

Pennsylvania

The Lempert Company, Inc.[2]
111 Presidential Boulevard
Suite 224
Bala Cynwyd, Pennsylvania 19004
215-667-7442

California

Levine, Huntley, Schmidt & Beaver, Inc.[1]
2505 Port Street
P. O. Box 985
West Sacramento, California 95691

Colorado

Levine, Huntley, Schmidt & Beaver, Inc.[1]
15000 East 39th Avenue
Aurora, Colorado 80011

Florida

Levine, Huntley, Schmidt & Beaver, Inc.[1]
1685 Florida Mango Road N.
P. O. Box 3007
West Palm Beach, Florida 33402

Illinois

Levine, Huntley, Schmidt & Beaver, Inc.[1]
301 Mitchell Court
Addison, Illinois 60101

New York

Levine, Huntley, Schmidt & Beaver, Inc.
250 Park Avenue
New York, New York 10177
212-557-0900

Texas

Levine, Huntley, Schmidt & Beaver, Inc.[1]
12615 San Pedro Avenue
P. O. Box 32906
San Antonio, Texas 78216

Washington DC

Levine, Huntley, Schmidt & Beaver, Inc.[1]
8611 Larkin Road
P. O. Box 427
Savage, Maryland 20763

Levy, King & White Companies, Inc.

Florida

Pearson, Thomas/Levy King & White Advertising[2]
Bayport Plaza
6200 Courtney-Campbell Causeway
Suite 800
Tampa, Florida 33607
813-885-2219

New York

Levy, King & White Advertising[2]
620 Main Street
Buffalo, New York 14202
716-853-6755

William Collins Assoc.
Public Relations[2]
620 Main Street
Buffalo, New York 14202
716-842-6260

Quantum Analysis/LKW[2]
620 Main Street
Buffalo, New York 14202
716-842-2560

LK&W Direct[4]
620 Main Street
Buffalo, New York 14202
716-853-6755

QA Research Centers[4]
Fayetteville Mall
5351 Burdick Street
Fayetteville, New York 13066
315-637-3169

Long, Haymes & Carr Incorporated

North Carolina

Long, Haymes & Carr Incorporated
140 Charlois Boulevard
Winston Salem,
North Carolina 27113
919-765-3630

Lord, Geller, Federico, Einstein, Inc.

New York

Lord, Geller, Federico, Einstein, Inc.
655 Madison Avenue
New York, New York 10021
212-421-6050

LGFE/Direct Marketing[4]
655 Madison Avenue
New York, New York 10021
212-421-6050

Luckie & Forney, Inc.

Alabama

Luckie & Forney, Inc.
120 Office Park Drive
Birmingham, Alabama 35223
205-879-2121

MARC Advertising

Pennsylvania

MARC Advertising
Four Station Square
Suite 500
Pittsburgh, Pennsylvania 15219
412-562-2000

McCaffery & Ratner, Inc.

New York

McCaffery & Ratner, Inc.
370 Lexington Avenue
New York, New York 10017
212-661-8940

McCaffrey and McCall, Inc.

California

McCaffrey and McCall West[1]
1875 Century Park East
Suite 1165
Century City, California 90067
213-201-5025

New York

McCaffrey and McCall, Inc.
575 Lexington Avenue
New York, New York 10022
212-421-7500

McCaffrey and McCall Direct Marketing[4]
575 Lexington Avenue
New York, New York 10022
212-303-6000

McCann-Erickson Worldwide

California

McCann-Erickson Los Angeles
6420 Wilshire Boulevard
Los Angeles, California 90048
213-655-9420

1 Branch
2 Subsidiary
3 Affiliate
4 Division

Location Index

Agency
State
Address

La Agencia de McCann-Erickson
6420 Wilshire Boulevard
Los Angeles, California 90048
213-655-9420

McCann-Erickson San Francisco
201 California Street
San Francisco, California 94111
415-981-2262

Georgia

McCann-Erickson Atlanta
615 Peachtree Street, N.E.
Atlanta, Georgia 30365
404-873-2321

Kentucky

McCann-Erickson Louisville
1469 South Fourth Street
P. O. Box 1137
Louisville, Kentucky 40208
502-636-0441

Michigan

McCann-Erickson Detroit
755 W. Big Beaver Road
Troy, Michigan 48084
313-362-4800

New York

McCann-Erickson New York
485 Lexington Avenue
New York, New York 10017
212-697-6000

McCann Direct
485 Lexington Avenue
New York, New York 10017
212-286-0460

Texas

McCann-Erickson Houston
520 Post Oak Boulevard
Houston, Texas 77027
713-965-0303

Washington

McCann-Erickson Seattle
1011 Western Avenue
Suite 600
Seattle, Washington 98104
206-682-6360

Nationwide Advertising Service Inc.

Arizona

Nationwide Advertising Service Inc.
3737 North 7th Street
Suite 108
Phoenix, Arizona 85014
602-263-8894

California

Nationwide Advertising Service Inc.
7750 Pardee Lane
Suite 210
Oakland, California 94621
415-632-7721

Nationwide Advertising Service Inc.
591 Camino De La Reina
Suite 606
San Diego, California 92108
619-299-8661

Nationwide Advertising Service Inc.
400 North Tustin Avenue
Santa Ana, California 92705
714-543-1544

Nationwide Advertising Service Inc.
The Galleria Garden Offices
15301 Ventura Boulevard
Suite 240
Sherman Oaks, California 91403
818-906-3313

Colorado

Nationwide Advertising Service Inc.
1325 S. Colorado Boulevard
Suite 503
Denver, Colorado 80222
303-759-9970

Florida

Nationwide Advertising Service Inc.
1001 N.W. 62nd Street
Suite 305
Ft. Lauderdale, Florida 33309
305-776-0285

Nationwide Advertising Service Inc.
3510 Bay to Bay Boulevard
Tampa, Florida 33629
813-831-1085

Georgia

Nationwide Advertising Service Inc.
229 Peachtree St., N.E.
Suite 1111
Atlanta, Georgia 30303
404-522-4047

Illinois

Nationwide Advertising Service Inc.
The Tower
35 East Wacker Drive
Chicago, Illinois 60601
312-332-6550

Kansas

Nationwide Advertising Service Inc.
9730 Rosehill Road
Lenexa, Kansas 66215
913-541-0914

Nationwide Advertising Service Inc.
Executive Park East
215 Lakeside Plaza
250 N. Rock Road
Wichita, Kansas 67206
316-682-4576

Maryland

Nationwide Advertising Service Inc.
American City Building
Suite 300
10227 Wincopin Circle
Columbia, Maryland 21044
301-964-9440

Massachusetts

Nationwide Advertising Service Inc.
44 School Street
Suite 408
Boston, Massachusetts 02108
617-723-1875

Michigan

Nationwide Advertising Service Inc.
1056 Penobscot Building
Detroit, Michigan 48226
313-961-6785

Minnesota

Nationwide Advertising Service Inc.
One Appletree Square
Suite 946
Minneapolis, Minnesota 55420
612-854-4091

Missouri

Nationwide Advertising Service Inc.
10137 Old Olive Street Road
P. O. Box 27322
St. Louis, Missouri 63141
314-432-3221

New Mexico

Nationwide Advertising Service Inc.
4700 Montgomery Boulevard, N.E.
Suite 200
Albuquerque, New Mexico 87109
505-888-4991

Location Index

Agency
State
Address

New York

Nationwide Advertising Service Inc.
419 Park Avenue South
New York, New York 10016
212-696-4400

Nationwide Advertising Service Inc.
1147 Sibley Tower Building
25 Franklin Street
Rochester, New York 14604
716-454-2520

North Carolina

Nationwide Advertising Service Inc.
3117 Poplarwood Court
Suite 322
Raleigh, North Carolina 27625
919-872-6800

Ohio

Nationwide Advertising Service Inc.
617 Vine Street
Suite 1401
Cincinnati, Ohio 45202
513-241-3121

Nationwide Advertising Service Inc.
Corporate Headquarters
The Penthouse, Statler Office Tower
Euclid Avenue at E. 12th Street
Cleveland, Ohio 44115
216-579-0300

Nationwide Advertising Service Inc.
2000 W. Henderson Road
Suite 230
Columbus, Ohio 43220
614-459-3556

Pennsylvania

Nationwide Advertising Service Inc.
1500 Chestnut Street
Suite 303
Philadelphia, Pennsylvania 19102
215-568-5000

Nationwide Advertising Service Inc.
Three Gateway Center
Suite 1751
Pittsburgh, Pennsylvania 15222
412-391-3915

Texas

Nationwide Advertising Service Inc.
9330 LBJ Freeway
Suite 260
Dallas, Texas 75243
214-690-4400

Nationwide Advertising Service Inc.
5805 Richmond Avenue
Houston, Texas 77057
713-780-0770

Washington DC

Nationwide Advertising Service Inc.
American City Building
Suite 300
10227 Wincopin Circle
Columbia, Maryland 21044
301-621-4986

Needham Harper Worldwide, Inc.

Arizona

Needham Harper Worldwide, Inc.[1]
2111 East Highland Avenue
Phoenix, Arizona 85016
602-969-5000

California

Needham Harper Worldwide, Inc.[1]
11601 Wilshire Boulevard
Los Angeles, California 90025
213-208-5000

Needham Porter Novelli[2]
11601 Wilshire Boulevard
Los Angeles, California 90025
213-824-0401

Needham Harper Worldwide, Inc.[1]
1303 J Street
Sacramento, California 95814
916-441-1935

Needham Harper Worldwide, Inc.[1]
707 Broadway
San Diego, California 92101
619-234-5101

Illinois

Needham Harper Worldwide, Inc.[1]
Three Illinois Center
Chicago, Illinois 60601
312-861-0200

PRB: A Needham Porter Novelli Company[2]
150 East Huron Street
Chicago, Illinois 60611
312-266-7200

Maryland

Needham Harper Worldwide, Inc.[1]
400 East Pratt Street
Suite 814
Baltimore, Maryland 21202
301-727-6717

Massachusetts

The DR Group[2]
10 Post Office Square
Boston, Massachusetts
617-482-7300

New York

Needham Harper Worldwide, Inc.[1]
909 Third Avenue
New York, New York 10022
212-758-7600

The DR Group[2]
522 Fifth Avenue
New York, New York 10036
212-391-8600

Needham Porter Novelli[2]
909 Third Avenue
New York, New York 10022
212-758-7600

Virginia

Needham Harper Worldwide, Inc.[1]
8300 Greensboro Drive
Suite 1200
McLean, Virginia 22102
703-790-4800

Washington DC

Needham Porter Novelli[2]
3240 Prospect Street, N.W.
Washington, D.C. 20007
202-342-7000

Posey & Quest, Inc.

Connecticut

Posey & Quest, Inc.
6 Glenville Street
Greenwich, Connecticut 06830
203-531-4900

New York

Posey & Quest, Inc.[2]
307 East 56th Street
New York, New York 10022
212-750-5566

Richardson, Myers & Donofrio, Inc.

Maryland

Richardson, Myers & Donofrio, Inc.
120 West Fayette Street
Baltimore, Maryland 21201
301-576-9000

RM&D/Public Relations[4]
120 West Fayette Street
Baltimore, Maryland 21201
301-576-9000

SP&CS, Graphic Arts Production[4]
120 West Fayette Street
Baltimore, Maryland 21201
301-576-9000

---

1 Branch
2 Subsidiary
3 Affiliate
4 Division

Location Index

Agency
State
Address

MacDantz Direct[3]
120 West Fayette Street
Baltimore, Maryland 21201
301-837-4966

Pennsylvania

Richardson, Myers &
Donofrio, Inc.[1]
1608 Walnut Street
Philadelphia, Pennsylvania 19103
215-545-0200

RM&D/Public Relations[4]
1608 Walnut Street
Philadelphia, Pennsylvania 19103
215-545-0200

RM&D/Sales Promotion[4]
1608 Walnut Street
Philadelphia, Pennsylvania 19103
215-545-0200

Rosenfeld, Sirowitz & Lawson, Inc.

New York

Rosenfeld, Sirowitz & Lawson, Inc.
111 Fifth Avenue
New York, New York 10003
212-505-0200

Rumrill-Hoyt, Inc.

New York

Rumrill-Hoyt, Inc.
635 Madison Avenue
New York, New York 10022
212-872-4000

Rumrill-Hoyt, Rochester[2]
1895 Mt. Hope Avenue
P. O. Box 1011
Rochester, New York 14603
716-227-2150

Saatchi & Saatchi Compton Inc.

California

Saatchi & Saatchi Compton Inc.[1]
8383 Wilshire Boulevard
Beverly Hills, California 90211
213-852-1415

BTD Directory Management, Inc.[2]
12900 Garden Grove Boulevard
Suite 120
P. O. Box 3200
Garden Grove, California 92643
714-636-5800

Cochran Chase, Livingston &
Company, Inc.[2]
5 Civic Plaza
P. O. Box 8710
Newport Beach, California
92658-8710
714-720-0330

Fairfax, Inc.[2]
4770 Campus Drive
Suite 200
Newport Beach, California 92660
714-476-2992

Indiana

Fairfax, Inc.[2]
25 East Cedar Street
Zionsville, Indiana 46077
317-873-5900

Michigan

Saatchi & Saatchi Compton Inc.[1]
American Center Building
Southfield, Michigan 48034
313-354-5400

New York

Saatchi & Saatchi Compton Inc.
625 Madison Avenue
New York, New York 10022
212-754-1100

Cadwell Davis Partners[3]
625 Madison Avenue
New York, New York 10022
212-350-1500

Fairfax, Inc.[2]
635 Madison Avenue
New York, New York 10022
212-350-1800

Irv Koons Advertising[2]
625 Madison Avenue
New York, New York 10022
212-752-4130

Klemtner Advertising Inc.[2]
625 Madison Avenue
New York, New York 10022
212-350-0400

Mayo-Infurna Design Incorporated[2]
635 Madison Avenue
New York, New York 10022
212-888-7883

Rumrill-Hoyt, Inc.[2]
635 Madison Avenue
New York, New York 10022
212-872-4000

Computer Marketing
Services, Inc.[2]
2000 Winton Road South
Rochester, New York 14618
716-272-2500

Rumrill-Hoyt, Inc.[2]
1895 Mt. Hope Avenue
Rochester, New York 14620
716-271-2150

Texas

BTD Directory Management, Inc.[2]
716 Skillman
Dallas, Texas 75243
214-349-0001

Wisconsin

Hoffman York & Compton[2]
Plaza Two East
330 East Kilbourn Avenue
Suite 650
Milwaukee, Wisconsin 53202
414-289-9700

Scali, McCabe, Sloves, Inc.

California

Scali, McCabe, Sloves/West[2]
2401 Colorado Avenue
Suite 280
Santa Monica, California 90404
213-207-7340

Georgia

Scali, McCabe, Sloves/South[2]
Atlanta Plaza
950 East Paces Ferry Road
Atlanta, Georgia 30326
404-233-7733

New York

Scali, McCabe, Sloves, Inc.
800 Third Avenue
New York, New York 10022
212-421-2050

Texas

Scali, McCabe, Sloves/Southwest[2]
2919 Allen Parkway
Houston, Texas 77019
713-522-1711

Schneider Parker Jakuc, Inc.

Massachusetts

Schneider Parker Jakuc, Inc.
31 St. James Avenue
Boston, Massachusetts 02116
617-542-3444

Location Index

Agency
State
Address

Scott Lancaster Mills Atha

California

Scott Lancaster Mills Atha
2049 Century Park East
Los Angeles, California 90067
213-552-6050

Sudler & Hennessey Incorporated

New York

Sudler & Hennessey Incorporated
1633 Broadway
New York, New York 10019
212-265-8000

Sudler & Hennessey
Consumer Group[2]
1180 Avenue of the Americas
New York, New York 10036
212-869-2121

Intramed Communications[2]
1180 Avenue of the Americas
New York, New York 10036
212-869-2121

J. Walter Thompson U.S.A., Inc.

California

The Entertainment Group[4]
10100 Santa Monica Boulevard
Suite 1365
Los Angeles, California 90067
213-553-8383

New York

J. Walter Thompson U.S.A.
466 Lexington Avenue
New York, New York 10017
212-210-7000

Hispania Advertising, Inc.[2]
420 Lexington Avenue
New York, New York 10017
212-210-8970

[1] Branch
[2] Subsidiary
[3] Affiliate
[4] Division

Deltakos U.S.A.[4]
420 Lexington Avenue
New York, New York 10017
212-210-8910

J. Walter Thompson Direct Network[4]
420 Lexington Avenue
New York, New York 10017
212-210-8440

Tracy-Locke, Inc.

California

Tracy-Locke, Los Angeles[1]
12100 Wilshire Boulevard
Suite 1800
Los Angeles, California 90025
213-207-1002

Colorado

Tracy-Locke, Denver[1]
5600 South Quebec Street
Suite B
Englewood, Colorado 80111
303-773-3100

Pennsylvania

Geographic Marketing Group[2]
2000 Market Street
Philadelphia, Pennsylvania 19103
215-751-9811

Texas

Tracy-Locke, Inc.
Plaza of the Americas
South Tower
P. O. Box 50129
Dallas, Texas 75250
214-969-9000

Promotional Services Group[2]
Plaza of the Americas
South Tower
P. O. Box 50129
Dallas, Texas 75250
214-742-7170

Tracy-Locke/BBDO Public Relations[2]
Plaza of the Americas
South Tower
P. O. Box 50129
Dallas, Texas 75250
214-742-1063

Tracy-Locke Direct[2]
Plaza of the Americas
South Tower
P. O. Box 50129
Dallas, Texas 75250
214-969-9000

VanSant, Dugdale & Co., Inc.

Maryland

VanSant, Dugdale & Co., Inc.
The World Trade Center
11th floor
Baltimore, Maryland 21202
301-539-5400

Pennsylvania

VanSant, Dugdale & Co., Inc.[1]
1845 Walnut Street
Philadelphia, Pennsylvania 19103
215-567-7662

Waring & LaRosa, Inc.

New York

Waring & LaRosa, Inc.
555 Madison Avenue
New York, New York 10022
212-755-0700

Zechman and Associates

Illinois

Zechman and Associates
333 N. Michigan Avenue
Chicago, Illinois 60601
312-346-0551

Location Index

State
City
Agency

Alabama

Birmingham

Luckie & Forney, Inc.
120 Office Park Drive
Birmingham, Alabama 35223
205-879-2121

Arizona

Phoenix

Bozell, Jacobs, Kenyon & Eckhardt
100 West Clarendon
Suite 2206
Phoenix, Arizona 85013
602-264-9100

Nationwide Advertising Service Inc.
3737 North 7th Street
Suite 108
Phoenix, Arizona 85014
602-263-8894

Needham Harper Worldwide, Inc.
2111 East Highland Avenue
Phoenix, Arizona 85016
602-969-5000

California

Beverly Hills

Saatchi & Saatchi Compton Inc.
8383 Wilshire Boulevard
Beverly Hills, California 90211
213-852-1415

Century City

McCaffrey and McCall West
1875 Century Park East
Suite 1165
Century City, California 90067
213-201-5025

El Monte

Smith-Hemmings-Gosden, Inc.
(Foote, Cone & Belding Communications, Inc.)
3360 Flair Drive
El Monte, California 91731
818-571-6600

Garden Grove

BTD Directory Management, Inc.
(Saatchi & Saatchi Compton Inc.)
12900 Garden Grove Boulevard
Suite 120
P. O. Box 3200
Garden Grove, California 92643
714-636-5800

Huntington Beach

Backer & Spielvogel
7711 Center Avenue
Huntington Beach, California 92647
714-895-9926

Los Angeles

Ad Latina
(Davis, Johnson, Mogul & Colombatto, Inc.)
3435 Wilshire Boulevard
Suite 720
Los Angeles, California 90010
213-251-4400

N W Ayer Inc.
707 Wilshire Boulevard
Los Angeles, California 90017
213-621-1400

Bozell, Jacobs, Kenyon & Eckhardt
1100 Glendon Avenue
Los Angeles, California 90024
213-208-0220

Bozell, Jacobs, Kenyon & Eckhardt
10850 Wilshire Boulevard
Los Angeles, California 90024
213-879-1800

Bozell, Jacobs, Kenyon & Eckhardt
Public Relations
10850 Wilshire Boulevard
Los Angeles, California 90024
213-879-1800

Bozell, Jacobs, Kenyon & Eckhardt
Yellow Pages
10850 Wilshire Boulevard
Los Angeles, California 90024
213-879-1800

Campbell-Ewald Company
10920 Wilshire Boulevard
Suite 1100
Los Angeles, California 90024
213-824-1922

Chiat/Day inc. Advertising
517 South Olive Street
Los Angeles, California 90013
213-622-7454

Cole & Weber
2029 Century Park East
Suite 920
Los Angeles, California 90067
213-879-7979

Davis, Johnson, Mogul & Colombatto, Inc.
3435 Wilshire Boulevard
Los Angeles, California 90010
213-251-4500

Della Femina, Travisano & Partners of California, Inc.
5900 Wilshire Boulevard
Los Angeles, California 90036
213-937-8540

Doremus/Los Angeles
10960 Wilshire Boulevard
Suite 1422
Los Angeles, California 90024
213-478-3071

DDB/Los Angeles
5900 Wilshire Boulevard
Los Angeles, California 90036
213-937-5100

The Entertainment Group
(J. Walter Thompson U.S.A., Inc.)
10100 Santa Monica Boulevard
Suite 1365
Los Angeles, California 90067
213-553-8383

Foote, Cone & Belding
11601 Wilshire Boulevard
Los Angeles, California 90025-1772
213-312-7000

FCB/Telecom
520 South Lafayette Park Place
Suite 201
Los Angeles, California 90057
213-389-1551

FCB/Entertainment
11601 Wilshire Boulevard
Los Angeles, California 90025-1772
213-312-7000

Gelman & Gray Communications, Inc.
Public Relations
(Davis, Johnson, Mogul & Colombatto, Inc.)
3435 Wilshire Boulevard
Suite 908
Los Angeles, California 90010
213-251-4600

Johnston Thoen & Lindh
(The Johnston & Johnston Group)
5455 Wilshire Boulevard
Los Angeles, California 90036
213-933-7577

keye/donna/pearlstein
11080 Olympic Boulevard
Los Angeles, California 90064
213-477-0061

Kresser, Craig/D.I.K.
(Doyle Dane Bernbach Group Inc.)
2029 Century Park East
Los Angeles, California 90067
213-553-8254

La Agencia de McCann-Erickson
6420 Wilshire Boulevard
Los Angeles, California 90048
213-655-9420

Location Index

State
City
Agency

McCann-Erickson Los Angeles
6420 Wilshire Boulevard
Los Angeles, California 90048
213-655-9420

Needham Harper Worldwide, Inc.
11601 Wilshire Boulevard
Los Angeles, California 90025
213-208-5000

Needham Porter Novelli
11601 Wilshire Boulevard
Los Angeles, California 90025
213-824-0401

Rapp & Collins, Inc.
(Doyle Dane Bernbach)
5900 Wilshire Boulevard
Los Angeles, California 90036
213-936-9600

Scott Lancaster Mills Atha
2049 Century Park East
Los Angeles, California 90067
213-552-6050

Tracy-Locke, Los Angeles
12100 Wilshire Boulevard
Suite 1800
Los Angeles, California 90025
213-207-1002

York Alpern/DDB
(Doyle Dane Bernbach Group)
5757 Wilshire Boulevard
Los Angeles, California 90036
213-931-9000

Newport Beach

Basso & Associates, Inc.
P. O. Box 8030
3198 Airport Loop Drive
Newport Beach, California 92660
714-641-0111

Cochran Chase, Livingston &
Company, Inc.
(Saatchi & Saatchi Compton Inc.)
5 Civic Plaza
P. O. Box 8710
Newport Beach, California
92658-8710
714-720-0330

Fairfax, Inc.
(Saatchi & Saatchi Compton Inc.)
4770 Campus Drive
Suite 200
Newport Beach, California 92660
714-476-2992

Oakland

Nationwide Advertising Service Inc.
7750 Pardee Lane
Suite 210
Oakland, California 94621
415-632-7721

Sacramento

Levine, Huntley, Schmidt &
Beaver, Inc.
2505 Port Street
P. O. Box 985
West Sacramento, California 95691

Needham Harper Worldwide, Inc.
1303 J Street
Sacramento, California 95814
916-441-1935

San Diego

Nationwide Advertising Service Inc.
591 Camino De La Reina
Suite 606
San Diego, California 92108
619-299-8661

Needham Harper Worldwide, Inc.
707 Broadway
San Diego, California 92101
619-234-5101

San Francisco

Albert-Frank Guenther Law
Incorporated
244 California Street
San Francisco, California 94111
415-989-7020

Chiat/Day inc. Advertising
77 Maiden Lane
San Francisco, California 94109
415-445-3000

Cole & Weber
10 Lombard Street
San Francisco, California 94111
415-393-2455

Dancer Fitzgerald Sample
San Francisco
1010 Battery Street
San Francisco, California 94111
415-982-8400

Davis, Johnson, Mogul &
Colombatto, Inc.
731 Market Street
San Francisco, California 94103
415-546-1100

Deutsch, Shea & Evans
(Foote, Cone & Belding
Communications, Inc.)
605 Market Street
Suite 706
San Francisco, California 94105
415-543-7222

Doremus/San Francisco
825 Battery Street
San Francisco, California 94111
415-981-4020

Doyle Dane Bernbach/San
Francisco
530 Bush Street
San Francisco, California 94108
415-398-2669

Foote, Cone & Belding
1255 Battery Street
San Francisco, California 94111
415-398-5200

McCann-Erickson San Francisco
201 California Street
San Francisco, California 94111
415-981-2262

Vicom Associates, Inc.
(Foote, Cone & Belding
Communications, Inc.)
901 Battery Street
San Francisco, California 94111
415-391-8700

Santa Ana

Nationwide Advertising Service Inc.
400 North Tustin Avenue
Santa Ana, California 92705
714-543-1544

Santa Monica

Scali, McCabe, Sloves/West
2401 Colorado Avenue
Suite 280
Santa Monica, California 90404
213-207-7340

Sherman Oaks

Nationwide Advertising Service Inc.
The Galleria Garden Offices
15301 Ventura Boulevard
Suite 240
Sherman Oaks, California 91403
818-906-3313

Torrance

Dancer Fitzgerald Sample
Southern California
3878 Carson Street
Torrance, California 90503
213-540-2554

Colorado

Aurora

Levine, Huntley, Schmidt &
Beaver, Inc.
15000 East 39th Avenue
Aurora, Colorado 80011

Location Index

State
City
Agency

Denver

Doyle Dane Bernbach/Denver
#2 Tamarac Square
Suite 416
7535 E. Hampden Avenue
Denver, Colorado 80231
303-337-3500

Nationwide Advertising Service Inc.
1325 S. Colorado Boulevard
Suite 503
Denver, Colorado 80222
303-759-9970

Englewood

Tracy-Locke, Denver
5600 South Quebec Street
Suite B
Englewood, Colorado 80111
303-773-3100

Connecticut

Greenwich

North Castle Partners
(Foote, Cone & Belding
Communications, Inc.)
20 Bridge Street
Greenwich, Connecticut 06830
203-622-1122

Posey & Quest, Inc.
6 Glenville Street
Greenwich, Connecticut 06830
203-531-4900

Hartford

HBM/CREAMER, Inc.
100 Constitution Plaza
Hartford, Connecticut 16103
203-278-1500

Stamford

Knudsen Moore Schropfer, Inc.
666 Glenbrook Road
Stamford, Connecticut 06906
203-967-7200

Wahlstrom & Co.
(Foote, Cone & Belding
Communications, Inc.)
Holly Pond Plaza
1281 Main Street
Stamford, Connecticut 06902
203-348-7347

Florida

Ft. Lauderdale

Nationwide Advertising Service Inc.
1001 N.W. 62nd Street
Suite 305
Ft. Lauderdale, Florida 33309
305-776-0285

Miami

Campbell-Ewald Latina
Koger Executive Center
8525 NW 53rd Terrace
Suite 101
Miami, Florida 33166
305-592-7135

Tampa

Nationwide Advertising Service Inc.
3510 Bay to Bay Boulevard
Tampa, Florida 33629
813-831-1085

Pearson, Thomas/Levy King &
White Advertising
Bayport Plaza
6200 Courtney-Campbell Causeway
Suite 800
Tampa, Florida 33607
813-885-2219

West Palm Beach

Levine, Huntley, Schmidt &
Beaver, Inc.
1685 Florida Mango Road N.
P. O. Box 3007
West Palm Beach, Florida 33402

Georgia

Atlanta

Bozell, Jacobs, Kenyon & Eckhardt
One Securities Center
3490 Piedmont Road
Atlanta, Georgia 30305
404-266-2221

Bozell, Jacobs, Kenyon & Eckhardt
Yellow Pages
One Securities Center
3490 Piedmont Road
Atlanta, Georgia 30305
404-226-2221

Bozell, Jacobs, Kenyon & Eckhardt
Public Relations
One Securities Center
3490 Piedmont Road
Atlanta, Georgia 30305
404-226-2221

Burrell Advertising Inc./Atlanta
100 Colony Square-Suite 200
Atlanta, Georgia 30361
404-875-1683

Cargill, Wilson & Acree Inc.
(Doyle Dane Bernbach Group)
Suite 1150 Tower Place
3340 Peachtree Road, N.E.
Atlanta, Georgia 30026
404-261-8700

Fletcher/Mayo/Associates, Inc.
(Doyle Dane Bernbach Group)
Five Piedmont Center
Suite 710
Atlanta, Georgia 30305
404-261-0831

Group 2 Atlanta
(Bozell, Jacobs, Kenyon &
Eckhardt)
3500 Piedmont Road
Atlanta, Georgia 30305
404-262-3239

McCann-Erickson Atlanta
615 Peachtree Street, N.E.
Atlanta, Georgia 30365
404-873-2321

Nationwide Advertising Service Inc.
229 Peachtree St., N.E.
Suite 1111
Atlanta, Georgia 30303
404-522-4047

Scali, McCabe, Sloves/South
Atlanta Plaza
950 East Paces Ferry Road
Atlanta, Georgia 30326
404-233-7733

Norcross

Della Femina, Travisano &
Partners/Atlanta
Waterford Centre
555 Triangle Parkway
Suite 200
Norcross, Georgia 30092
404-263-0500

Hawaii

Honolulu

Milici Valenti Smith Park
Advertising, Inc.
(Doyle Dane Bernbach Group)
12th Floor
700 Bishop Street
Honolulu, Hawaii 98613
808-536-0881

Illinois

Addison

Levine, Huntley, Schmidt &
Beaver, Inc.
301 Mitchell Court
Addison, Illinois 60101

Chicago

N W Ayer Inc.
One Illinois Center
111 East Wacker Drive
Chicago, Illinois 60601
312-645-8800

Location Index

State
City
Agency

Backer & Spielvogel Chicago, Inc.
479 Merchandise Mart Plaza
Chicago, Illinois 60654
312-222-2511

Bozell, Jacobs, Kenyon & Eckhardt
625 North Michigan Avenue
Chicago, Illinois 60611
312-988-2000

Bozell, Jacobs, Kenyon & Eckhardt
Direct
625 North Michigan Avenue
Chicago, Illinois 60611
312-988-2000

Bozell, Jacobs, Kenyon & Eckhardt
Public Relations
625 North Michigan Avenue
Chicago, Illinois 60611
312-988-2000

Bozell, Jacobs, Kenyon & Eckhardt
Yellow Pages
625 North Michigan Avenue
Chicago, Illinois 60611
312-988-2000

Leo Burnett Company, Inc.
Prudential Plaza
Chicago, Illinois 60601
312-565-5959

Burrell Advertising Inc.
625 N. Michigan Avenue
Chicago, Illinois 60611
312-266-4600

Campbell-Ewald Company
120 S. Riverside Plaza
Chicago, Illinois 60606
312-454-1752

Campbell-Mithun Advertising
737 North Michigan Avenue
Chicago, Illinois 60611
312-565-3800

Doremus/Chicago
500 North Michigan Avenue
Suite 400
Chicago, Illinois 60611
312-321-1377

Fletcher/Mayo/Associates, Inc.
(Doyle Dane Bernbach Group)
211 E. Ontario
15th floor
Chicago, Illinois 60611
312-266-1717

Foote, Cone & Belding
401 N. Michigan Avenue
Chicago, Illinois 60611
312-467-9200

FCB Direct Marketing
401 N. Michigan Avenue
Chicago, Illinois 60611
312-467-9200

Golin/Harris Communications
(Foote, Cone & Belding
Communications, Inc.)
500 N. Michigan Avenue
Chicago, Illinois 60611
312-836-7100

Grant/Jacoby, Inc.
500 N. Michigan Avenue
Chicago, Illinois 60611
312-664-2055

Graphic TypeTech
(Bozell, Jacobs, Kenyon &
Eckhardt)
57 West Grand Avenue
Chicago, Illinois 60601
312-744-0003

Haddon Advertising, Inc.
919 N. Michigan Avenue
Chicago, Illinois 60611
312-943-6266

Haddon, Lynch and Baughman, Inc.
919 N. Michigan Avenue
Chicago, Illinois 60611
312-649-0371

HBM/CREAMER, Inc.
410 North Michigan Avenue
Chicago, Illinois 60611
312-222-4900

IMPACT/Chicago
(Foote, Cone & Belding
Communications, Inc.)
401 N. Michigan Avenue
Chicago, Illinois 60611
312-467-9200

Nationwide Advertising Service Inc.
The Tower
35 East Wacker Drive
Chicago, Illinois 60601
312-332-6550

Needham Harper Worldwide, Inc.
Three Illinois Center
Chicago, Illinois 60601
312-861-0200

PRB: A Needham Porter Novelli
Company
150 East Huron Street
Chicago, Illinois 60611
312-266-7200

Zechman and Associates
333 N. Michigan Avenue
Chicago, Illinois 60601
312-346-0551

Indiana

Zionsville

Fairfax, Inc.
(Saatchi & Saatchi Compton Inc.)
25 East Cedar Street
Zionsville, Indiana 46077
317-873-5900

Kansas

Lenexa

Nationwide Advertising Service Inc.
9730 Rosehill Road
Lenexa, Kansas 66215
913-541-0914

Wichita

Nationwide Advertising Service Inc.
Executive Park East
215 Lakeside Plaza
250 N. Rock Road
Wichita, Kansas 67206
316-682-4576

Kentucky

Louisville

McCann-Erickson Louisville
1469 South Fourth Street
P. O. Box 1137
Louisville, Kentucky 40208
502-636-0441

Louisiana

New Orleans

Fitzgerald Advertising Inc.
1055 St. Charles Avenue
New Orleans, Louisiana 70130
504-529-3161

Maryland

Baltimore

The Earle Palmer Brown
Companies
100 Saint Paul Plaza Building
Suite 500
Baltimore, Maryland 21202
301-576-8420

MacDantz Direct
(Richardson, Myers
& Donofrio, Inc.)
120 West Fayette Street
Baltimore, Maryland 21201
301-837-4966

Nationwide Advertising Service Inc.
American City Building
Suite 300
10227 Wincopin Circle
Columbia, Maryland 21044
301-964-9440

Location Index

State
City
Agency

Needham Harper Worldwide, Inc.
400 East Pratt Street
Suite 814
Baltimore, Maryland 21202
301-727-6717

Richardson, Myers &
Donofrio, Inc.
120 West Fayette Street
Baltimore, Maryland 21201
301-576-9000

RM&D/Public Relations
120 West Fayette Street
Baltimore, Maryland 21201
301-576-9000

SP&CS, Graphic Arts Production
(Richardson, Myers
& Donofrio, Inc.)
120 West Fayette Street
Baltimore, Maryland 21201
301-576-9000

VanSant, Dugdale & Co., Inc.
The World Trade Center
11th floor
Baltimore, Maryland 21202
301-539-5400

Bethesda

The Earle Palmer Brown
Companies
6935 Arlington Road
Bethesda, Maryland 20814
301-986-0510

Lutherville

Davis, Johnson, Mogul &
Colombatto, Inc.
1615 York Road
Suite 305
Lutherville, Maryland 21093
301-823-7500

Massachusetts

Boston

Bozell, Jacobs, Kenyon & Eckhardt
One Boston Place
Boston, Massachusetts 02108
617-367-7300

Bozell, Jacobs, Kenyon & Eckhardt
Direct
One Boston Place
Boston, Massachusetts 02108
617-367-7300

Campbell-Ewald Company
88 Broad Street
Boston, Massachusetts 02110
617-423-0121

Doremus/Boston
535 Boylston Street
Boston, Massachusetts 02116
617-266-2600

The DR Group
(Needham Harper Worldwide, Inc.)
10 Post Office Square
Boston, Massachusetts
617-482-7300

HBM/CREAMER, Inc.
One Beacon Street
Boston, Massachusetts 02108
617-723-7770

Nationwide Advertising Service Inc.
44 School Street
Suite 408
Boston, Massachusetts 02108
617-723-1875

Schneider Parker Jakuc, Inc.
31 St. James Avenue
Boston, Massachusetts 02116
617-542-3444

Michigan

Birmingham

Bozell, Jacobs, Kenyon & Eckhardt
30600 Telegraph Road
Birmingham, Michigan 48010
313-645-6170

Detroit

N W Ayer Inc.
2000 Fisher Building
Detroit, Michigan 48202
313-874-8500

Nationwide Advertising Service Inc.
1056 Penobscot Building
Detroit, Michigan 48226
313-961-6785

Southfield

Saatchi & Saatchi Compton Inc.
American Center Building
Southfield, Michigan 48034
313-354-5400

Troy

Doyle Dane Bernbach/Detroit
Top of Troy Building
755 W. Big Beaver Road
Suite 900
Troy, Michigan 48084
313-362-2339

McCann-Erickson Detroit
755 W. Big Beaver Road
Troy, Michigan 48084
313-362-4800

Warren

Campbell-Ewald Company
30400 Van Dyke
Warren, Michigan 48093
313-574-3400

CeCo Communications, Inc.
(Campbell-Ewald Company)
30400 Van Dyke
Warren, Michigan 48093
313-575-9400

Minnesota

Minneapolis

Bozell, Jacobs, Kenyon & Eckhardt
100 North 6th Street
Minneapolis, Minnesota 55403
612-371-7500

Bozell, Jacobs, Kenyon & Eckhardt
Direct
100 North 6th Street
Minneapolis, Minnesota 55403
612-371-7500

Bozell, Jacobs, Kenyon & Eckhardt
Public Relations
100 North 6th Street
Minneapolis, Minnesota 55403
612-371-5500

Bozell, Jacobs, Kenyon & Eckhardt
Yellow Pages
100 North 6th Street
Minneapolis, Minnesota 55403
612-371-7500

Campbell-Mithun Advertising
222 South Ninth Street
Minneapolis, Minnesota 55402
612-347-1000

Cash Plus
(Campbell-Mithun Advertising)
222 South Ninth Street
Minneapolis, Minnesota 55402
612-347-6901

Custom Production Service, Inc.
(Bozell, Jacobs, Kenyon &
Eckhardt)
100 North 6th Street
Minneapolis, Minnesota 55403
612-371-5555

Nationwide Advertising Service Inc.
One Appletree Square
Suite 946
Minneapolis, Minnesota 55420
612-854-4091

Location Index

State
City
Agency

Promotion Works
(Campbell-Mithun Advertising)
222 South Ninth Street
Minneapolis, Minnesota 55402
612-347-1495

Missouri

Kansas City

Fletcher/Mayo/Associates, Inc.
(Doyle Dane Bernbach Group)
427 West 12th Street
Kansas City, Missouri 64105
816-421-1000

St. Joseph

Fletcher/Mayo/Associates, Inc.
(Doyle Dane Bernbach Group)
R.R. #3 John Glenn Road
P. O. Box B, Station E
St. Joseph, Missouri 64505
816-233-8261

St. Louis

Kerlick, Switzer & Johnson
Advertising
727 N. First Street
St. Louis, Missouri 63102
314-241-4656

KS & J Direct
727 N. First Street
St. Louis, Missouri 63102
314-241-4656

KS & J Public Relations
727 N. First Street
St. Louis, Missouri 63102
314-241-4656

KS & J Entertainment
727 N. First Street
St. Louis, Missouri 63102
314-241-4656

Nationwide Advertising Service Inc.
10137 Old Olive Street Road
P. O. Box 27322
St. Louis, Missouri 63141
314-432-3221

Nebraska

Omaha

Bozell, Jacobs, Kenyon & Eckhardt
10250 Regency Circle
Omaha, Nebraska 68114
402-397-8660

Bozell, Jacobs, Kenyon & Eckhardt
Visual Communications Center
730 North 109th Court
Omaha, Nebraska 68114
402-397-8660

Bozell, Jacobs, Kenyon & Eckhardt
Agricultural
10250 Regency Circle
Omaha, Nebraska 68114
402-397-8660

Bozell, Jacobs, Kenyon & Eckhardt
Co-op Services
10250 Regency Circle
Omaha, Nebraska 68114
402-397-8660

Bozell, Jacobs, Kenyon & Eckhardt
Public Relations
10250 Regency Circle
Omaha, Nebraska 68114
402-397-8660

Bozell, Jacobs, Kenyon & Eckhardt
Yellow Pages
10250 Regency Circle
Omaha, Nebraska 68114
402-397-8660

Dudycha Group
(Bozell, Jacobs, Kenyon &
Eckhardt)
407 South 27th Avenue
Omaha, Nebraska 68131
402-346-3100

New Jersey

Belleville

The Lempert Company, Inc.
202 Belleville Avenue
Belleville, New Jersey 07109
201-759-2927

Union

Bozell, Jacobs, Kenyon & Eckhardt
2700 Route 22
Union, New Jersey 07083
201-688-2700

Bozell, Jacobs, Kenyon & Eckhardt
Public Relations
2700 Route 22
Union, New Jersey 07083
201-688-2700

Custom Production Service, Inc.
(Bozell, Jacobs, Kenyon &
Eckhardt)
2700 Route 22
Union, New Jersey 07083
201-688-2700

New Mexico

Albuquerque

Nationwide Advertising Service Inc.
4700 Montgomery Boulevard, N.E.
Suite 200
Albuquerque, New Mexico 87109
505-888-4991

New York

Buffalo

William Collins Assoc. Public
Relations
(Levy, King & White
Companies, Inc.)
620 Main Street
Buffalo, New York 14202
716-842-6260

Healy-Schutte & Company
1207 Delaware Avenue
Buffalo, New York 14209
716-884-2120

Levy, King & White Advertising
620 Main Street
Buffalo, New York 14202
716-853-6755

LK&W Direct
620 Main Street
Buffalo, New York 14202
716-853-6755

Quantum Analysis/LKW
(Levy, King & White
Companies, Inc.)
620 Main Street
Buffalo, New York 14202
716-842-2560

Fayetteville

QA Research Centers
(Levy, King & White
Companies, Inc.)
Fayetteville Mall
5351 Burdick Street
Fayetteville, New York 13066
315-637-3169

Melville

Greenstone & Rabasca
Advertising, Inc.
1 Huntington Quadrangle
Melville, New York 11746
516-249-2121

New York

AC&R Advertising, Inc.
16 East 32nd Street
New York, New York 10016
212-685-2500

AC&R Direct
16 East 32nd Street
New York, New York 10016
212-685-2500

AC&R Public Relations
136 Madison Avenue
New York, New York 10016
212-685-8000

AC&R Rossi
136 Madison Avenue
New York, New York 10016
212-532-1411

Location Index

State
City
Agency

Albert Frank-Guenther Law
(Foote, Cone & Belding
Communications, Inc.)
71 Broadway
New York, New York 10006
212-248-5200

The Alden Group
535 Fifth Avenue
New York, New York 10017
212-867-6400

J.S. Alden Public Relations Inc.
535 Fifth Avenue
New York, New York 10017
212-867-6400

Ally & Gargano, Inc.
805 Third Avenue
New York, New York 10022
212-688-5300

N W Ayer Inc.
1345 Avenue of the Americas
New York, New York 10105
212-708-5000

Ayer Design
1345 Avenue of the Americas
New York, New York 10105
212-708-5188

Ayer Direct
1345 Avenue of the Americas
New York, New York 10105
212-708-6350

Ayer International
1345 Avenue of the Americas
New York, New York 10105
212-708-5670

Ayer Public Relations
1345 Avenue of the Americas
New York, New York 10105
212-708-5461

Backer & Spielvogel, Inc.
11 West 42nd Street
New York, New York 10036
212-556-5200

Barnum Communications, Inc.
500 Fifth Avenue
New York, New York 10110
212-221-7363

Betacom, Inc.
(Biederman & Co.)
100 Fifth Avenue
New York, New York 10011
212-929-7200

Biederman & Co.
100 Fifth Avenue
New York, New York 10011
212-929-7200

Bozell, Jacobs, Kenyon &
Eckhardt, Inc.
One Dag Hammarskjold Plaza
New York, New York 10017
212-705-6000

Bozell, Jacobs, Kenyon &
Eckhardt Direct
40 West 23rd Street
New York, New York 10010
212-206-5000

Bozell, Jacobs, Kenyon &
Eckhardt Co-op Services
6 East 43rd Street
New York, New York 10017
212-916-8500

Bozell, Jacobs, Kenyon &
Eckhardt Healthcare
6 East 43rd Street
New York, New York 10017
212-867-1670

Bozell, Jacobs, Kenyon &
Eckhardt Public Relations
6 East 43rd Street
New York, New York 10017
212-916-8500

Bozell, Jacobs, Kenyon &
Eckhardt Yellow Pages
6 East 43rd Street
New York, New York 10017
212-916-8500

Carl Byoir & Associates
(Foote, Cone & Belding
Communications, Inc.)
380 Madison Avenue
New York, New York 10017
212-986-6100

Cadwell Davis Partners
(Saatchi & Saatchi Compton Inc.)
625 Madison Avenue
New York, New York 10022
212-350-1500

Calvillo, Shevack & Partners, Inc.
1350 Avenue of the Americas
New York, New York 10019
212-245-7300

Campbell-Ewald of New York, Inc.
1345 Avenue of the Americas
New York, New York 10105
212-489-6200

Chiat/Day inc. Advertising
79 Fifth Avenue
New York, New York 10003
212-807-4000

Custom Production Service, Inc.
(Bozell, Jacobs, Kenyon &
Eckhardt)
40 West 23rd Street
New York, New York 10010
212-206-5000

The DR Group
(Needham Harper Worldwide, Inc.)
522 Fifth Avenue
New York, New York 10036
212-391-8600

Dancer Fitzgerald Sample, Inc.
405 Lexington Avenue
New York, New York 10174
212-661-0800

Della Femina, Travisano &
Partners Inc.
625 Madison Avenue
New York, New York 10022
212-421-7180

Della Femina, Travisano, Sherman
& Olken, Inc.
625 Madison Avenue
New York, New York 10022
212-421-7180

Deltakos U.S.A.
(J. Walter Thompson U.S.A., Inc.)
420 Lexington Avenue
New York, New York 10017
212-210-8910

David Deutsch Associates
655 Third Avenue
New York, New York 10017
212-867-0044

Doremus & Company
120 Broadway
New York, New York 10271
212-964-0700

Doremus/Marketshare
41 Madison Avenue
New York, New York 10010
212-725-8400

Doyle Dane Bernbach/New York
437 Madison Avenue
New York, New York 10022
212-415-2000

William Esty Company, Inc.
100 East 42nd Street
New York, New York 10017
212-692-6200

Fairfax, Inc.
(Saatchi & Saatchi Compton Inc.)
635 Madison Avenue
New York, New York 10022
212-350-1800

Font & Vaamonde Associates, Inc.
183 Madison Avenue
Suite 1402
New York, New York 10016
212-679-9170

Foote, Cone & Belding
101 Park Avenue
New York, New York 10178
212-907-1000

Location Index

State
City
Agency

FCB Direct East
101 Park Avenue
New York, New York 10078
212-907-1007

HBM/CREAMER, Inc.
1633 Broadway
New York, New York 10019
212-887-8000

Hispania Advertising, Inc.
(J. Walter Thompson U.S.A., Inc.)
420 Lexington Avenue
New York, New York 10017
212-210-8970

Bernard Hodes Advertising
(Doyle Dane Bernbach Group)
555 Madison Avenue
New York, New York 10022
212-758-2600

IMPACT/New York
(Foote, Cone & Belding
Communications, Inc.)
101 Park Avenue
New York, New York 10178
212-907-1000

Intramed Communications
(Sudler & Hennessey Incorporated)
1180 Avenue of the Americas
New York, New York 10036
212-869-2121

Jim Johnston Advertising, Inc.
551 Fifth Avenue
New York, New York 10176
212-490-2121

Kallir, Philips, Ross, Inc.
(Doyle Dane Bernbach Group)
605 Third Avenue
New York, New York 10158
212-878-3700

Klemtner Advertising Inc.
(Saatchi & Saatchi Compton Inc.)
625 Madison Avenue
New York, New York 10022
212-350-0400

Irv Koons Advertising
(Saatchi & Saatchi Compton Inc.)
625 Madison Avenue
New York, New York 10022
212-752-4130

Laurence, Charles, Free &
Lawson, Inc.
261 Madison Avenue
New York, New York 10016
212-661-0200

Levine, Huntley, Schmidt &
Beaver, Inc.
250 Park Avenue
New York, New York 10177
212-557-0900

Lord, Geller, Federico,
Einstein, Inc.
655 Madison Avenue
New York, New York 10021
212-421-6050

LGFE/Direct Marketing
655 Madison Avenue
New York, New York 10021
212-421-6050

Mayo-Infurna Design Incorporated
(Saatchi & Saatchi Compton Inc.)
635 Madison Avenue
New York, New York 10022
212-888-7883

McCaffery & Ratner, Inc.
370 Lexington Avenue
New York, New York 10017
212-661-8940

McCaffrey and McCall, Inc.
575 Lexington Avenue
New York, New York 10022
212-421-7500

McCaffrey and McCall Direct
Marketing
575 Lexington Avenue
New York, New York 10022
212-303-6000

McCann-Erickson New York
485 Lexington Avenue
New York, New York 10017
212-697-6000

McCann Direct
485 Lexington Avenue
New York, New York 10017
212-286-0460

Nationwide Advertising Service Inc.
419 Park Avenue South
New York, New York 10016
212-696-4400

Needham Harper Worldwide, Inc.
909 Third Avenue
New York, New York 10022
212-758-7600

Needham Porter Novelli
909 Third Avenue
New York, New York 10022
212-758-7600

Posey & Quest, Inc.
307 East 56th Street
New York, New York 10022
212-750-5566

Rapp & Collins Inc.
(Doyle Dane Bernbach Group)
475 Park Avenue South
New York, New York 10016
212-725-8100

Respond Productions
(AC&R Advertising, Inc.)
16 East 32nd Street
New York, New York 10016
212-685-2500

Rosenfeld, Sirowitz & Lawson, Inc.
111 Fifth Avenue
New York, New York 10003
212-505-0200

Rumrill-Hoyt, Inc.
(Saatchi & Saatchi Compton Inc.)
635 Madison Avenue
New York, New York 10022
212-872-4000

Saatchi & Saatchi Compton Inc.
625 Madison Avenue
New York, New York 10022
212-754-1100

Scali, McCabe, Sloves, Inc.
800 Third Avenue
New York, New York 10022
212-421-2050

Sudler & Hennessey Incorporated
1633 Broadway
New York, New York 10019
212-265-8000

Sudler & Hennessey Consumer
Group
1180 Avenue of the Americas
New York, New York 10036
212-869-2121

J. Walter Thompson U.S.A.
466 Lexington Avenue
New York, New York 10017
212-210-7000

J. Walter Thompson Direct Network
420 Lexington Avenue
New York, New York 10017
212-210-8440

Waring & LaRosa, Inc.
555 Madison Avenue
New York, New York 10022
212-755-0700

Rochester

Computer Marketing
Services, Inc.
(Saatchi & Saatchi Compton)
2000 Winton Road South
Rochester, New York 14618
716-272-2500

Healy-Schutte & Company
Harro East
400 Andrews Street
Rochester, New York 14604
716-325-6830

Location Index

State
City
Agency

Nationwide Advertising Service Inc.
1147 Sibley Tower Building
25 Franklin Street
Rochester, New York 14604
716-454-2520

Rumrill-Hoyt, Rochester
(Saatchi & Saatchi Compton Inc.)
1895 Mt. Hope Avenue
P. O. Box 1011
Rochester, New York 14603
716-227-2150

North Carolina

Chapel Hill

The Carolina Partnership
(The Johnston & Johnston Group)
P. O. Box 2839
Chapel Hill, North Carolina 27514
919-967-8282

Raleigh

Nationwide Advertising Service Inc.
3117 Poplarwood Court
Suite 322
Raleigh, North Carolina 27625
919-872-6800

Winston Salem

Long, Haymes & Carr Incorporated
140 Charlois Boulevard
Winston Salem, North Carolina
27113
919-765-3630

Ohio

Cincinnati

Nationwide Advertising Service Inc.
617 Vine Street
Suite 1401
Cincinnati, Ohio 45202
513-241-3121

Cleveland

The BoardRoom Design &
Promotion
(The Jayme Organization, Inc.)
23200 Chagrin Boulevard
One Commerce Park Square
Cleveland, Ohio 44122
216-831-0204

The Jayme Organization, Inc.
23200 Chagrin Boulevard
One Commerce Park Square
Cleveland, Ohio 44122
216-831-0110

MacDantz Direct
(The Jayme Organization, Inc.)
23200 Chagrin Boulevard
One Commerce Park Square
Cleveland, Ohio 44122
216-831-0110

Nationwide Advertising Service Inc.
Corporate Headquarters
The Penthouse, Statler Office
Tower
Euclid Avenue at E. 12th Street
Cleveland, Ohio 44115
216-579-0300

Publicom Public Relations
(The Jayme Organization, Inc.)
23200 Chagrin Boulevard
One Commerce Park Square
Cleveland, Ohio 44122
216-831-0400

Strategic Research Center
(The Jayme Organization, Inc.)
23200 Chagrin Boulevard
One Commerce Park Square
Cleveland, Ohio 44122
216-831-2410

Columbus

Nationwide Advertising Service Inc.
2000 W. Henderson Road
Suite 230
Columbus, Ohio 43220
614-459-3556

Oregon

Portland

Cole & Weber
55 S.W. Yamhill Street
Portland, Oregon 97204
503-226-2821

Davis, Johnson, Mogul &
Colombatto, Inc.
101 SW Main Street
Suite 1200
Portland, Oregon 97204
503-241-7781

Pennsylvania

Philadelphia

Albert Frank-Guenther Law
Incorporated
2000 Market Street
Philadelphia, Pennsylvania 19103
215-564-2345

The Earle Palmer Brown
Companies
1845 Walnut Street
Philadelphia, Pennsylvania 19103
215-299-3800

Geographic Marketing Group
(Tracy-Locke, Inc.)
2000 Market Street
Philadelphia, Pennsylvania 19103
215-751-9811

HealthCom
(Foote, Cone & Belding
Communications, Inc.)
1700 Market Street
Philadelphia, Pennsylvania 19103
215-568-3775

The Lempert Company, Inc.
111 Presidential Boulevard
Suite 224
Bala Cynwyd, Pennsylvania 19004
215-667-7442

Lewis, Gilman & Kynett
(Foote, Cone & Belding
Communications, Inc.)
1700 Market Street
Philadelphia, Pennsylvania 19103
215-543-3775

Nationwide Advertising Service Inc.
1500 Chestnut Street
Suite 303
Philadelphia, Pennsylvania 19102
215-568-5000

Richardson, Myers &
Donofrio, Inc.
1608 Walnut Street
Philadelphia, Pennsylvania 19103
215-545-0200

RM&D/Public Relations
1608 Walnut Street
Philadelphia, Pennsylvania 19103
215-545-0200

RM&D/Sales Promotion
1608 Walnut Street
Philadelphia, Pennsylvania 19103
215-545-0200

VanSant, Dugdale & Co., Inc.
1845 Walnut Street
Philadelphia, Pennsylvania 19103
215-567-7662

Pittsburgh

Campbell-Ewald Company
Porter Building
Suite 1101
601 Grant Street
Pittsburgh, Pennsylvania 15219
412-765-1200

HBM/CREAMER, Inc.
600 Grant Street
Pittsburgh, Pennsylvania 15219
412-456-4500

MARC Advertising
Four Station Square
Suite 500
Pittsburgh, Pennsylvania 15219
412-562-2000

Location Index

State
City
Agency

Nationwide Advertising Service Inc.
Three Gateway Center
Suite 1751
Pittsburgh, Pennsylvania 15222
412-391-3915

Rhode Island

Providence

HBM/CREAMER, Inc.
800 Turks Head Building
Providence, Rhode Island 02903
401-456-1500

Texas

Dallas

BTD Directory Management, Inc.
(Saatchi & Saatchi Compton Inc.)
716 Skillman
Dallas, Texas 75243
214-349-0001

Bozell, Jacobs, Kenyon & Eckhardt
201 E. Carpenter Freeway
P. O. Box 619200
Dallas/Ft. Worth Airport, Texas
75261-9200
214-556-1100

Bozell, Jacobs, Kenyon & Eckhardt
Co-op Services
201 East Carpenter Freeway
P. O. Box 619200
Dallas/Ft. Worth Airport, Texas
75261-9200
214-556-1100

Bozell, Jacobs, Kenyon &
Eckhardt Direct
201 East Carpenter Freeway
P. O. Box 619200
Dallas/Ft. Worth Airport, Texas
75261-9200
214-556-3427

Bozell, Jacobs, Kenyon & Eckhardt
Industrial/Technical
201 East Carpenter Freeway
P. O. Box 619200
Dallas/Ft. Worth Airport, Texas
75261-9200
214-830-2432

Bozell, Jacobs, Kenyon & Eckhardt
Public Relations
201 East Carpenter Freeway
P. O. Box 619200
Dallas/Ft. Worth Airport, Texas
75261-9200
214-556-1000

Bozell, Jacobs, Kenyon & Eckhardt
Recruitment Advertising
201 East Carpenter Freeway
P. O. Box 619200
Dallas/Ft. Worth Airport, Texas
75261-9200
214-830-2428

Bozell, Jacobs, Kenyon & Eckhardt
Yellow Pages
201 East Carpenter Freeway
P. O. Box 619200
Dallas/Ft. Worth Airport, Texas
75261-9200
214-556-1100

Custom Production Service, Inc.
(Bozell, Jacobs, Kenyon &
Eckhardt)
201 East Carpenter Freeway
P. O. Box 619200
Dallas/Ft. Worth Airport, Texas
75261-9200
214-830-2432

CPS Camera
(Bozell, Jacobs, Kenyon &
Eckhardt)
201 East Carpenter Freeway
P. O. Box 619200
Dallas/Ft. Worth Airport, Texas
75261-9200
214-830-2490

Direct Response Group, Inc.
(Doyle Dane Bernbach Group)
8701 Carpenter Freeway
Dallas, Texas 75247
214-631-5111

Graphic Typography
(Bozell, Jacobs, Kenyon &
Eckhardt)
1451 Empire Central, Suite 110
Dallas, Texas 75247
214-630-5661

Group 2
(Bozell, Jacobs, Kenyon &
Eckhardt)
201 East Carpenter Freeway
P. O. Box 619200
Dallas/Ft. Worth Airport, Texas
75261-9200
214-830-2432

Nationwide Advertising Service Inc.
9330 LBJ Freeway
Suite 260
Dallas, Texas 75243
214-690-4400

Promotional Services Group
(Tracy-Locke, Inc.)
Plaza of the Americas
South Tower
P. O. Box 50129
Dallas, Texas 75250
214-742-7170

Tracy-Locke, Inc.
Plaza of the Americas
South Tower
P. O. Box 50129
Dallas, Texas 75250
214-969-9000

Tracy-Locke/BBDO
Public Relations
Plaza of the Americas
South Tower
P. O. Box 50129
Dallas, Texas 75250
214-742-1063

Tracy-Locke Direct
Plaza of the Americas
South Tower
P. O. Box 50129
Dallas, Texas 75250
214-969-9000

Houston

Bozell, Jacobs, Kenyon & Eckhardt
RepublicBank Center, Suite 3300
700 Louisiana Street
Houston, Texas 77002
713-228-9551

Bozell, Jacbos, Kenyon & Eckhardt
Public Relations
RepublicBank Center, Suite 3300
700 Louisiana Street
Houston, Texas 77002
713-228-9551

McCann-Erickson Houston
520 Post Oak Boulevard
Houston, Texas 77027
713-965-0303

Nationwide Advertising Service Inc.
5805 Richmond Avenue
Houston, Texas 77057
713-780-0770

Scali, McCabe, Sloves/Southwest
2919 Allen Parkway
Houston, Texas 77019
713-522-1711

San Antonio

Levine, Huntley, Schmidt &
Beaver, Inc.
12615 San Pedro Avenue
P. O. Box 32906
San Antonio, Texas 78216

Location Index

State
City
Agency

Utah

Salt Lake City

Bozell, Jacobs, Kenyon & Eckhardt
First Interstate Plaza
170 South Main Street, Suite 1230
Salt Lake City, Utah 84101
801-531-6106

TPC/Cole & Weber
375 W. 2nd South
Salt Lake City, Utah 84101
801-364-2740

Virginia

McLean

Needham Harper Worldwide, Inc.
8300 Greensboro Drive
Suite 1200
McLean, Virginia 22102
703-790-4800

Richmond

The Earle Palmer Brown
Companies
7814 Carousel Lane
Suite 300
Richmond, Virginia 23229
804-747-7666

Washington

Seattle

Cole & Weber
Riverview Plaza
16040 Christensen Road S.
Seattle, Washington 98188
206-433-6200

McCann-Erickson Seattle
1011 Western Avenue
Suite 600
Seattle, Washington 98104
206-682-6360

Washington DC

Bozell, Jacobs, Kenyon & Eckhardt
1199 North Fairfax Street
Alexandria, Virginia 22314
703-549-0600

Doremus/Washington
1090 Vermont Avenue, N.W.
Washington, D.C. 20005
202-842-3666

HBM/CREAMER, Inc.
1612 K Street, N.W.
Suite 706
Washington, D.C. 20006
202-775-9320

Levine, Huntley, Schmidt &
Beaver, Inc.
8611 Larkin Road
P. O. Box 427
Savage, Maryland 20763

Nationwide Advertising Service Inc.
American City Building
Suite 300
10227 Wincopin Circle
Columbia, Maryland 21044
301-621-4986

Needham Porter Novelli
3240 Prospect Street, N.W.
Washington, D.C. 20007
202-342-7000

Wisconsin

Milwaukee

Hoffman York & Compton
(Saatchi & Saatchi Compton Inc.)
Plaza Two East
330 East Kilbourn Avenue
Suite 650
Milwaukee, Wisconsin 53202
414-289-9700

If none of the advertising agencies in this book can solve your problems, call us at (212) 704-0430.

Lemont Consulting Group

1515 Broadway
New York, NY 10036

Request for Information on the 1987 Edition

✂------

The Agency Book 1986
Want to advertise in the next issue?
Please contact me with more information on the Agency Section☐ or the Supplier Section☐ (check one).

Name

Title

Company

Address

City　　　　　　　　　State　　　　　Zip

Phone (　)

☐ Ad Agency　　☐ Supplier　　☐ Other (please state)
The Agency Book, 540 Madison Avenue, New York, NY 10022

✂------

The Agency Book 1986
Want to advertise in the next issue?
Please contact me with more information on the Agency Section☐ or the Supplier Section☐ (check one).

Name

Title

Company

Address

City　　　　　　　　　State　　　　　Zip

Phone (　)

☐ Ad Agency　　☐ Supplier　　☐ Other (please state)
The Agency Book, 540 Madison Avenue, New York, NY 10022

Request Forms for Additional Copies

✂ —

The Agency Book 1986
Extra copies? Yes!
Please rush me _____ copy(s) at $60. plus $5. postage and handling.
New York residents please add $4.95 sales tax.
Order two copies and receive the third free!

Name _____

Title _____

Company _____

Address _____ Home☐ Business☐

City _____ State _____ Zip _____

Phone ( ) _____

Payment by (circle one) Enclosed Check   VISA   MasterCard   AmEx

Account Number _____ Expiration Date _____

Signature _____
Checks should be made payable to: The Agency Book
The Agency Book, 540 Madison Avenue, New York, NY 10022

✂ —

The Agency Book 1986
Extra copies? Yes!
Please rush me _____ copy(s) at $60. plus $5. postage and handling.
New York residents please add $4.95 sales tax.
Order two copies and receive the third free!

Name _____

Title _____

Company _____

Address _____ Home☐ Business☐

City _____ State _____ Zip _____

Phone ( ) _____

Payment by (circle one) Enclosed Check   VISA   MasterCard   AmEx

Account Number _____ Expiration Date _____

Signature _____
Checks should be made payable to: The Agency Book
The Agency Book, 540 Madison Avenue, New York, NY 10022